FROM CYRANO TO MAGOO:

MY YEARS WITH

JOSÉ FERRER AND JIM BACKUS

BY JACK LLOYD

From Cyrano to Magoo:
My Years with José Ferrer and Jim Backus
©2011 Jack Lloyd

All rights reserved.

No part of this book may be reproduced or distributed, in print, recorded, live or digital form, without express written permission of the copyright holder. However, excerpts of up to 500 words may be reproduced online if they include the following information, "This is an excerpt from From Cyrano to Magoo: My Years With José Ferrer and Jim Backus.

Published in the USA by:

BearManor Media
P.O. Box 71426
Albany, Georgia 31708
www.BearManorMedia.com

All photographs and illustrations are from the personal collection of Jack Lloyd.

All program titles and program descriptions are used in editorial fashion with no intention of infringement of intellectual property rights.

ISBN-10: 1-59393-632-X (alk. paper)
ISBN-13: 973-1-59393-632-7 (alk. paper)

Printed in the United States of America.

Copy Editor: David W. Menefee

Book design and layout by Valerie Thompson

TABLE OF CONTENTS

Acknowledgments . . . 1

Introduction by Peter Marshall . . . 2

Chapter 1 . . . . Music Tours and Then Some . . . 4
Getting Up to Speed . . . 5
Steve Gold Expands My Duties . . . 7
I Begin to Pull My Weight . . . 9

Chapter 2 . . . . Music Tours Become a Way of Life . . . 10
A Straight Accountant Becomes Our Banker . . . 11
We Build a Staff . . . 12
Drugs Take Me . . . 13
Burt Needs Help . . . 16

Chapter 3 . . . . Things Occasionally Work Out for the Best . . . 17
José Ferrer Becomes Part of My Life . . . 19
I Make Friends With an Englishman . . . 21

Chapter 4 . . . . My Prophecy About My Job Becomes a Reality . . . 23
My Life Begins to Change Again . . . 24
Eric Burdon Goes American . . . 25
Steve Gold 1, MGM 0 . . . 25

Chapter 5 . . . . It's Bernie to the Rescue Again . . . 28
My Second Drug Encounter . . . 28
I See A Possibility of Many Dollars Fade Away . . . 31

Chapter 6 . . . . The End Grows Closer . . . 34
Another Beginning . . . 36
Even More About Steve Tolin . . . 37

Chapter 7 . . . . A New Beginning . . . 40
Better Than I Could Say It . . . 42

Chapter 8 . . . . My Circle of Friends Grows . . . 45
Our Relationship and How It Grew . . . 47
There Are Other Opinions . . . 48

	No, He Wasn't Perfect . . . **48**
	Tom Korman Speaks . . . **50**
	Omar Sharif . . . **51**
	More About Omar . . . **53**
Chapter 9	Starting to Act Like a Manager . . . **55**
	How to Get Wanted in a Hurry . . . **56**
	You Don't Have to Be Famous to Get My Attention . . . **57**
	Being Around Joe Made for Some Fun . . . **59**
	Joe is Available for Friends . . . **61**
	Other Plans . . . **62**
Chapter 10	Competition Intensifies for Joe . . . **63**
	More Fun and Games . . . **66**
Chapter 11	Life With Stella . . . **68**
	A Story That is Now Famous . . . **69**
	I Get Around to Some Serious Managing . . . **70**
	I Take a Chance to Spout Off . . . **73**
	We Will Go to Almost Any Extreme . . . **75**
	We All Make a New Friend . . . **76**
	Joe Will Do Almost Anything If It Helps His Kids . . . **78**
Chapter 12	The (Bing) Crosby Clambake . . . **80**
	There's Always Something Else . . . **83**
	Joe is in the Rose Parade on New Year's Day . . . **85**
	Joe, the Lover . . . **85**
	How to be Ready for Whatever Comes . . . **87**
	A Bit About Me . . . **89**
Chapter 13	Some Odds and Ends . . . **90**
	I Do My Part for Charities, Etc. . . . **90**

Portrait Gallery #1: José Ferrer . . . 95

Chapter 14	Jim Backus Calls Me . . . **109**
	A Very Hollywood Story . . . **112**
	Joe Conducts Business Without Me . . . **113**
	We Decide Not to Drink This Trip . . . **114**
	Something Different . . . **115**
	Old Friends . . . **115**
	Reflections on Reading Dr. Mario Stopes Book on Birth Control . . . **117**
Chapter 15	Backus Becomes a Full-Time Client . . . **118**
	You Sometimes Hurt the One You Like . . . **118**
	Investigating Jim's Problems . . . **120**
	Breaks Start Coming Our Way . . . **121**

	We Expand Our Horizons . . . **122**
	We Get Into Routines . . . **125**
Chapter 16	We Begin to Tour and Build a TVQ . . . **126**
	A Bad Rep Debunked . . . **127**
	Interviews Go National . . . **129**
Chapter 17	We Hit the Road Again . . . **133**
	Being Social Isn't Always Fun . . . **133**
	Beverly Hills Doesn't Always Have the Best . . . **135**
	It's Great Getting Popular Again . . . **136**
	The Work Starts Rolling In . . . **139**
	Things Have a Way of Getting Odd . . . **140**
	A Fun Trip and Commercial Shoot . . . **142**
Chapter 18	Jim Gets Desired . . . **145**
	We Return to Philly For a Week . . . **147**
	Jim Greets a Long List of Friends . . . **149**
	Downington is Different . . . **151**
	Jim Lays an Egg, But is Saved . . . **152**
Chapter 19	Backus Becomes My Main Client . . . **154**
	Something About Henny . . . **155**
	What in the World is Troy? . . . **157**
	Golf is More Than a Game . . . **158**
	It's a Different Hollywood Now . . . **159**
	I Go Social . . . **162**
Chapter 20	Jim's Hypochondria Gets Real . . . **165**
	Back Working In Clubs . . . **168**
	It's Good to Be a Star . . . **171**
	I Get Serious About Having Our Own Club . . . **171**
	Everyone Needs a Little Help Sometime . . . **173**
Chapter 21	We Go on the Road Again . . . **176**
	Jim Scores—Just Not On Stage . . . **177**
	Seattle is Different . . . **178**
Chapter 22	Charlie Goldring . . . **181**
	I Meet With the "Owner" of Mr. Magoo . . . **182**
	Things Get Contentious . . . **183**
	How Things Can Get Confused in Hollywood . . . **185**
	Almost the Beginning of an End . . . **187**
Chapter 23	I Start a New Phase of My Life . . . **190**
	We Go Country . . . **191**
	Not All Is Evident . . . **192**
Chapter 24	Change is the Only Constant . . . **193**
	The Peking Opera Gig is Short-Lived . . . **195**

Chapter 25 . . . . Backus and I Re-Connect . . . **196**
It Could Have Been Great . . . **197**

Chapter 26 . . . . A Florida "Vacation" For Jim and Me . . . **199**
Jim Forgets to be Sick . . . **201**
Jim Gets Away from Me . . . **201**
Jim Has Another Movie Offer . . . **202**
Mooch . . . **205**

Chapter 27 . . . . I'm Weaned Off Management . . . **207**
Morocco Comes Calling . . . **207**
My Last Trip for the King . . . **209**

Chapter 28 . . . . I Kind of Wrap Things Up . . . **212**
It Gets Harder for Jim . . . **213**
All Things Must End . . . **215**
I Get a New Hobby—Celebrity Golf . . . **218**
So, I'm Not Quite Done . . . **221**

Portrait Gallery #2: Jim Backus . . . 222

Epilogue . . . 239

Index . . . 243

Acknowledgments

Once you acknowledge the help you are given for a first book, you (I) need to search around for different ways to say pretty much the same things for a subsequent book. It has been my good fortune to be assigned to author David W. Menefee as my editor and guide. Not only has he kept me on the straight and narrow, but he has and is teaching me how to use my computer. Other people to whom I owe many thanks include my son, Robert Lloyd, a columnist for the *Los Angeles Times*, who has gone through this manuscript putting proper diacritical marks where they belong, correcting some grammatical errors, and showing me how to use the "Style" book. My daughter, Alison, and my ever-encouraging wife, Phyllis, have put up with me through this entire project. I also owe a debt of gratitude to author Robert Mills (*The Laugh Makers*) who pushed me to actually get this material published. Of course, I cannot forget the many friends on whom I have, over the years, foisted the many anecdotes in these pages and let me live to put the words on paper.

INTRODUCTION

Jack Lloyd has asked me to write an Introduction to his second book, and while I have never quite understood the necessity for an Introduction to a book I have, as you can see, done it. It seems to me that if the subject matter is of any interest to the reader, nothing anyone can write in a few lines is going to convince anyone to read what he or she is recommending. That said, this particular book deals most with actors José Ferrer and Jim Backus. If you don't know who they were, you probably won't have an interest in reading much farther. However, I'll take a chance and give you a very brief idea.

José Ferrer graduated from Princeton University too many years ago to be of interest to anyone other than an elderly alumnus of that school. He had intended to become an architect, but got sidetracked when Josh Logan—a school chum—talked him into appearing in a school production. I could expand on that, but then you'd have no reason to read the book. Just as a teaser, suffice it to say he won seven Tony Awards and one "Oscar," in addition to a few more nominations.

Jim Backus is, unfortunately, mostly known by two of the characters he played on radio, on television, and even on the big screen. I say "unfortunately" because his reputation as a funny person kept him from being known as the fine actor he was. Some of you may remember him as the voice of Mr. Magoo, the bumbling, near sighted little fellow of the cartoon series. Some of you older folk might recall him as the original Hubert Updyke III, the "richest man in the world," from the old Alan Young radio show (if you even remember Alan Young). Later, Hubert morphed into Thurston Howell III, still the richest man in the world, on *Gilligan's Island*.

Of course, there are more than a few names contained within these pages that may pique your interest, but you'll either have to buy the book or steal it from a friend who managed to obtain a copy by hook or by crook.

PETER MARSHALL

Chapter 1
Music Tours and Then Some

Never one to stay where I felt unloved or where I had ceased to be useful, I left my job of a year as the head of American Productions, the concert production unit of The Beach Boys. All in all, I had worked with them for more than three years, when I walked out the door and into the next phase of my life.

Before I get into that phase, I suppose a very brief résumé should go here. The first time I was asked to write a biography, I opened with: "In the beginning, darkness was upon the face of the earth," immediately skipping ahead to being discharged from the U.S. Navy after WWII. From there, I leaped forward somewhat to matriculating and finally graduating from the University of Southern California.

My first after college job was as a Junior Executive Trainee for a large clothing chain, rising to the second highest, non-family executive before telling the owner's son to "go fuck yourself," leaving with no idea where I'd end up. Obviously, I did end up with a couple of "end ups," including work as an inspector for insurance companies (a sort of detective job), running a chrome replating company, a life insurance salesman (fired for canceling more policies than I sold, and rehired when no one else would work in Watts, the scene of a famous riot), working with a friend in the concert business, and then with The Beach Boys, which more or less brings me to the onset of this book.

After leaving The Beach Boys, I joined a company owned by music producer Jerry Goldstein and his partner, Steve Gold, which operated under the name Music Tours. We had come together when I was contacted by Jerry Goldstein, when he approached The Beach Boys about doing some business together. Jerry and I had actually met earlier, when I hired his rock group, *The Sheep*, for one of our concerts.

Their primary business, and only money-making activity at that time, was producing and selling souvenir posters for music acts, mostly rock and rollers. Later, they changed the name to The Visual Thing and began producing hard cover souvenir books, also for music acts, in addition to the posters. They eventually formed a partnership with the English blues singer, Eric Burdon, and called that division, Far Out Productions.

As I walked in the front door at 250 North Canon Drive on my first day of my new job, Steve Gold was walking out of his office, accompanied by a very sexy, extremely well-endowed blonde. He turned to her and said, "Laura, meet Jack Lloyd, he's an Aries."

She squealed, ran across the room, jumped up, and threw her legs around my waist. I thought, *This is going to be better than I imagined.* I had no idea then that Laura was Steve's girl friend.

By way of explaining Steve and his girl friend, for which I guess the technical term would be "mistress," let me relate the story he told me about their relationship: Steve was still married, with a young daughter, which didn't seem to get in his way when it came to having Laura for his mistress. It never seemed to bother Laura, either.

The New Year's Eve before I joined the company, Steve took his wife out to a posh restaurant for dinner, and when they arrived, Laura was already waiting at the table. Ann was obviously taken aback, having no idea who this gorgeous blonde might be. Steve turned to her and said, "Honey, I'd like you to meet my mistress." And he got away with it.

GETTING UP TO SPEED

One thing about starting a new job is that more often than not, you have no idea just what you're supposed to do. Steve and Jerry showed me to an office that had been the province of a singer-musician everyone called The Elephant, for obvious physical reasons. He was ostensibly in charge of the poster selling operation and spent a good part of his time on the road.

The truth of the matter was that The Elephant was not really in charge of anything, but Steve gave people titles to keep them happy—in lieu of money. For example: after things started going well and the company actually was netting money, Steve and Jerry came into my office and handed me some business cards that read, "Vice President."

I said, "Does this mean more money?"

Together they said, "Of course not."

I suggested they keep the cards and make some that had no title whatever. That way, I could give myself whatever title I felt I needed for that particular moment. I could be the President if I wanted.

Showing me the room that was about to become my office, Steve said, "This is yours, but for now plan to spend some time with us in our office, at least until you get to know the operation." Steve and Jerry shared two sides of the same desk; for anyone else, there was a large leather chair, where I planted myself, and a couch for visitors. In the beginning, it seemed I was destined to hang out and do a lot of laughing at and with Steve and Jerry. Work seemed to be something I would do eventually, if not at that particular moment. It looked as though I had lucked into a job that was going to be a lot of fun, and for more money than I had been making with The Beach Boys.

Until I came on board at The Visual Thing, there seemed to be very little in the way of financial control. I guess they were willing to trade some stealing for some loyalty. Salespeople had been pretty much on their own in that respect. The company bought them an airline ticket and they took their expense money from receipts, which probably actually encouraged—let me call it "misreporting of funds."

It was obvious that an awful lot of money was being wasted by sending our own salespeople out no matter how short or long the tour. I changed that as quickly as I could by utilizing salespeople already located in almost every city. That meant that either the building management, concessionaires, or individuals I met or to whom I was referred by other people in the book business. Of course, there were times I had to send someone on the road, but it was rare.

STEVE GOLD EXPANDS MY DUTIES

At the end of my second or third week at Music Tours, Steve called me into his office with a request. Actually, more like an order.

"We've got a couple of money men coming in from New York, who might be willing to put a million dollars into the company, and I want to do something to impress them. I want you to get me sixteen hookers for an orgy."

"I don't know *any* hookers," I protested. "Where am I going to get sixteen of them?"

"That's your job, go do it."

I knew that some of my friends used hookers, either for themselves or for customers. I called them, got numbers, and made appointments. Every one of the women was less than attractive, a couple downright ugly, and certainly not anyone I would want to give to a couple of guys willing to put up a million dollars. I was beginning to run out of hope when a thought struck me. *Hookers all have answering services.*

So, I called ours, asked for the owner, and pleaded, "I know you must have hookers and call girls on your service, and I desperately need sixteen of them."

She answered that even if they did have some hookers on their service, and she wouldn't admit it, they most likely didn't have sixteen.

"Can you get me *one*?" I begged.

She said she would call me back or have someone contact me.

An hour or so later, a person named Kelly (we won't mention her last name) called and questioned me closely. When she determined I was not a cop and that I was an Aries, (she was a Libra), she agreed to come to the office and discuss the situation. Kelly arrived a couple of hours later, and I took her into my office, where she talked about me being Aries and she being Libra, which meant I could be trusted, or something. Steve finished whatever he was doing, and rang me to bring her to his office. Steve and Kelly got on right away, because, as she later explained to me, he was a Leo, and Leos and Libras also go very well together.

Kelly and I eventually became great friends, even though, or maybe because I was not invited to the orgy. I was also non-judgmental about her work, and I accepted her for herself. Kelly was not your average street hooker. She was a call girl, who charged lots of money for an evening out. Mostly, she dated very important people, charging $200 just to go to dinner. Sex was extra.

She looked a little like Ann-Margret, only not quite as pretty, and got occasional work as an actress. I knew her agent, which seemed to embarrass him somewhat when we ran into one another at a party Kelly threw, but it made no difference to me. He probably didn't want it nosed around that he was representing a prostitute. I tried to help her with her acting career, and every time she felt blue or depressed, she called my house and talked for a couple of hours. If for some reason I wasn't home, she talked to my wife. Kelly was about five-foot six or seven, with a reasonably nice figure, later enhanced a little with silicone that was not particularly obvious. She did have nice legs and a good ass, and she worked a lot. Just not in movies or television.

The end result of her conversation with Steve and Jerry was that Kelly said she could supply seven women in addition to herself. She couldn't bring in the other eight. However, help came from an unexpected quarter. The wife of a friend of Steve's offered to bring seven of her married friends and herself to complete the field.

Being the "company straight," as Steve described me to people, meant that I was not allowed to participate in their drug scenes, which was certainly no problem because practically the only drug I ever used was alcohol, and by that point in my life, only socially. Therefore, I surely could not take part in any debauchery. I was sorry because I had never been to an orgy, other than Spokane, Washington, when I was still with The Beach Boys, and even then I didn't stick around to take part in the actual event. I just delivered my dinner date and split.

While it seems that everyone in attendance at Steve's orgy had a great time, the potential investors never came through with their million dollars.

I BEGIN TO PULL MY WEIGHT

After my so-so success with the hookers, Steve once again called me into his office and said, "So, what have you done so far? When are you going to make changes?"

"Actually," I said, "today is the day. I'm planning to dump about twenty of your employees. I don't see what they do around here except collect a pay check for occasionally rolling posters."

Steve told me to go ahead and do what I wanted, but that I couldn't fire The Elephant because he was also under contract to the company as a musician, or their friend Burt McC., who had been with them from the onset. I argued that in checking all the past records it appeared that they were both stealing, but Steve said, "They don't steal that much. Keep them."

Chapter 2
Music Tours Become a Way of Life

In 1969, following the success of Woodstock, music festivals had become the rage of the rock and roll business, or were in the process of becoming so. In the spring of that year, a Los Angeles group put together a festival they called Newport '69, which would be held at the north campus of the California State University at Northridge, known familiarly as Devonshire Downs from the days when the grandstands and race track were used for the San Fernando Valley Fair.

We rented a booth to sell posters, and did extremely well. Without going into detail about the concert, I will say that never had, nor have I, seen so many people freaked-out on drugs; so many bad trips in one place, although a Blind Faith concert a few months later in Santa Barbara at the Earl Warren show grounds came pretty close. The first aid tent was near our booth, and there was a steady stream of people being led, carried, or dragged there.

Burt McC. was there every day and worked the booth along with me, my son, and a few others from the company, including the company secretary/do everything, Lois, and Bob Gordon, one of our two photographers. The other photographer, Ron Rafaelli, eventually achieved a minor notoriety as a producer of pornographic stills and movies.

Next to our space was a booth selling battery-powered yo-yos, which lit up when you spun them. Burt bought a couple, and spent the night in front of our booth spinning them. He probably sold more yo-yos than posters.

He eventually got a job with them when he went to a rock festival in Atlanta for us, from which, incidentally, he failed to return until several months later, and of course, without any money from poster sales. I'll get to his return somewhere down the line.

By show time, the organizers seemed to have taken a powder with the receipts and were nowhere to be found. A five-foot one-inch twenty-year-old girl, who must have weighed about ninety pounds, was left alone on the stage to get the whole thing going. Jackie Balzano, a tough little Italian from Brooklyn's Red Hook District, just stepped forward and took over. She shoved big equipment men around, took no shit from anyone, and ran the whole show. She impressed the heck out of me. The whole fiasco was dubbed by Steve Gold "The Devonshire Downer," for obvious reasons.

A STRAIGHT ACCOUNTANT BECOMES OUR BANKER

Steve and Jerry had eyes to lease an office building on Sunset Boulevard, a two-story edifice they eventually hoped to buy. The company—really only our division of it—was bringing in very good money by then, but because they had no credit rating and certainly no legitimate financial statement, they needed help.

Help came in the form of Bernard S., a very successful and wealthy CPA with offices in Beverly Hills. Steve Gold had once been a very straight, three-button-suit CPA until he discovered LSD. Bernie was made-to-order for him.

Oddly enough, I knew Bernie from my wife's high school days. He was going with a girl friend of hers, and we had become friendly. Bernie was now the financial advisor to one of the most famous cowboy actors, a job he took, I believe, right out of college, working for a percentage of the star's income. Bernie had become so wealthy that he was then a patron of the arts, and at least the part-owner, of a record company.

The building Steve coveted was a combination of offices and sound stage, although the stage hadn't been used in some time. The offices were on both floors across the front with the entire back portion of the building relegated to the stage. They planned to turn the sound stage into a recording studio for Far Out Productions.

One night a month or so after the move to Sunset Boulevard, Steve, Jerry, Lois, and I, and probably a few others from the company, were at The Whisky A-Go-Go, where I ran into Jackie from "The Devonshire Downer." She wasn't working, and I said, "I told you that if I ever had a chance to hire you, I'd do it. Do you want to go to work for me?" She did.

WE BUILD A STAFF

For a time, Jackie and I did everything ourselves, contacting concessionaires and individual booksellers in various cities, and letting them handle our sales. That change alone cut expenses enormously. We even did all the shipping ourselves, and Jackie kept on top of the sellers to make sure we got not only our money, but all the unsold posters. It seems that the salespeople who worked for Music Tours rarely bothered bringing the posters back; too much trouble. They were generally "lost in shipping." Jackie never lost a dime or a poster for the company.

Not too long after Jackie went to work for me, I hired a fellow named Wes, the boyfriend of Pat B., one of the women I worked with at The Beach Boys' office. He needed work desperately, and I knew he could be trusted.

The last member of my staff was a secretary. Loree was a beautiful girl with very prominent breasts, which were two of the reasons I hired her. However, the primary reason was that she was highly qualified, more than capable of handling the work, and even had a connection to the music business in a way.

At that time, Loree was dating Cory Wells, a member of Three Dog Night, and the job kept her close to the music business and her boyfriend. Jackie and I kept telling her she should wear a bra, or by the time she was thirty, her breasts would be down around her knees, but she preferred to skip the advice and the support.

A couple of months after we had our complete staff, I confided to Jackie that I might have made a mistake in coming to that company because "In six months, I'll have worked myself out of a job."

Jackie was already capable of making the deals with sellers around the country, and because of her personality, she had as good, if not better, relationship with some of them than I.

A brief description of some of the company's staff may be in order. I have mentioned Bob Gordon and Rafaelli. Bob was a big man, heavier than I, at about 250 pounds, and he was soft-spoken. He was very laid back, a gentle man and an outstanding photographer, who did most of the photography for the posters. Rafaelli, who did much of the work for the souvenir books when we expanded from the poster business, was not exactly on staff. In exchange for the photographic equipment Steve and Jerry got him, he was available for any work at no charge. I used to wonder if they ever paid anyone for the equipment, or if they somehow stiffed some poor purveyor.

Up to that point, I was never invited to the parties in the hills for the simple reason that I was always going to be the company straight. I have no idea whether or not the company secretary, Lois, was into using drugs like Eric Burdon did. Eric had joined with Steve and Jerry to form Far Out Productions, but I don't think Jerry was much into LSD, certainly not like Steve, who told me he frequently dropped acid eight or nine times a day. He explained, ". . . only every other day," because the day after he was on acid, it didn't work; it just kept him awake.

I was at a company party at Steve and Jerry's home in the hills the first time Lois dropped acid. She and Bob Gordon left the party together, and went down to Griffith Park. They were both into "pretty" things, so acid was never going to give either of them a bad trip. The next day, Lois described the "rivers of paisley flowing under the grass in the park."

DRUGS TAKE ME

Lois's first experiment with LSD, as it turned out, was also mine. I was not, as I have said, into any drug other than booze, and really never had any particular interest until I read about Huxley's use of LSD and how psychiatrists were using it to get deeper into the minds of their patients. That made me a little curious. I was also a lot afraid. One day, I said to Steve, "I'd like to try acid, but I'd only do it if you were with me."

A month or so later, Steve said, "Tonight's the night."

"For what?" I asked.

"We're having a party at the house, and you're invited, and tonight you can have your first acid trip. I'll be near by all night."

With some serious trepidation, I arrived at the house a little earlier than everyone else, as Steve had asked. He gave me a little tablet, which I swallowed. I waited. Nothing happened for an hour, and he suggested we take one more. I did, and within minutes, some hallucinations began. What appeared to be the molecules of Steve's eyeglasses started revolving around his head. I thought that was nice. Colors began to intensify, and I was satisfied I could handle the drug.

Then, Steve said, "I think we should drop one more time. You're a pretty big guy and can handle it."

I did, but shouldn't have. Within a few minutes, I felt so weary I could hardly stand.

Steve explained that "acid" intensified your emotions, or in this case, the fact that I was already tired.

I went to the couch in the living room and stretched out on my side. I felt a chill, and someone brought me a blanket. Then, my hallucinations took an odd form. I began introspecting like crazy. My whole life was playing on a record spinning in front of me. Every so often, I could jog myself back to reality, and once, I looked up to see Beach Boy Mike Love's wife, Susan, sitting on the couch next to me. She sat down just to see how I was doing.

"I didn't know you did drugs," she said.

"I don't. Can't you tell?"

I learned later that she was a regular at Steve's drug parties.

"Now you know why kids should never take drugs," Steve said when he, too, stopped by the check on me. "You know your mind is being affected temporarily by a chemical. Kids don't realize that and that's why they freak out. You *know* it will wear off."

Bob Gordon sat down at the end of the couch, and right then I learned something about myself, something of which I was not proud. I had suspected Bob was a homosexual. Don't ask why. I have no idea, except perhaps that he was such a soft-spoken, gentle man. As I watched him, he seemed to be moving closer to me, although I realized he hadn't moved at all. I said, "Stay over there."

Bob replied, "Don't worry, Jack. I'm not a fag."

The next day, when I recovered from my drug-induced condition, I went to Bob and apologized. I told him about being approached when I was in the navy and never realized that it left me with an uncomfortable feeling about homosexuals. Drugs brought that navy experience back to mind, and it cured me of ever having those feelings again.

I don't know how long I lay there thinking about myself, but at some point I felt an overwhelming urge to urinate, and didn't particularly care to do it on the couch. Steve was nearby—he checked on me every five minutes or so—and I said, "Steve, I've got to go—bad. I don't think I can walk that far."

"Sure you can. Get up and do it."

"Are you sure?"

"Positive. You can do anything you want. Do it."

I stood up and felt as though I was about fifteen feet tall, top heavy and about to keel over. However, I believed Steve and stepped over and around people, as I made my way across the room to the john.

I thought I was pissing for an hour and that it would never stop. I also began to feel sick to my stomach, so I walked out of the house to get some air.

I saw an old car, a Jaguar I think, with a square trunk and big rubber bumper guards. The trunk was slightly ajar, and my mind converted it to a hippopotamus with its mouth opening and closing. "Great," I thought. "I wonder if Disney knows about this." I decided not to go back into the house, but to stay out in the air. Being still tired, I lay down in the front seat of my car. As people left, they stopped to see me and ask how I felt. By then, I felt fine, just tired, and said so.

After an hour or so, the nausea had gone completely, and I went back into the house to find the party over and all the guests gone. Steve was sitting in a chair watching television. The colors on the screen were wild and out of whack. I said, "I hope that's the television and not me."

Steve assured me it was the television. "Well," he said, what did you think of it?"

"I found it very interesting, except when I got sick to my stomach."

"I think this acid had some strychnine in it, that's why you got sick. I didn't know. It was supposed to be pure."

I said, "I think once was enough. I did see some funny things though. I even thought I saw midgets running around the room."

"That's because there *were* midgets running around the room," he said.

At some point during the evening, Bob and Lois had gone down to Sunset Boulevard to recruit more merry-makers. There were lots of people doing drugs then and it wasn't hard to round up a bunch of people interested in dropping acid or speed, especially for free. That's where they found the two dwarfs.

"Speed," methamphetamine, is how they got posters rolled then. We didn't own a rolling machine yet, so someone would go to the Boulevard, round up a few speed freaks, and get them rolling and stuffing posters into cellophane sleeves.

BURT NEEDS HELP

Oh, yes. Burt's return. We hadn't heard from him for a few months following his trip to Atlanta. One night, some time after midnight, the telephone rang at my home. It was Burt. It seemed he had returned to Los Angeles a few days earlier, but that night, he was stopped by the Beverly Hills police for running a red light or something. A routine check revealed several outstanding tickets and a couple of warrants, so he was arrested. He needed someone to come bail him out.

Phyllis and I drove to the station, where I ran into another friend, who was also named Burt, and he was my trainer way back a "lifetime" before when I was an insurance inspector. He was then a civilian employee of the Beverly Hills Police Department, working as a desk sergeant. He loved the job because he got to wear a uniform and carry a gun. His being there helped smooth the way for the other Burt's release. I put up the bail money, which I got back the next day from Steve Gold, and waited while he retrieved his belongings. I watched as the envelope was opened and the contents dumped on the counter. Burt's entire personal effects consisted of six electric yo-yos and about 60¢ in cash.

Chapter 3
Things Occasionally Work Out for the Best

While I was busy having misgivings about taking the job, which I now realized for certain had a finite future, moving from The Beach Boys to Music Tours proved to be one of the smartest, or most fortunate, things I ever did. Also, things began to move quickly in a couple of other directions for me after the first five or six months with Music Tours. The forerunner of my next change actually began shortly after we moved to the Sunset Boulevard offices, although I had no inkling of it at the time.

I was teaching Wes how to work with concessionaires and other on-site book-sellers, but felt the need to take him on the road and have him actually sell posters himself and meet some concessionaires face to face. The opportunity arose, when Glen Campbell booked some dates in the Midwest. We decided to join him for three of them, starting in Chicago. Then, we'd go on to two more in Wisconsin, before we returned to Los Angeles.

I reserved first class airline seats to Chicago and rooms at the Water Tower Inn. As we settled in our seats, I noticed that directly across the aisle was the great American actor, José Ferrer. He was in the window seat with the aisle seat vacant.

Back in 1950, when I was still a student at USC, Mr. Ferrer came to lecture the film school on the making of *Cyrano de Bergerac* as a motion picture as opposed to the stage production in which he also starred and for which he earned the Best Actor Tony Award. The lecture was scheduled for a 600-seat auditorium, but about 2,000 people showed up. They had to move everyone over to Bovard Auditorium, which rapidly filled to capacity. I found a place in the front row of the balcony.

Cyrano de Bergerac had been my favorite play since reading it almost by accident in high school. José Ferrer's lecture was fascinating, and when he recited some of the dramatic speeches from the play, standing alone in a pin spot on an otherwise dark stage, I was practically overcome with emotion. It was the single most impressive acting job I had ever seen. I had an urge to tell him that, but he seemed very preoccupied with a book in one hand and a stenographer's notebook in which he was busily writing in the other. I later learned that he was translating *Siegfried* from English to German, "just to keep my hand in."

After being fed, Wes and I were in conversation with two stewardesses working in the coach section, hoping to get lucky, of course, but without success. José had gone to the toilet, and I noticed him coming back. As he was not writing or reading, I took advantage of his vulnerability and stopped him. I related my USC story to him, and he asked me to join him in the empty seat. I did, and then I brought Wes over.

As men will do, within a few moments, we were discussing our businesses, the reasons we were on the plane, and women. I offered to drive him into downtown Chicago if he needed a lift, as we had to rent a car for the trip to Wisconsin anyway. I told him we'd be at the National Car Rental desk.

"Maybe I'll see you there," he replied.

Wes and I were filling out rental papers when José approached. He decided to take us up on our offer, and I said, "I've never been to O'Hare (Chicago's main airport). It wasn't built when I left town, so you'll have to navigate."

"Not a problem," he said, "I've been here many times."

He was in Chicago to re-join the national company of *Man of La Mancha* in which he was, of course, starring. He had taken the weekend off to attend his youngest son's confirmation in Los Angeles and was returning for Tuesday's performance.

José's directions from the airport to downtown were so good that it took us two hours to make what should have been a twenty to thirty-minute trip. We dropped him at the Ambassador East Hotel, and went on to our own hotel, fully expecting that I would never hear from him again, even though he asked me for, and I gave him, my card, one without a title.

Wes and I did our work in Chicago and Wisconsin, and then we returned to Los Angeles, and I thought no more about José Ferrer except to tell my wife all about it.

JOSÉ FERRER BECOMES PART OF MY LIFE

Three weeks later, I received a telephone call from Stella Magee. Stella was a good friend dating back to my days in the concert business when I worked with Irving Granz, the younger brother of famed jazz impresario Norman Granz. She was executive secretary to Jerry Perenchio, then one of the top rock and roll agents in Los Angeles, from whom we used to buy acts. Whenever there were problems, I would go directly to Stella, who always managed to straighten out everything.

A little more than a year earlier, while I was still with Irving, she had moved back to New York. Although I had her telephone number, I was never able to contact her when I was going to be or already was in New York. I was surprised to hear from her.

"Where are you?" I almost shouted. I told her how often I had tried to contact her and she explained only that she went out of town on weekends.

"We have a mutual friend," she said.

"Who?"

"Someone you met on an airplane."

"Stella, you know me. I'm always on an airplane and I meet a lot of people. Who is it?"

"José Ferrer."

"José Ferrer! How do you know him?"

"I live with him," she said simply.

She related the following story: when José returned to their room in Chicago, he told her about meeting "a young concert promoter" on the airplane (I was forty-two then, and fifteen years younger than he) and went on to describe me. Stella said, "Oh, you must mean Jack Lloyd." He practically went into shock.

Now that the *La Mancha* had moved to Los Angeles, he had Stella call and invite us to a performance. Stella said she would leave tickets at the box office.

The night of the show, there was nothing under my name, José's, or Stella's. I found Gordon Davidson, the director of the Music Center, and asked if he knew anything about it. He didn't.

"Why don't you go down to the dressing rooms and ask Mr. Ferrer?"

"It's all right with you?" I asked, somewhat surprised.

"Sure. Go ahead."

I went down below the theater and sent my card back to José's dressing room. A few seconds later, his booming baritone echoed down the hall. "Hey Jack, come on back." At the time, he was busy applying his own makeup, and it really astounded me that he would let anyone in the dressing room while he was getting ready for a performance.

After he told me Stella had the tickets and should arrive momentarily, we exchanged pleasantries for awhile. I really didn't know what to say to him other than to thank him for inviting us. Before I returned to Phyllis, I asked, "What do I call you, 'José' or 'Mr. Ferrer?'"

"My friends call me 'Joe,'" he answered.

"Okay," I said, "*what* do I call you?"

"Call me Joe."

"Why don't you let me take you to lunch while you're here? Just to thank you for the tickets," I said finally.

"Great. Give me a call." He wrote down a telephone number of the house he was renting for the length of the run. I called on Monday, and José said, "Instead of going out, bring your swim suit over and we can go for a dip in the pool. Besides, I have a great cook and she can make lunch for us."

I did go to lunch at the house. We swam for a long time, and I met some of his children, who came to use the pool because theirs was full of leaves and hadn't been filled with water since Joe and Rosemary Clooney divorced. We shared some drinks and talked about his plans to produce *Cyrano de Bergerac* on Broadway as a musical.

Joe had already employed the men who had written the lyrics and did the film score for the motion picture version of *Song of Norway*. They had produced a masterful score for his "book," a new translation of the Rostand play. Joe spoke perfect French. One night, he called from Florida to play me a tape of the entire score over the telephone.

We decided we would both try to find possible angels, which is the show business term for someone who puts money into a new venture such as our musical. Joe and I saw each other frequently during the time *Man of La Mancha* was in Los Angeles, and from that time, kept in close touch by telephone until he returned for a television role.

During that entire time, I was still working with Steve and Jerry, who by then had changed the name of the poster company to The Visual Thing. Because I had not yet become Joe's manager—that was to come a little later—I made just one more short trip for the company.

I MAKE FRIENDS WITH AN ENGLISHMAN

With less and less to do selling posters, I started spending more time in Steve and Jerry's office, but never too long. I had long since learned that you didn't have to *be* busy, you just had to *appear* busy when you worked for someone else. I began casting around for something else to do and to create a new position of some kind for myself.

There was one other employee with the company with whom I became friendly: an Englishman named Nick Hague. Several months before I joined the company, Goldstein and Gold had struck a deal with guitarist Jimi Hendrix to produce a film of his European concert tour. With Steve's girlfriend, Laura, in tow, they did so much drugs and so much partying that, as they neared the end of the tour, they had little or no usable footage in the can. The London concert would be their last opportunity. Someone had them contact Nick Hague.

Nick was then a producer and director for Rediffusion Television and had directed many segments of *Top Of The Pops*, the #1 rock and roll show in England. He also had won awards for music documentaries. Nick was able to produce enough good footage to edit into a film, when combined with a few cuts from the balance of the tour.

Steve Gold convinced Nick he should come to Los Angeles, become a part of the company, and edit the film. They bought him a one-way ticket.

He was then living in the Hollywood Hills above Sunset Boulevard, and I picked him up on my way to the office from my home in the San Fernando Valley. Oh, yes, *he* got to go to the orgy.

Four or five months passed, and Nick still had nothing to do because Steve decided he wanted to shoot additional studio footage, and he wanted his girl friend, Laura, to produce it. It was taking forever, largely, I suppose, because he and Laura were so involved sexually that there wasn't much time for anything else; that, a shortage of funds, and some difficulty with Warner Bros. Music, which claimed ownership of the rights to Jimi Hendrix' music.

Nick decided to do something about the sound stage to occupy *his* time that was otherwise relegated to going out to lunch with me and hanging around Steve and Jerry's office hoping something would happen.

When I was with them in the office, life seemed to be one continual good time. Something was always happening to give us a laugh. For example, Steve had been given a whiskey decanter, topped with a replica of that famous statue located, I think, in Belgium—the one of a little boy pissing in a fountain. You pressed down on his head and a stream of booze would pour from the spout which represented a penis.

One day, a visitor helped himself to a drink. He took one swig and spit it out. "Christ," he said, this is piss!"

"Of course, it is," said Steve, "what do expect to come out of a cock?"

CHAPTER 4
My Prophecy About My Job Becomes Reality

In my book, *Endless Summer: My Life With The Beach Boys*, I mentioned that when Irving Granz and I were producing *The Beach Boys Summer Spectacular* in San Francisco, I was approached by a young man, Steve Tolin, who wanted me to hear a singer he was managing. I liked Steve and his client, but we had very little contact after that, and none at all in perhaps six months, when out of the blue, he called. He had moved to Los Angeles to work with impresario Dick Clark.

Steve, who was always hustling, met Clark and ended up doing some work for him in San Francisco. Clark was sufficiently impressed that he hired him on a full-time basis to develop new ideas for his company.

It didn't take Steve very long to realize that Clark was taking credit for everything he did, and that he was never going to get any personal recognition, which was not what he had in mind when he took the job. Steve had been hoping to build a reputation for himself in Los Angeles and broaden his own horizons.

Another reason Steve came to Los Angeles was to make enough money to publish a show business annual that he planned to call *The Official Talent and Booking Directory*. In it, he would list all the agents, managers, record labels, all the acts, and whatever else he could think of. It was going to take considerable time and money, mostly because of the research involved. By working for someone else, and getting a regular paycheck, he figured he would be able to work on the book part-time.

I introduced him to Steve and Jerry, and they offered him office space, an assistant, and a telephone in exchange for a partnership in the book. It seemed like a good deal for Steve.

Unfortunately, Steve never got the research help he was promised, because Goldstein and Gold were very long on promises, but very short on delivery. They were experts at putting things off with a laugh.

Steve Tolin ended up working days and nights, until he realized there was no future for him with Goldstein and Gold. If he wasn't going to make any money, he could do that anywhere and not have to give away half his project.

One night, after Steve found someone who would work with him on "spec," he dropped by my office to let me know he was moving out—right then. He found a small place where he could work, and to finance his project, he planned to publish a magazine on the order of *Where* and the other throwaway publications available in hotels and restaurants everywhere.

MY LIFE BEGINS TO CHANGE AGAIN

Steve called the magazine, *What's Happening*, and it would cover all facets of entertainment in Los Angeles and Orange Counties. He wanted me to join him, although there would be no salary for either of us until we developed some advertising income. One thing could always be said about Steve: he was persistent and he was thorough. He had already investigated the advertising potential and created a "dummy" magazine to use in conjunction with advertising sales, and he kept after me to go with him. It looked good, and I told him I would consider it.

The Visual Thing was going strong, and I was still making money for the corporation, and in fact, more than earning my keep with the poster sales business. I was not yet ready to turn it over to my assistants.

Besides, this was the perfect job in that whenever Joe Ferrer was in town, I could be with him. In fact, Steve and Jerry encouraged it because they wanted to do a photo-driven book about him. They even sent their chief photographer, Ron Rafaelli, to the house Joe was renting to do a preliminary photo shoot. A huge picture he took of Joe and me hangs in my office today.

ERIC BURDON GOES AMERICAN

Because there were always drugs around, there were also young women around, mostly at Steve and Jerry's, which may have been what attracted the English blues singer, Eric Burdon, formerly of Eric Burdon and The Animals, a very popular English blues group, to Steve and Jerry in the first place.

Eric had moved to Los Angeles more or less permanently, and Jerry was hot to produce a record album for him. They started combing the area for a back-up band, sort of an American version of The Animals, if they could find one.

Peter Rosen, another employee of the company, really a musician who worked with Jerry, discovered a group called The Night Riders, an eleven-piece rock, blues, and soul group working in the San Fernando Valley.

Steve and Jerry met with the band and the group was reduced to seven. Steve re-named them War, because liked the idea of using the slogan "War is Coming."

Peter and I eventually were involved in managing a group that could have had gigantic success if they hadn't started experimenting. I'll get to that later.

STEVE GOLD 1, MGM 0

MGM Records and its president Mike Curb were more than anxious to sign Eric, who was still a prestigious name. Mike Lloyd, Curb's top producer, once told me that Curb had put more than a hundred rock groups under contract, all of whom were given signing bonuses, and none of whom were ever recorded. Eventually, they were all released.

Steve, as stoned on acid as he was much of the time, could be—and was—a great negotiator. The funny thing was that he was so outrageous all the time that everyone presumed he was stoned even when he wasn't. As a result, he could get away with being straight just as long as he maintained his act of insanity. For all his weirdness, Steve was the sanest crazy man I ever met; self destructive, yes, but incredible to watch.

Steve Gold, to my way of thinking, eventually pulled off the contract of the century, perhaps of all time, with MGM. Mike Curb, head of the label, had been vacillating about signing Eric for several weeks when Steve demanded a meeting in Curb's office. I believe that Mike Curb was terrified of him, and so he signed the contract rather than having to deal with him any more.

The story is told by people who witnessed the event that Steve Gold grabbed Curb by the shirt, backed him against the wall, and demanded, "Sign the contract, you fucking faggot!"

Curb said, "Why do you always call me a fucking faggot?"

Steve replied, "Because you're a fucking faggot. Now sign the contract."

I know that MGM's head attorney was in Mike's office when the deal was signed. Mike asked him what to do and Dick Whitehouse said, in essence, "Go ahead and sign it."

MGM agreed to produce two albums a year for Eric and guarantee sales of 100,000 units on each one. Instead of paying Eric a performer's royalty on actual sales, they had to pay Far Out Productions for the LP jackets. In that way, Steve maintained absolute control of sales. MGM couldn't sell merchandise "out the back door," as some record labels were known to do. By doing it that way, Eric and Far Out very likely made more than they would have from royalties.

In addition, if MGM wanted to release a single, they had to buy the paper sleeves from Far Out. Steve, still the accountant and ever the con man, had already met and convinced the owner of a paper goods manufacturing business to make and print the jackets for a ridiculously low price.

Not only did MGM have to buy 200,000 album covers a year, they had to make payments every thirty days, which gave Steve, Jerry, and Eric a steady income. Jerry once told me that not only did the payments have to arrive by a certain date, but if MGM was ten days late, they had to pay a penalty of 10,000 additional jackets.

A week or two later, Steve received a call from Dick Whitehouse, MGM's head counsel. He wanted to modify the tape sales deal with regard to Canada. It seems that the way it was structured, MGM would lose 50¢ on every tape they sold there. On top of that, they suddenly came to the realization that the contract they signed was for Eric Burdon only. War's name did not appear anywhere.

Steve said, and I am absolutely paraphrasing him here, "Why should it? You bought Eric Burdon." They presumed that Eric and War came as a unit, like Eric Burdon and The Animals. Steve said in essence, "Whatever gave you that idea? I never mentioned anything about War. He was already in negotiations with United Artists Records for the band. Eric Burdon and War fit like hand to glove, and Jerry had a good feel for producing the group. Eric and the band appeared together a few times at the Whisky and The Troubadour where Jerry taped a live album, which, while sensational, was never released. There was no doubt they were going to be successful.

War, as I said, consisted of seven musicians, six black and one white. The white musician was Lee Oskar, an outstanding blues harmonica player, who went on to more and greater success as a single act a year or two later. The band, all seven of them, wanted to call themselves the Seven Man Nigger Band, but got no favorable votes from Steve or Jerry. Besides, whatever Steve Gold wanted, Steve Gold generally got.

Chapter 5
It's Bernie to the Rescue Again

As a full-fledged musical entrepreneur, Steve Gold felt the need for a prestigious residence. He located a mansion in Beverly Hills, but as there was no way he and Jerry could pass muster on a lease. Once more, Bernie S. rode to the rescue. I believe the lease was made in his name, which I'd bet he eventually came to regret. As I have no proof of that last remark, it's purely speculation.

My recollection of the place was that it was fenced completely, with a fairly long and steep driveway up to the house. There was a gigantic living room with adjacent wet bar and den, and a full dining room. The bedrooms were all on the second floor. It seemed to be the perfect party house. I went there only twice.

The first time was a party in celebration of Eric Burdon's contract with MGM Records. The house was overflowing with people. By then, Jon Parks from The Beach Boys office had taken my place, and for some reason, he was there, probably having something to do with the poster deal. As they say, booze and wine were flowing like water, and drugs were flowing in equal abundance.

MY SECOND DRUG ENCOUNTER

A new friend, "Stretch" Adler, formerly President of a major television network, was there and was already about two sheets out of three to the wind by the time I arrived. He was the first to greet me.

Someone brought out a huge sheet cake, and everyone dug in. Actually, Stretch handed me a big piece. "Spice cake," he said. I loved spice cake, so I ate it all. Shortly thereafter, someone said to me, "You know it's loaded, don't you?"

I didn't. The people who made the cake supposedly dumped a kilo—2.2 pounds—of grass into the mixture. Although that seemed fairly impossible, I am in no position to question the word of someone who actually knew something about marijuana. An hour or so went by, and since nothing was happening, I presumed I was immune to pot. I knew it must have been potent because Stretch came up to me, practically weeping, and he exclaimed, "Here, take this. I know those bastards don't pay you enough money." With that, he stuffed two $100 dollar bills in my hand.

I tried to refuse it, but he kept insisting. Finally, I said, "Okay, Stretch, but I'll give it back to you tomorrow."

The hour was growing late and Jon and I had to leave. Since I had come to the party in his car, I left with him, returning to the office for mine. About half a mile from the mansion, the drug hit us simultaneously. The only way I can describe the feeling is that the world almost came to a stop. It certainly came to an extremely *slow*.

I remembered Bruce Johnston of The Beach Boys telling me how marijuana affected him when he first tried it, and I felt the same way. It seemed as though it was taking us forever to reach a stoplight, which actually seemed to be receding and getting closer at the same time. I looked at Jon's speedometer and although it felt like we were driving five miles an hour, we were actually doing thirty-five.

I'm not stupid, and while I was worried about driving under the influence of a drug, I was reasonably certain I would be able to handle it because I discovered I could force myself back to reality, even if for only a few minutes at a stretch. I was fully aware that being drugged, my reactions would be very much impaired, and I would have to compensate for that. Fear sometimes makes you smart, too.

I made sure to stay in only one lane as I drove home. I kept the speedometer exactly at thirty-five whenever traffic allowed me to get up to that speed. I started and stopped in relationship to the vehicles in front of me, and even though stoplights seemed to recede as I approached them, I was intelligent enough to realize that they were not. When I reached the freeway, I got into the right hand lane and stayed there, maintaining an even fifty-five miles per hour.

However, I had one other small problem. It was also my anniversary, or some other special event for which I had to purchase a present for my wife. I stopped in Van Nuys to buy a gift. I once more realized the potency of the drug, when I was approached by a saleslady to see if I needed help. I had been standing still for almost ten minutes, staring at the object I held in my hand.

Once more forcing myself back to reality, I made the purchase, drove home, showered, dressed, and went out for the evening with no one, I'm sure, the wiser. I discovered that marijuana ingested takes up to eight hours to leave the system, at least out of mine.

The other party I attended at the mansion, this time with Phyllis (my wife if you've forgotten), was either on Christmas or New Year's Eve. Everyone in the company except Steve Gold, Eric Burdon, and my young assistant, Jackie, was in the living room when we arrived, all pretty much stoned or well on the way. By the time the trio came downstairs and joined the party on the first floor, Eric and Steve had in one way or another ingested just about every form of drug in the house. Jackie brought some small orange tablets she called "Peace Pills."

At one point, Steve Gold was lying supine on the living room floor and exclaiming, "My god, I can't move."

Phyllis and I spent what little time we stayed at the party in the bar area, where we sipped a glass or two of very good champagne and watched everyone else scattered about the living room floor, stoned out of their gourds. If they were communicating with one another, it had to be telepathically. I suppose they were, or thought they were, having a good time, but to me they were just boring.

There was one other huge party there. I think it was mostly for musicians and Eric's friends. I wasn't invited, which didn't disturb me in the least. My young assistant, Jackie, was stationed at the bottom of the driveway with a clipboard, checking names. It was a very exclusive invitation list.

People in that scene have a way of finding out about parties like that, and often show up uninvited. Eric and Steve didn't want the place overrun by too many weirdoes. One carload of musicians drove up to the gate and tried to get in, but Jackie wouldn't let them because she didn't have their names on her list. She knew who they were, but to her, orders were orders.

Mick Jagger yelled, "We're the Rolling Stones, for god's sake . . . let us in."

Jackie told him, "Get fucked. You're not on the list, you don't get in." She later told me, "If it had been The Jefferson Airplane, I would have let them in. Them, I like." Finally, she asked the rent-a-cop to check with Eric before she relented and let them in.

I SEE A POSSIBILITY OF MANY DOLLARS FADE AWAY

I mentioned earlier that Peter Rosen and I once formed a management team. He had been playing around town with a jazz combo, featuring himself and Darius Brubeck, son of famed pianist Dave Brubeck, and he thought that we might be able to market them. Peter later replaced himself with an acoustic bassist, who was a *Down Beat* winner.

He also found a drummer who formerly worked with Edgar Winter's band, and who just might have been one of the ten best drummers I ever heard, and I have heard most of the greats, including Gene Krupa, Louis Bellson, Buddy Rich, and others such as Philly Joe Jones, Cozy Cole, and Max Roach.

"Maruga," as he was calling himself—his real name was Steve Bookvich—could do unbelievable things on the drums. Not like today's rock and roll drummers, who are basically mono-dimensional. The trio was so good that when I went to Joe Smith, then head of Elektra Records, he gave them a studio to rehearse in for as long as they wanted, and guaranteed them an album whenever they felt ready to record.

One night, when Rosemary Clooney and José Ferrer were at least temporarily back on good terms, I took them all to play at Rosemary's home on Roxbury Drive in Beverly Hills. Joe and Rosey declared the group to have an enormous future.

Joe said to me, "You know, the piano Darius was using was the one George Gershwin used when he composed *Rhapsody in Blue*. He probably used it to compose a lot of other songs, because the house had belonged to Gershwin before Joe bought it. George's brother, Ira, lived in the house next door."

Peter and I had visions of making big money with that group. He was so happy that one day he decided to celebrate our good fortune with heroin, a drug he used back in New York, but which he hadn't done since his marriage more than a year earlier. His wife found him on the floor, not quite blue, and rushed him to the hospital barely in time to save his life. He did it once more, but that time, she didn't get home soon enough. One of the saddest things I ever did in my life was to deliver a eulogy at the grave.

Oh, yes . . . the group. Whatever happened to them? Well, I booked them at Donte's, a popular jazz club in North Hollywood. The owners were very excited to have a jazz group fronted by the son of Dave Brubeck. Elektra Records sent a couple of A & R men to the gig.

I arrived at the club to find that "Maruga's" drums were nowhere in sight. I found him and asked him what was going on. He said, "I'm going to play finger drums tonight. Don't worry, it'll be great." Having heard him play finger drums before, I knew he could create a very exciting sound, and while I had some minor reservations, there was nothing I could do about it at that late hour. I thought, *Okay, maybe it'll work out.*

One of the club owners and I sat down at the bar waiting to hear what I knew was going to be incredible music, only what came out was totally unfamiliar to me. Sunny asked, "What the hell is that?"

I could only answer, "I have no idea."

What I didn't know until later was that "Maruga" had gotten himself involved in some sort of east Indian mysticism, and had in the week before the gig converted the bass player. Darius, who was already heavily into Scientology, was immune to this new philosophy. The "music," or whatever it was they were playing, was apparently a reflection of "Maruga's" suddenly change in thinking, I guess. They were no longer playing what got them there in the first place. Darius, sweet guy that he was, just went along with them. He was, I imagined, happy just to be playing. In fact, what made the music even stranger was that he seemed to be playing jazz, while everyone else was on a different page—or planet.

That night was the end of the group. There was no way I could book them anywhere the way they were playing, I didn't even want to try. Elektra withdrew their offer, and I withdrew from the group.

The next day, I called Stretch Adler and said, "Stretch, come on over, I want to give you back the $200 you gave me."

"What money?" He was beside himself.

I reminded him of the $200 he forced me to take, but he refused to believe me.

"I don't remember giving you any money. I *wouldn't* have given you any money. I *never* give away money."

I said, "Okay, but I've got a couple hundred bucks here that belong to you, and if you want it, come on over."

He came over, I gave him the money, and he took me out for a four-martini lunch at the Villa Nova Restaurant by way of thanks.

Chapter 6
The End Grows Closer

As I predicted, my own work load was continuing to decrease, and I was certain my future with The Visual Thing/Far Out Productions was very limited. To keep myself busy when no one was on tour, I got involved with Nick Hague in running the sound stage. Not that there was enough work for us both; there was barely enough for Nick, but we created enough "busy work," and we were enjoying each other's company.

One day, there was a commercial shoot on the stage, and following filming, the sound man came upstairs to my office. He introduced himself and showed me a card indicating that he had won an Academy Award for developing magnetic recording for the movie industry. He told me the cinematographer on the shoot, a good friend of his, was an award winner for films like *Downhill Racer* and *Ice Station Zebra.*

"What would you think about shooting a porno film on this stage?" he asked.

"Personally, I'd love it," I answered, "providing Nick and I get to watch."

"Do you think we can get the stage at night . . . for nothing?"

I indicated that I didn't know why not. I was certain Steve and Jerry would go along. I thought Steve might even want to be in it.

Unfortunately, nothing ever came of it.

Nick was beginning to get tired of waiting around to edit the Hendrix film, which was seemingly never going to be finished. He started hinting to Steve that he might like to get his promised return ticket to England if something didn't happen soon. Steve stalled him, and then he somehow managed to put together enough money to shoot the additional scenes that Steve and his girl friend, Laura, wanted. The money probably came from Bernie S. again, but that's another guess.

I never saw the filming, but Nick told me that it involved Laura thrashing around on a bed with a Jimi Hendrix doll; that it was just short of pornographic. In the end, Laura did the actual editing of the film without Nick, even though she had absolutely no experience, or any concept of how film should be cut. They finally had a private showing to which I was not invited. Both Nick and Stretch Adler told me the film was so terrible it would never be shown.

Nick started getting some outside work on his own, editing mostly, and finally made enough to pay his own way back to England. I doubt that Steve and Jerry ever came up with the money they promised him. Their reasoning would have been something to the effect that as long as he was earning money from them he should have been satisfied. I'm not saying that was the way it actually went down, but I'm surmising it might have been that way.

That wasn't the end of my relationship with Nick, however. Back in England, he produced a concert film using many top-flight musicians from rock and roll, blues, and jazz, and he managed to sell it in Europe. I tried to sell it here, but with no luck because, I was told, "the audience was too polite."

About eight months after I started with Goldstein and Gold, my paycheck bounced. It was the first of several. Steve found a way of making them good for awhile, but then about two months before I finally left the company, they not only bounced, they stayed bounced. Then, I discovered the company was not even making payments to the government, even though the check stubs indicated FICA and income taxes were being withheld. Deductions were certainly being made, but the government never got the dough.

I wasn't smart enough to keep check stubs, but my assistant, Jackie Balzano, was, and later when she needed money, she confronted Steve and Jerry and offered them the option of giving her some cash or possibly going to jail. She got her money.

ANOTHER BEGINNING

Steve Tolin had long since packed up and moved, but continued pressing me to join him. By then, it seemed the prudent thing to do, because if he and I actually made any money, at least I would get paid *something*. I finally did quit and joined Steve. I was making less gross than I got from Gold and Goldstein, but the checks were good and we made up the difference by trading out ads for goods and services. Steve even traded out for his apartment rent, and with an ad for AAMCO, I had a new transmission installed in my old Toyota. Through ads with an auto body shop, we both got our cars painted.

What's Happening turned out to be a very good little publication. In the beginning, I wrote all of the copy and did most of the research, while Steve went out and sold the bulk of the ads. He and I did the layout work together and I did all the paste-up. The world hadn't converted to computers yet.

Fairly early on, we hired a secretary, a very pretty young woman, whom I suspected Steve thought he could take to bed even though she was married. She was very attractive, but not, in my opinion, terribly efficient. She almost never got her work done on time, but whenever Steve fired her, she'd start to cry. Steve would relent and rehire her. Every few days, she'd say to me, "You really ought to meet my husband; he's in the music business just like you were."

"Why would I want to meet a twenty-year-old kid?" I always responded. However, one late afternoon, when her work for the upcoming edition was nowhere near complete, she called on him and some of his friends to come to our office to help her.

So, meet we did. I found him very bright, and wondered what he saw in Yolanda, other than a cute figure. Later, I learned that she pursued and caught him, mostly I suspect, because she knew he had a very wealthy father. After some conversation with Michael, I decided to go visit him at his office in Hollywood.

Michael Zugsmith and his high school friends were into booking bands for local clubs. They had no contractual arrangements with any performers, but sold several clubs on the idea of utilizing their services. They were making a little money and having a lot of fun. Mike's father, movie producer Albert Zugsmith, was never a fast man with a buck when it came to Michael, always insisting that Michael work for the things he wanted. Through friends, he got jobs with a couple of record companies, enough to pay for his Corvette, at any rate.

After several meetings, Mike and I decided we would produce some dances and concerts together while I was still working with Steve. I figured I might pick up a few extra dollars, which certainly wouldn't hurt, considering the irregularity of our magazine income. After I left Steve to devote all my time to management, Mike Zugsmith and I managed a singer and a couple of rock bands together, while continuing to produce a dance every now and then.

EVEN MORE ABOUT STEVE TOLIN

As I have previously mentioned, Steve Tolin was an interesting character, very aggressive and very money and career oriented. He was possibly the best salesman I ever met, and it was through his own energies and drive that *The Official Talent and Booking Directory* got off the ground, grew, and became a virtual necessity in the music industry. *Billboard* eventually "ripped off" practically the entire publication and sold it as their *Blue Book*.

After I left *What's Happening*, Steve and I worked together on several projects, including the *The Official Talent and Booking Directory*. One year, using my own records, we added the section on facilities in the major cities in the US and Canada. His research people kept the book up to date after that.

Steve had a boyish way with females that always attracted them. He never liked losing when he wanted a girl, and persisted until she ended up in his bed. After the conquest, his interest would start to wane and the relationships always ended within a few months.

I recall one time when we were in Washington, DC, for the National Education Alliance (NEA) meeting, which was one of the jobs I did for him after I left the company. The NEA was an organization of some 900 colleges that held a convention every year to audition acts for student promotions. Anyone, any act, any agency wanting to book those schools had to take a booth for the week of the convention. Some acts were showcased on stage by the NEA, while others rented their own facilities to produce their own show.

We were there to sell ads in *The Official Talent and Booking Directory* to the acts, agents, managers, record companies, and anyone else who had reason to be at the convention. We met a very beautiful young woman, who was Dean of Students at a girls' school somewhere back east. She was only twenty-seven years old then, and we were both very much taken with her intelligence and her looks. We both flirted outrageously with her, although nothing came of it. At least, not then. However, a year later at the next convention, Steve ran into her again.

The next year, Steve made a deal with the NEA to produce a "program" for the convention. He sold them on the idea of a tabloid-size newspaper containing a great many articles about the NEA, the acts who would be performing, as well as the other acts who would be represented there. It would also contain the agendas and schedules for the convention. Steve's deal was that he would sell the ads and keep the money, while the NEA got the "program" for nothing.

He hired me to write most of it and edit all of it. In order to conduct research and interviews, I flew to Columbia, South Carolina, where the NEA offices were located at the University of South Carolina. I spent a week there gathering information and writing material for the paper, which ended up being something like 128 pages. The job took several months and paid well.

I didn't go back to Washington that year, mostly because I was too busy with José, but I continued writing for Steve whenever he had special projects. That second year, Steve ran into the beautiful young Dean of Students again, and that time, he pursued her in earnest.

He called to tell me, "This time, I'm really in love." Within a few months, she was in California, thinking that she and Steve were altar-bound. Steve made two mistakes with her. First, he didn't take down the pictures in his bedroom. He had posters made from photographs of several former girl friends and decorated the walls with them. Second, he failed to make it clear that he was not the marrying kind. Being in love had nothing to do with leaving the single scene.

I got a call from him a few days after she arrived. "I don't know what to do," he said. "I'm having problems getting it up. That's never happened to me before. You know about these things."

I don't know how he figured that except that I was considerably older. I sure wasn't having trouble getting it up back then. "When did it start?" I asked.

"A couple of days ago. Listen, she expects to get married, and I'm not ready for that."

"Okay," I said, "go tell her that you don't want to get married, and see what happens."

So, he told her. His erection returned immediately, he convinced her to stay for the week, and they went right on sleeping together.

About that same time, he was also seeing a girl named Vicki and became very good friends with her husband even though they were more or less separated. Steve would go to her apartment at night and they'd head straight for the bedroom. Their relationship was purely sexual, and that was just they way they both wanted it.

Vicki was a very beautiful girl, and I got her placed with a commercial acting agency. However, as time went on, she kept losing weight, which she attributed to a vegetarian diet, but which I attributed to drugs. She lost her looks along with her weight, and the agency dropped her.

Chapter 7
A New Beginning

José Ferrer and I were spending so much time together whenever he was in town that I finally had to decide whether to be a full-time editor, or leave Steve Tolin and *What's Happening* and become José's full-time personal manager. Being a personal manager was a lot more appealing, although the money was sure to be irregular.

Joe, as I called him, came to Los Angeles for a month-long television project, and once again, he rented a house in Beverly Hills. I met Joe at the airport, and we drove to the house that real estate maven Elaine Young had leased for him on Beverly Glen. On the way, Joe said out of the blue, "I'd like you to be my personal manager."

On his previous trip to Los Angeles, Joe had signed a management contract with a fairly well known personal manager so I was taken completely by surprise. "You just signed with a manager, didn't you?"

"Yes, but I've already fired him. We had some serious disagreements. Do me a favor and pick up my pictures from his office."

I agreed to get the pictures, but deferred any decision about becoming his manager. I said, "Let me think about it," which I did, until several days later, when we ended up flying back to Chicago together.

We were flying to Chicago together because of another in a series of coincidences in our life. First, there was Stella, and that trip was the result of the second coincidence.

I had joined Joe on the set of whatever he was shooting, and he said, "I've got to fly to Chicago tonight." It was Friday and he wasn't scheduled to work over the weekend.

"What's doing in Chicago?" I asked.

"I've got a lead on some money for the *Cyrano* musical. There's someone there who's financed a couple of film projects, and a friend of mine knows his money man. He set up a meeting."

"What's his name?" I asked. "I'm from Chicago. There's only about four million people there—I must know him."

He pulled a scrap of paper from his pocket and handed it to me. "This is the guy."

I walked over to a pay telephone, saying to Joe, "Come with me." I dialed the number using my calling card, and when the male voice answered, I said, "Zev, this is Jack Lloyd. We went to high school together." Zev Braun was a year behind me, but our school was very small and everyone pretty much knew everyone else. Zev's father made his money in the container business, manufacturing bottles of all kinds and sizes, and Zev used some of it to finance a small film, which won an award at the Cannes Film Festival. Zev was on the brink of becoming a full-fledged motion picture producer.

I brought him up to date about my relationship with Joe, and he suggested that I come to Chicago, too, and stay with him while we were there. I could hardly stay with Joe because he had already arranged to stay with a long-time female friend with whom he once had a serious sexual relationship. She picked us up at the airport.

I was sitting in the back seat with the luggage and a couple of spare tires listening to Joe and Anne talk, when something she said struck a memory chord. I interrupted their conversation. "Excuse me, what did you say your name was?"

"Anne. Anne Brake."

"Do you know a woman named Laura Silver? (not her real name)."

"Yes," she answered, obviously a little surprised.

"Do you remember a time about six months ago when she called you and asked you to go to dinner with a friend of hers? I think she got engaged, or her husband came home, or something, and couldn't see this friend."

"Yes," I do," she said warily.

"Well, do you recall that you got a call from that person, but you couldn't go out with him because you were too busy in your restaurant?"

"I remember that."

"Well," I said, "that guy was me."

So, there were then three coincidental ties to Joe. A love for golf, and an inability to play with any degree of expertise was a fourth. We also shared a love for good wines, spirits, and conversation.

Joe spent Saturday with Anne, and I spent the day with Zev at the bottling works, and in the evening, we went to dinner with Zev and his "money man." We pitched the project, and returned on Sunday to Los Angeles, not very enthusiastic about our prospects. Zev's "money man" was more interested in funding motion picture projects.

Unfortunately, nothing ever came of the meeting. Even more unfortunately, we were never able to raise the money, and worse yet, Christopher Plummer performed someone else's musical version of *Cyrano* at the Tyrone Guthrie Theater in Minneapolis, Minnesota.

Plummer's play, with a very unmemorable score, moved to Broadway and closed quickly. He won a Tony Award for his performance, but the play was a bomb. Joe's "book" should have made it to Broadway, and Joe should have won his second Tony for portraying Cyrano, because no one before or since has come close to his interpretation.

BETTER THAN I COULD SAY IT

This might be a good place to say something about Joe Ferrer, and just who he is. Quoting from a biography:

"He first attracted attention while appearing in University Theater productions at Princeton. He made his Broadway debut with a bit part in *A Slight Case of Murder* in 1935, followed by a featured role in *Brother Rat*. His portrayal of Lord Fancourt Babberly in the 1940 revival of *Charley's Aunt* provided his first Broadway conquest. His first try at Shakespeare came with his starring role as Iago to Paul Robeson's title role of *Othello*. In 1946, he made his first appearance in the role now generally considered 'his,' when he starred in Rostand's classic play, *Cyrano de Bergerac*. He subsequently reprised his Antoinette Perry ('Tony') Award winning performance on both the motion picture and television screens, and again in another Broadway revival.

"Mr. Ferrer's other memorable Broadway credits include starring in *The Silver Whistle*; directing and starring as Oscar Jaffe in *Twentieth Century*; directing *Stalag 17* (which he also produced), and *The Four Poster*, each of which garnered Tony Awards for his directing; directing and staring as Jim Downs in *The Shrike*, the Pulitzer Prize-winning play for which he received three Critics' Circle Awards and two more Tony Awards for his direction and performance; directing *My Three Angels*, and *The Andersonville Trial*; starring in *The Girl Who Came to Supper*, and *Man of La Mancha*, in which he replaced Richard Kiley in New York, and then started the first national company in which he made more than eight hundred appearances. He most recently starred in *A Life in the Theater*, in New York.

"He made his operatic debut in the title role of *Gianni Schicchi* at the Santa Fe Opera; sang the title role at the Brooklyn Academy of Music; sang Amonasro (Aida's father) for the Beverly Hills Opera, and in Dallas, directed Mozart's *Don Giovanni*. He has also directed ballet in several cities.

"José Ferrer's first motion picture portrayal was as the Dauphin to Ingrid Bergman's *Joan of Arc*, for which he received his first Oscar nomination. Other notable screen appearances, in addition to his Academy Award winning performance in *Cyrano*, include a third Oscar nomination of his portrayal of Toulouse-Lautrec (and as Lautrec's father) in *Moulin Rouge*, *Miss Sadie Thompson*, an absolutely memorable performance as Barney Greenwald in *The Caine Mutiny, The Shrike, Lawrence of Arabia, Nine Hours to Rama, The Greatest Story Ever Told, The Great Man, Ship of Fools*, and *Enter Laughing*. He directed *Return to Peyton Place*, and the remake of *State Fair*, and served as both director and star in *The High Cost of Loving* with Gena Rowlands. He also directed the aforementioned *The Great Man*, and *I Accuse*, in which he starred as Dreyfus. More recently, he appeared in *Behind the Iron Mask*, and *Fedora*, for Billy Wilder.

"On television, he has narrated documentaries, starred in two productions of Cyrano de Bergerac, and many specials including *The Marcus-Nelson Murders* (the pilot for *Kojak*), *Kismet, A Case of Libel*, Arthur Miller's *Fame, Gideon,* in which he co-starred with Peter Ustinov, and recently as Justice Abe Fortas in the Hallmark production of *Gideon's Trumpet*. His most recent television appearances included a mini series of little note, entitled *The French Atlantic Affair*, in which he starred as the President of France; as Spiros Skouros in *The Dream Merchants* with an all-star cast, and *Pleasure Palace*, with Omar Sharif." For *Gideon's Trumpet*, I believe that he *should* have been nominated for an Emmy.

I ask you, has there ever been a more complete Renaissance man? He wrote (a new version of *Cyrano*, which would have been made as a musical had we been able to raise the funds in time). He was a singer, a dancer, an excellent pianist and a linguist, and among his other accomplishments I include the fact that he did the *Sunday New York Times Magazine* crossword puzzle in ink (and didn't have to make corrections).

I would also like to quote a small portion of a review of *White Pelicans*, a two-man, "off Broadway" production in which he starred with Morgan Freeman. The play, incidentally, was not a hit, but if you believe the *New Yorker* magazine review, it wasn't because of its stars, Joe or Morgan.

I quote: "That the attempt (the play) is somewhat successful is more a matter of the performances than of the script, since the miners are played by José Ferrer and Morgan Freeman, two of the most powerful actors we have."

Joe had put a lot of his own money into *White Pelicans*, and asked me if I would consider buying a share. I had read the play and was convinced that while it was an excellent "read," it wouldn't be a great success on the stage, but I did put up money for one share. It did fail after running three weeks, and as an investor, I got one hundred dollars back, so it wasn't a *total* loss.

Chapter 8
My Circle of Friends Grows

Whenever Joe Ferrer was in Los Angeles, we tried to find time for a round or two of golf, not that either of us was particularly good at the game, but we both loved it and played wherever we could scrounge our way on to a country club course. Fame brings with it many perks including Starters and General Managers at private clubs, who were only too happy to let Joe play, which generally meant me, too. Not that Joe (and certainly not I) was a snob about playing on public courses, but public courses generally require reservations and we normally squeezed in a game when he had the time.

Joe was frequently invited to play at places like Hillcrest Country Club, or some other equally prestigious courses, where I was not invited. After all, to some of the people who wanted to play golf with Joe, I wasn't famous or important. It didn't bother me at all. Actually, I did play Hillcrest twice with Joe, as a guest of Todd Fisher, son of Debbie Reynolds and Eddie Fisher. Todd's stepfather, the late Harry Karl, had belonged, and Todd was allowed to keep the membership.

Joe once called me from New York to let me know he joined Sleepy Hollow Country Club near his home in Ossining. "I'm ashamed to tell you this, but it's restricted," he said. Then he added, "On the other hand, they don't know I'm Puerto Rican."

Joe introduced me to his friend, singer/actor Francesco Sorienello, who at that time, was calling himself Frank Sorel because it was easier to remember than Sorienello. Frank had an outstanding singing voice that was not quite good enough for grand opera, although he kept trying. I worked with Frank from time to time, got him a theatrical agent, and even tried to help with his singing career, but there was not much market for his kind of voice except maybe in stage musicals, and there weren't a lot of them around. He would have been terrific in Operettas, but no one was producing them in the 1960s and 1970s.

Later, Frank went back to singing full time; sang in churches, worked with some local opera companies, and once toured with Juliet Prowse in *Sweet Charity*, in which he had a major, but oddly enough, non-singing role. He changed his name back to Sorienello about the time he appeared with Joe in a revival of *Man of La Mancha* in Sacramento, California.

Fred Holliday (née: Grossinger) was another actor who became part of our circle. One day, Joe and I had a date for golf, and I picked him up at the Sunset Marquis, the hotel where he generally stayed. They always tried to give him the same suite and had a private telephone line installed that they would connect whenever he arrived.

Joe said we had to stop by a television show as a favor to Fred, who was substituting as co-host on *Mid-Morning LA*, with regular host Meredith McRae. Joe, who was never ostentatious in his dress, was wearing golf slacks, shirt, and his ever-present golfing hat. He wasn't about to dress up for a television show and then change for golf.

When the show ended, Fred asked, "Why don't I join you?" and proceeded to get a staring time for the three of us at Lakeside Country Club, the home club of comedian Bob Hope. Afterwards, we went to Fred's home in Toluca Lake, where I had left my car. Before we could leave, Fred asked us to go into his bedroom to watch a short video clip. Joe was always polite in situations like that, and besides, Fred did get us on a good course. The tape was of a sketch Fred did on *The Tonight Show*, or as it was more familiarly known, "The Johnny Carson Show." Subsequently, Carson repeated the skit several times, and always showed it on his "anniversary" programs. It featured Johnny Carson as President Ronald Reagan and Fred as Reagan's Press Secretary. It was by all accounts, Carson's favorite bit.

On the way home, Joe asked, "Why did he show us that tape?"

I said, "Joe . . . that was Fred."

"No kidding. He was very funny."

I thought that Joe and Fred had been friends for a long time considering the ease of their relationship. When I conveyed that to Joe, he told me that they met only a short time before Joe asked me to be his manager.

Fred, who died too young, a week before his sixtieth birthday, was one of the nicest and most respected men in commercial television, as well as one of the hardest working. He remained one of my closest and dearest friends. You've seen him in hundreds of commercials and infomercials, not to mention the many roles he has portrayed on dramatic and serial television.

OUR RELATIONSHIP AND HOW IT GREW

Joe became closer to me than a brother could have been. Stella once told me that "Joe has only three real friends, you, Frank, and Bob Merrill." Bob was an opera singer, and considering the number of famous and some not so famous people Joe was close to, I suspect the number was considerably higher than three.

When I finally agreed to manage Joe, he told me he hadn't made a Hollywood film in four years. Obviously, he worked, but mostly in the east or Europe. It seemed almost impossible to me that Joe hadn't even been *offered* a job. He was arguably one of the all-time best, and to my thinking, the most complete American actor, and I'm fully cognizant of Marlon Brando and all the other Actors' Studio people. Just his work in *Cyrano de Bergerac*, for which he won the Oscar, and *Moulin Rouge*, for which he was nominated, and *The Great Man*, which he directed, as well, should have generated dozens, if not hundreds of offers. I have given a lot of thought over the years to possible reasons.

Some people have accused Joe of being difficult to work with. There may have been a modicum of truth in that, but only when you consider that he resented actors who were not prepared to work. I found that when I questioned anyone who carped about his being "difficult," it was generally hearsay and they had ever actually worked with him. Either that, or I suspect they felt compelled to put someone else down, and if they were going to put someone down, they might as well pick on the best.

THERE ARE OTHER OPINIONS

On the other hand, if you spoke with anyone who ever performed with him on stage or film, or was directed by him, you heard nothing but the highest praise.

Harvey Lembeck, the late, wonderful comedic actor Joe directed in *Stalag 17* on Broadway, told me that Joe taught him everything he knew about acting. Obviously an exaggeration, but you get the point. Ray Walston, another marvelous actor, also directed by Joe on Broadway, spent forty-five minutes extolling Joe as an actor, director, producer, and human being.

I ran into Hume Cronyn, one of Joe's oldest friends (see, I told you there were more than three), in an airport one day. He said, "Joe is the greatest actor I ever worked with." The list of people who respected—even loved—his work, is endless. Good actors, I discovered, thought Joe was a *great* actor. When Joe presented Hume his award at the Kennedy Center Honors, Hume whispered into his ear, "I should be giving this to you."

One of the great injustices in the American theater is that José Ferrer has rarely received the public honors he deserved. Privately, his peers spoke of his talent, and he was one of the first twelve to receive the National Medal of Honor, presented by President Ronald Reagan. José Ferrer was, without doubt, one of the finest producers, directors, and actors of the American stage.

NO, HE WASN'T PERFECT

I am one of the first to admit that there were times Joe "walked" through a part, and I told him so, but those were television roles with no great substance on shows of no particular merit, but those times were rare, indeed.

However, even when Joe walked through a role, other actors conceded that he was terrific. Even his performance in the title role of a mini-series as banal as *The Return of Captain Nemo*, drew raves from the director and from actors Burgess Meredith and Horst Buchholz, who co-starred.

Irwin Allen was producing a show called *The Swarm*, a stinker about killer bees, on a nearby set at the same time *The Return of Captain Nemo* was in production. He heard that Joe was working nearby and begged him to play a one-day cameo in his film. Because it was Irwin Allen, Joe agreed, working that role around his scenes in *The Return of Captain Nemo*.

Perhaps one of the reasons Joe encountered some sort of resentment in Hollywood, if that's what it was, and then only from a very few members of the acting community, was that he always came prepared to work. No one ever had to wait for him. For some actors, he may have set a bad example; one they could not or did not want to live up to. He *always* knew his lines, he was *always* on time, and he was ready and willing to take direction.

Joe had great respect for most directors, and unlike many people in the industry, never ever arbitrarily imposed his own interpretations on the director. He always asked his director how he wanted a certain role played, and I have heard directors answer back, "However you see the part, Joe. I know you'll do it right."

Another possibility was that among those in Hollywood, Joe was thought of as a "New York" actor, even though he lived in Beverly Hills for several years during his marriage to Rosemary Clooney. He moved back to New York only after their separation.

While he was in Hollywood, he produced some outstanding work, including *Cyrano de Bergerac, Moulin Rouge,* and *The Great Man,* in which he turned Ed Wynn, better known as "The Perfect Fool," into the perfect dramatic actor. Joe also portrayed Sigmund Romberg in *Deep In My Heart,* a very lightweight movie, but one made memorable by Joe's acting all the parts in a show that he, as Romberg. had written for Al Jolson. In that scene he danced, sang, and put the exclamation point to the skit by diving out a window.

Enter Laughing was by and about actor-director-comedian Carl Reiner, but once again, Joe virtually stole the movie. He also charmed American audiences in *Anything Can Happen,* the film adaptation of the book by Ludwig Bemelmens.

An example of Joe's commitment to even the smallest part was his recurring role on *Newhart,* as the rich father of the ingénue, played by Julia Duffy. Not much of a part, but he did it mostly as an excuse to spend some time in Los Angeles with his children. He asked Newhart, "How do you want me to play him?" meaning the role.

Newhart answered, "Joe, this isn't *Hamlet*, just find your mark and say the words." Joe couldn't do that even for as inane a role as this.

He never complained about sitting around for hours on location or a set, and he got along with everyone from wardrobe people and drivers to the least important member of the crew. Once, when he completed a role on *Columbo*, the Peter Falk series, I overheard the sound man asking him to please come to the wrap party. "We didn't invite Peter, but we all want you there," he said. After another *Columbo*, shot largely on location, Joe and I hung out with the crew at a nearby bar, at their invitation.

Joe once said to me, after his movie and television career got back on track, "Wouldn't it be odd if the only reason I haven't worked here is that no one has mentioned my name?"

TOM KORMAN SPEAKS

I am at this moment reminded of a story told to me by super-agent and manager Tom Korman, who was Joe's last agent. He had submitted Joe for the role of the President of France in *The French Atlantic Affair*, and was in either the director's or producer's office when they hesitated about using Joe. Whoever it was said, "I really had in mind using someone who could play a Frenchman, or at least a continental."

Tom was stunned for a moment, but before he walked out, he said, "I'm going to leave you with two words: Toulouse-Lautrec." Whoever it was appeared to have no idea what Tom was talking about.

Eventually, someone must have told the director or producer who Toulouse-Lautrec was and about Joe's portrayal, leading to a call to Tom. "Will he come in and read?" they asked.

"Are you out of your fucking mind?" countered Tom.

Obviously, he got the part, and as usual, was excellent. Just ask Corinne Calvet, who played his wife, or anyone else who worked the show.

OMAR SHARIF

That brings to mind a story about *Pleasure Palace*, with Joe and Omar Sharif. You can see how my mind works when a story about *The French Atlantic Affair* makes me think of Omar. They had been shooting the mini-series in Las Vegas, and when filming there was complete, the company moved to Los Angeles for the rest of the scenes. They shot on location in Burbank for three or four days in a penthouse apartment, but Joe was used very little.

One morning, I came by early for breakfast burritos with Joe at the mobile catering truck. We were eating them in the tiny cubicle that passed for a dressing room in the trailer, which is frequently called a "honey wagon." "Honey Wagon" is a term generally applied to the long trailer that houses the toilets and small dressing rooms on location. Joe or Omar could have asked for, and gotten individual motor homes if they wanted, but neither of them was demanding of their employers.

One of those days, when it looked as though Joe would sit around all day even though he had a call for six o'clock in the morning, Joe asked the First Assistant Director when he thought he would be needed. When he said that they probably wouldn't get to him for several hours, we took off for DeBell golf course (a public course) in Burbank and got in nine holes. When Joe was in town, I generally carried our clubs in my trunk; one never knew when we might run into enough free time.

The Biltmore Hotel in Los Angeles was then being used to represent the Las Vegas hotel where the action took place. A small ballroom had been converted into a gaming casino for the shoot. I dropped by for lunch and suggested Cooks, one of the best steak houses in Los Angeles, which was only a couple blocks from the Biltmore.

Joe, Omar, and I were seated and given menus. Joe saw "Baby Squid in its own ink" on the menu, and I thought the two of them would salivate to death. I declined to join them, saying I couldn't imagine anything less inviting. Omar, sitting next to me in the booth said, "Close your eyes and take one," stuffing the fork into my mouth.

"What do you think?" he asked.

"To tell the truth," I answered, "it isn't awful, but if it's all the same to you, I don't think I'll ever order it."

Following lunch, Omar insisted we finish with an after dinner drink. Whatever I ordered upset Omar terribly.

"How can you drink that? That's a *woman's* drink."

"Okay," I responded, "what should I drink?"

"You must drink alcohol."

"All right," I said, and turned to the waiter. "Bring me *alcohol*," trying to imitate Omar's accent. The waiter had no idea what I was talking about. "Cognac." I said. "Whatever it is they're drinking."

When filming was over, I went to get Joe at the CBS photo studio where they were taking publicity pictures of the two stars. I said to Omar, "You look like you're in pretty good shape. Do you work out a lot?"

"I am not in good shape; I never work out," he said, adding, "I don't have a hard muscle in my body, and that's the way I intend to keep it."

The "wrap dinner" for *Pleasure Palace* was actually a party thrown by Omar at Homer and Edie's Bistro, a New Orleans-style restaurant that Omar considered worthy of his taste in food. I once asked him if he ever ate in a less than three-star restaurant, to which he replied succinctly, "Why should I?"

Omar ordered fresh oysters from the east coast, and they were delivered directly from the airplane. Basically, the party was to celebrate the showing of *Gideon's Trumpet* in which Joe co-starred with Peter Ustinov. Incidentally, Joe told me that Ustinov used to get other actors upset because he had a habit of changing a "cue" line without telling anyone, which meant every other actor had to be on his toes. Not a kind thing to do to another actor.

In a private room on the second floor of the restaurant, Omar had the seating arranged in a horseshoe, the open end of which faced a large-screen television set on which we were all to watch Joe's show.

There was only one hitch. Joe and Stella didn't come. She was angry at Omar for once telling a story about the time he and Joe were in Spain filming *Lawrence of Arabia*. Everyone (or almost everyone) is familiar with Omar's success with women, and Joe was never considered a slouch in that department either. Omar had related a tale about Joe living in a brothel for the two weeks they were in Spain. It wasn't *quite* true, but Stella was very upset. Joe asked Stella, "What are you so mad about? I didn't even know you in 1962." At any rate, she never forgave Omar, and because she wouldn't come to the dinner, Joe wouldn't go either. In her defense, she was mad only because she thought it made Joe look bad. He was rather proud of the incident.

Incidentally, Joe did not live in a brothel. The madam had provided him and Omar with young ladies to keep them company during their stay there, but living in a brothel made a better story.

Regardless, at the appointed hour, the dinner was stopped, the television set turned on, and we all watched the show.

MORE ABOUT OMAR

Two stories about Omar come to mind. He was talking with my wife, Phyllis, about his love for gambling—mostly playing bridge—relating that one night in a club that I think was in Deauville, France, where he dropped a very large number. Rather than sulk about it, he returned to his home in Paris, made a few investments, and then went back and bought the casino. He told her, "Now I sit in my office and watch the money roll in on the television monitors."

Joe also told me that while they were in Las Vegas, Omar was behind a couple hundred thousand dollars, as they were sitting in limousines waiting for the trip to the airport. Suddenly, Omar said, "Wait a minute." He jumped out of the car, ran back into the casino, and won back, according to Joe, about $20,000.

He had, and rightly so, a reputation with the ladies. The script girl working *Pleasure Palace* told me that Omar and others of his type didn't really appeal to her; she went more for someone like Joe. On the night of the wrap dinner, she arrived with a girlfriend, and I watched as Omar deftly separated them, placing the girlfriend with my wife, me, and the script girl next to him.

Now, I don't know what Omar said or didn't say to her, but by the time the evening was drawing to a close, I looked across the "horseshoe" table and saw this gorgeous girl nibbling on his fingers. A few days later, I received a telephone call from her, very upset.

She told me that she had stayed with Omar for four nights following the dinner, but something happened the night before her call to me when they had been out to dinner. She had no idea what brought it on, but he suddenly stood up, threw some money down on the table, and walked out on her. She did not hear from him again, and wanted to know whether I might be able to find out what, if anything, she did. As it turned out, Omar had left town and I had no idea how to reach him.

A few days after I completed this chapter, my dear friend, Fred Holliday, died suddenly from a heart attack. He had just returned from a celebrity golf tournament in Orlando, Florida, and was seemingly in the best of health. He drove to a car wash and, waiting in line, died. He was my business associate, as well as my friend. From the day we met at the television show, we spent hundreds of hours together, socializing, working, eating out, and week-ending at their condo in Laguna Beach, all the normal things pals do together. When I won a trip to Fiji and turned it into a trip to Australia, Fred managed to find a one-day job in Sydney so that he, his wife, Judy, Phyllis, and I could spend three or four days together there. We had many plans for the coming year, but they are plans I can never fulfill with anyone else. As I miss José Ferrer, I will miss Fred Holliday. Neither can ever be replaced. They were one-of-a-kind people.

Chapter 9
Starting to Act Like a Manager

At the time I agreed to become his personal manager, Joe's agent was Jack Gilardi, a self-proclaimed giant in the industry.

I called him to introduce myself and to find out why Joe hadn't had an offer from him in four years.

Jack said, "That's impossible."

Well, it was possible and I told him so, and I also told him that as Joe's manager, I expected a call from him on a regular basis. Furthermore, not only did I want to know the roles for which he was being submitted, but I wanted to know any offers of any kind for any money being generated by his agency. I would make the decision whether or not to pursue the offer.

Weeks went by, and even though I did get an occasional call, all I ever got from Gilardi was what I refer to as "agent bullshit"—double talk and nonsense, but never any real reasons why Joe wasn't getting, at the very least, offers—even unacceptable ones.

I called once more and said, "Jack, I'm sending you a letter today firing you as Joe's agent."

"Why would you do that?" he asked.

"Because you haven't generated an offer of any kind in the past seventy-seven days, and your contract has been breached. In fact, I can't figure out when you last made a legitimate offer to Joe."

At that time, the Screen Actors Guild said, more or less, "If no legitimate offer of two weeks work has been tendered in any ninety consecutive day period, the contract can be terminated. At the end of seventy-seven days, you could not get two weeks work in before ninety days had passed.

Jack asked me to have lunch with him because, he said, "I value Joe as a client. He's very important to me." Having Joe's name on his roster of clients was very prestigious, even if Joe wasn't . . . .

I said, "Jack, I'm always available for a free lunch, but I don't think you can change my mind."

He insisted he wanted to talk to me, and we agreed to meet at the Villa Nova, a fine restaurant that was on Sunset Boulevard and within walking distance from my office. However, I let *him* drive.

Jack brought three or four of his henchmen and they plied me with drinks, which I gladly accepted as long as they were paying. The talk during lunch had virtually nothing to do with Joe, except for a couple more hours of agent bullshit.

Lunch over, I rose and said, "Jack, I want to thank you for the food and drink, but you're still fired."

HOW TO GET WANTED IN A HURRY

Somehow, word got around—as things have a way of doing in Hollywood—that "José Ferrer's manager was looking for a new agent." To use a well worn cliché, the telephone started ringing off the hook. Apparently, every agent in town wanted Joe, if only for his name value. I started interviewing agents.

Contemporary-Korman, a big-time independent agency called. They were just the kind of agency I had in mind. They were big enough to wield some power and small enough to pay attention to the client. I don't recall which agent called, but it was someone who had known Joe for several years, and I agreed to come to their office for a meeting. When I arrived at their building in Beverly Hill, I was immediately surrounded by half a dozen agents. I never felt so wanted.

They set up chairs and sat themselves in a semi-circle in front of me. Each of them enumcrated reasons why I should have Joe sign an exclusive agency agreement with them. "Exclusivity" is a very big thing in Hollywood, and understandably so. It sometimes saves a lot of headaches, which I will go into much later.

Someone handed me a list of their clients, which was pretty impressive. A quick check showed five or six other actors who would be in competition with Joe for the same kind of parts. I pointed this out and was told, "Oh, well, we'll give Joe top priority."

I said, "I'm kind of sorry to hear that, because if you're willing to treat the clients you already have that way, one day you'll do exactly the same thing to Joe."

A few years later, standing at urinals in the Men's Room of the Pantages Theater in Hollywood where we had gone to the opening of *Sugar Babies*, Jim Backus, Tom Korman, and I were talking. I had put Jim with Tom Korman because Tom agreed to handle him personally. Tom mentioned that he had always wanted to represent Joe, and I told him that he could have had him back when I first interviewed the people at his agency. All Tom had to do was come to the meeting and tell me that he would handle Joe personally. Tom was nonplussed, and asked if it was too late. I agreed to call Joe the next morning. I set up a telephone conversation and I think Tom flew east to meet with Joe. He did sign, and Tom and Joe remained close friends until Joe's death.

YOU DON'T HAVE TO BE FAMOUS TO GET MY ATTENTION

Getting back to the time I fired Gilardi: I knew a woman agent named Velvet Amber. That wasn't her real name—it was Vivian McMurtry—but she had been a dancer under the name of "Velvet," and that name opened many more doors than Vivian would have. A producer she didn't know once came out to meet her just because, as he said, "I've got to meet someone named Velvet Amber." I met her when she was working with an agency in West Hollywood and she called me just after she opened her own shop.

Through Darius Brubeck (son of Dave, in the event you've forgotten), I met an actor named Geoffrey Lewis with whom I developed a friendship and a working relationship that did not involve his acting initially. Geoffrey was a comparative newcomer to Los Angeles, but had already, on his own, managed to snag a few parts in some Westerns. His personality quickly made him a number of friends in the business.

In addition to his acting, Geoffrey worked with two friends, Jeff Levin and David Campbell, both excellent musicians. Jeff played guitar and banjo, and David played violin. They worked with Geoff as The Great American Entertainment Show, mostly at a place called Celebrity Center, which is where I went to hear them.

Geoff wrote most of their material. He played drums and sang/acted/recited the material.

I managed to get them a few bookings, but eventually their religious affiliation got in the way of our relationship; that and Geoff's acting career, which took more and more of his time.

They, like Darius Brubeck and his wife, Sheena, were Scientologists, and because I wasn't one, they may have been pressured to work with someone within the church.

Geoff needed a theatrical agent, and I was convinced that Velvet was ideal for him. They took an immediate liking to one another and she went to work in earnest. She got him work almost immediately and kept increasing his asking (and getting) price, but after a year or so, he was definitely pressured to leave her for a representative who was also a Scientologist.

Velvet had a valid contract with Geoff and took him to arbitration over commissions. The end result was that Geoff had to pay her for the balance of their contract, even though he probably paid his Scientologist agent, as well. Geoff, who has made dozens of features, is probably most recognizable as Clint Eastwood's sidekick in *Every Which Way But Loose* and *Any Which Way You Can*, the two pictures they made with the Orangutan.

Anyway, Velvet was in my mind as a possible agent for Joe, even though she was a comparative unknown. However, she did what a lot of "name" agents no longer did: she went out into the field every day and met with producers, directors, and casting directors. I knew if I turned her loose, she'd beat the doors down for Joe.

He had a habit of calling me at any hour of the night or day with a joke he just heard. Some of them were awful. I would tell him so and laugh. He'd say, "If it's so terrible, why are you laughing?" And I would answer, "*Because* it's so terrible."

We were in constant contact by telephone and the mails, although not always by letter. Joe sent "care packages" of articles he thought were worth my reading, especially Red Smith, the late great sports writer for the *New York Times*. He sent menus, photographs, post cards, copies of letters he received from people such as the writer

Richard Condon, or the great jazz bass player Chubby Jackson. I would send him articles from the Los Angeles papers on the rare occasion when I found something readable.

Joe and I never actually traveled much together. That's because he was living in New York, Florida, or Puerto Rico, and his traveling amounted mostly to coming to California. We went places together like Lexington, Kentucky, or Riverside and San Bernardino, California, or San Francisco; places like that, but they were mostly to play golf, except northern California, where we joined him for a revival of *Man of La Mancha*, and as I recall, his acting in a version of *A Christmas Carol*.

BEING AROUND JOE MADE FOR SOME FUN

Joe came from a very well-to-do Puerto Rican family, who spent every summer of his first fourteen years vacationing in Italy. It was there that he learned the language that he literally spoke like a native, as well as French, and of course, Spanish. He felt he was a "little light" in German, although as I have mentioned, he was busily translating *Siegfried* from English to German when we met.

Joe's facility with languages always stood us in good stead at ethnic restaurants. In a French restaurant, he spoke nothing but French. He spoke Italian in Italian joints, and of course, Spanish in Mexican or Spanish restaurants.

I recall one night at L'Auberge, a charming French restaurant that was once on Sunset Boulevard. My wife, Phyllis, and I had joined him for dinner. Joe was accompanied by a spectacularly beautiful woman, who just happened to be an outstanding golfer, which was, I suppose, one basis for their friendship. Of course, being beautiful didn't hurt either.

Naturally, Joe was recognized by the owner, Daniel, who immediately presented himself at our booth. Joe greeted him in French, and from that moment on, we were surrounded by waiters, the maitre d', and of course, Daniel, who insisted on ordering for us.

The food was memorable, from the Shad Roe and Oysters Rockefeller to the Crepes Suzette at the finish. We had Aquavit with the Shad Roe and a different French wine with each of the subsequent courses, topping off the Crepes with a cordial. One other thing I remember from the evening was that during dinner, Sydney, Joe's dinner companion, said to him, "Why don't we get married?"

To which Joe replied, "Lady, do you want to give me a permanent *tic*?"

Sitting in an adjacent booth was Paul Lynde, the brilliant comedian, who for several years held the center space on the television game show, *Hollywood Squares*. About half way through our meal, Paul shouted, jokingly I imagine, "They've got five waiters, and I can't even get a cup of coffee!"

Back to some background on Joe. Before he matriculated at Princeton, he attended a Prep school in Switzerland for a year. I believe he was only fifteen when he arrived at Princeton, which is why he laid out a year before finishing his studies. Among his friends were fellow architecture student James Stewart, who also gave up architecture for acting, and theater arts major, Josh Logan. It was Logan who persuaded Joe to try out for the Triangle Club's annual production. The unique quality of Joe's voice, something he attributed to being born without a uvula, and a natural flair for acting, won him the lead.

One day, I asked Joe, "When did you know you wanted to be an actor?"

He answered, "When I realized that I loved the drudgery of the theater." He explained that even sweeping the stage and helping build sets when he worked in summer stock thrilled him.

While he was still at Princeton, Joe formed a band, with himself as pianist and leader. José Ferrer and His Pied Pipers worked locally and on at least one trans-Atlantic liner during the summer. For a while, his boy singer was friend Jimmy Stewart.

Joe had a love for all kinds of music, and over the years became good friends with just about every great jazz musician. I think he would have gladly given up acting if he could have been a successful jazz pianist and night club performer.

He went to the extent of having a musical act written for him, and having band orchestrations created by some of the music world's top arrangers. Once, when he was staying at his penthouse in Santurce, Puerto Rico, he was called on to substitute for Jack Jones, who had taken ill. He may have been prouder of his good reviews than he was of his Academy Award for *Cyrano de Bergerac*.

Joe would sing at the drop of a hat, and not always well, even though he successfully portrayed Don Quixote in *Man of La Mancha*. When I became his manager, I introduced him to a vocal coach I had used with other actors. Lee Wintner worked with him for three weeks. They were singing operatic duets and singing them well.

JOE IS AVAILABLE FOR FRIENDS

Ricardo Montalban was at that time in the process of creating a group called *Nosotros*, aimed at securing work for and improving the image of Latino actors. Naturally, he wanted Joe as a charter member, an honor he gladly accepted. Because Joe was in New York or Florida most of the time, I represented him at many of the meetings.

The members of *Nosotros* decided to have a fund-raising event at the Hollywood Bowl, inviting major Latino performers and other top name acts. Since I had already presented two shows with Irving Granz at the Bowl, I was able to show them how to save money and utilize the facility to its best advantage. Joe, of course, returned to Los Angeles for the big event.

I don't recall everyone who appeared on the bill because it was very long, but I know Ricardo did a reading and several Mexican performers worked on the first half. On the second half of the show, Joe did a medley of "Dulcinea," "Man of La Mancha," and "The Impossible Dream."

I was backstage having a drink with Frank Sinatra just before Joe went on. I was having a drink with him because he came in while I was having one and I offered to make one for him. I introduced myself and mentioned that we had a mutual friend, Mo Ostin, who headed Frank's company, Reprise Records.

When Joe was introduced, Frank said, "We'll talk later. I want to hear Joe."

Dionne Warwick was next to closing and she wowed the audience. Frank turned to me and said, "I guess I'll have to go some to outdo her." And he did.

OTHER PLANS

Joe was given to taking lessons. He took navigation lessons in the hope that one day he, Frank Sorel (aka: Sorienello), and I would rent a boat and cast it more or less adrift in the Caribbean or Mediterranean Sea. We planned to pull into port only for food, wine, and if we needed money, to put Frank ashore so he could get a singing job. We were going to have a piano for Joe to play and a darkroom for me to develop and print the pictures he and I would take along the way.

We also planned to have a crew of no less than six women ". . . who would not be possessive of any of us . . . ." to do all the work and to make our lives more pleasant. Hey, if you're going to have a fantasy, I say, have a good one.

He was going to take flying lessons and may have actually taken one or two. His future wife, Stella Magee, took lessons, too, and did earn her pilot's license. He also took golf lessons.

Joe probably took more golf lessons than anyone who ever lived. I would get a call from New York or Miami, or wherever he happened to be at the moment, proclaiming, "I just took a lesson from (fill in the name of any pro), and he showed me something I never knew before. He made the game so simple. I'll show you as soon as I get out there."

Of course, when we next went to a driving range, there was no difference in his swing, and no improvement in his score. Score wasn't important to us, anyway. We just played to have a good time together and rarely kept count.

Chapter 10
Competition Intensifies for Joe

I was seriously considering "Velvet," Amber when I got a call from someone named Joan McC. I didn't know anyone by that name, and I had no idea how she found me. She had a small agency, and she, too, wanted to talk about representing Joe. Since it was a free lunch, I figured, *Why the heck not.* Joan showed up with an associate with whom she seemed to be living at the time. After getting to know him, I decided that it was a very strange relationship, one eventually doomed to failure. Long before she became an agent, Joan had been a trick rider in rodeos, an actress, and a writer.

At one point in my life, she became *my* agent when she opened a literary division. Again, I'm getting ahead of myself. Joan became more than a business associate. Eventually, we did a lot of things together, including some writing.

At lunch, she expressed her desire to represent Joe, and I explained that I was still interviewing agents and that right then, she had as much chance as anyone, but that I could promise nothing. Joan and I took an immediate liking to one another and talked every day for the next few weeks. She introduced me to a husband and wife writing team, Dana and Martin Weiss, with whom I was to become very close. Nothing makes you closer than failing at a lot of things together. They had a script they wanted me to read, ideal for José Ferrer. Actually, I loved the script and gave it to Joe. He would have done it in a minute except for one fact of Hollywood life: they couldn't raise the money. They would get someone to put up the "below the line" costs and then couldn't raise the "above the line" costs, or it would happen the other way. They could never get backers for both halves at the same time.

One day, Joan called and said she wanted me to meet a young lady who worked in the agency. She went to work with Joan on or about her twenty-first birthday and was then only twenty-three or four. The implication was that if I brought Joe into the agency, she'd get this young lady to grant me, and of course, Joe, certain favors. I told Joan that she ought to keep the thought in the back of her mind, and that some day she could introduce her protégé to Joe and me, and maybe let nature take its course. Unfortunately, after several years of very active heterosexual relationships, all casual, Anita informed Joan that she was switching to girls and was no longer interested in men. She eventually went to work for another agency, after Joan closed the doors of her own.

Anita and Joan were "members" of a place called The 101 Club, which was a swing club back when "swing" had nothing to do with music and dancing. I ended up with a lifetime membership when I designed a tasteful ad for *What's Happening* magazine. "Lifetime" amounted to about five months when their location was revealed in a *Newsweek* article on "swinging" and the club was forced to close its doors after the publicity.

I was an occasional visitor to the club, mostly during the day, when my friend, Joe Price, and I used to sit in the shade of the trees and write together. Joe particularly liked working there, although he was often distracted when the few females who lived there would walk around naked.

A few times during the very hot summer, my wife and I would go there at night during the week to swim. Parties were only on Friday and Saturday nights. They kept the grounds dark at night in order to save on electricity costs, and since we were the only people using the pool, we were able to go skinny-dipping. During party nights, nudity was required, but sex in the pool was prohibited.

Of course, all that had very little to do with Joe Ferrer, except that Joe was due back in Los Angeles to do a guest shot on *Columbo*, and Joan called me to see if she could meet him. I had not yet signed Joe to any agent, although I let Velvet and anyone else present offers. Joe had a day off, and Joan filled it by inviting us both to lunch.

We arrived at a very nice restaurant on Wilshire Boulevard to find that Joan, her live-in, and a very pretty young starlet who I knew from the agency were already seated. The starlet was to be, I gathered, a sort of offering to Joe as a potential inducement to sign with their agency.

About half way through lunch, the sweet young thing turned to me and whispered, "Should I be impressed by him?" She hadn't the foggiest notion who José Ferrer might be.

I said, "Yes, you should be impressed."

Joan had apparently arranged for the girl to go back to Joe's hotel if he wanted. Although Joe didn't commit one way or the other to Joan and her agency, the "offering" did go back to Joe's hotel with him. I have no idea what eventually happened to her other than a photo series I saw that included her in a very soft core "art" book by Rafaelli, who I mentioned earlier with reference to Steve Gold and Jerry Goldstein.

Oh, yes. Joe did have one minor involvement with the 101 Club, although not at the club itself, and then only with one of the members. There was a party in the Hollywood Hills above Sunset Boulevard to which Joan had invited us. After I picked up Joe at the airport, I told him about the party and asked if he wanted to go. He did. It was in a private home, and of course, Joan and Anita—before her "conversion"—were there. Joe did disappear with Anita for about half an hour, but he still didn't sign with the agency.

Very early on in my relationship with Joe, I received a telephone call from a Susan Christ, who identified herself as an "old friend" of Joe's. I had never heard the name, and she didn't sound very old, but then Joe and I hadn't been friends ourselves very long.

Susan, who had done many things over the years, was at that time involved with the HEAR Foundation, an organization working with deaf children. She wanted to know if Joe would appear at a benefit for them. The late Johnny Ray, who was famous for the song "Cry," was the host, and actor Michael Parks was scheduled to appear.

I called Joe and he confirmed that they were indeed very good friends. She had worked for him in New York as a secretary, and then for a playwright friend of his. He hadn't seen her in some time, and I'm not sure if he even knew she was living in California. I told him I thought it would be a pretty good idea, if only for the publicity, which he needed in California. He agreed, and we showed up early as requested, at the Pasadena Civic Auditorium.

Sue hadn't mentioned anything about a performance, and as Johnny Ray was already scheduled to sing, I thought that would be just a public appearance for Joe; he would say a few words extolling the HEAR Foundation, and we'd be off somewhere. However, when we arrived, some girl who was heavily involved with the charity asked me if Joe would sing something from *Man of La Mancha*. I said, "I really don't know how he could do it without a rehearsal or anything." She begged me to ask him.

He said, "If it'll help Sue, I'll give it a try." He talked to the band that would play for Johnny Ray and they decided they could do "The Impossible Dream." I admit that I had my doubts about it, mostly because of the high note at the end. While Joe was a more than adequate singer, I didn't want him to be embarrassed by a bad performance because he didn't rehearse or even have a chance to vocalize.

Anyway, he went on stage and did it, and I held my breath waiting for the high note at the end, figuring he would, under the circumstances, never go for it, only he did and he hit it, which proved something to me: Joe could do almost anything he set his mind to. I suspect that if someone asked him to perform emergency surgery, he'd give it a try and probably get away with it.

MORE FUN AND GAMES

One day I got a call from Joan—the agent—asking if I would bring Joe to a party she was throwing in Century City for some magazine. I asked, "Are there going to be girls there?"

Joan replied, "Have you ever been to one of my parties where there weren't girls?" Since I had been to a half dozen or so parties with Joan, no further answer was needed.

We showed up at the appointed hour, looked around, and realized that the gathering might be a pretty dull affair. If there were girls there, we didn't notice them. We figured we'd have a few drinks on Joan, eat some of her food, and then take off.

I told Joan that we were going to leave, and she said, "Wait just a minute."

Within a few seconds, she showed up with a beautiful girl in tow, one whom I knew from a stint running my friend, Beverly Hecht's, commercial talent agency while she was busy having a minor nervous breakdown. I had known Beverly from the first day I arrived in Los Angeles, when she was in my folk's living room.

Jean was a client of the agency and I hadn't seen her in almost a year. Joe was smitten instantly, and we stayed.

While Joe was in town, he called Jean frequently, they shared several lunches and a couple of dinners, and Joe sent her an album of the opera he directed. One day, I received a call from Jean, who asked, "What does he want from me? He sent me this album and I don't even like opera."

I said I'd be happy to tell him that, but also that I couldn't speak for him with regard to what he wanted from her. I didn't carry that any farther, but I thought it really should have been pretty obvious.

She replied, "Well, I like him and all that, but he's way too old for me."

I relayed the information to Joe, and he stopped calling immediately. He added, "Did you notice, she's got absolutely perfect breasts?"

I answered, "They should be. She paid enough for them."

Chapter 11
Life with Stella

Long before they were married, Joe's lovely wife to be, Stella Magee, a woman I consider one of the great ladies I have known, said to him, "I don't like it when you go to California without me. Jack is always getting you in trouble."

I hereby categorically deny that statement. I never once got Joe into any trouble. In fact, neither of us ever got the other in any "trouble." We did a lot of stuff together, some of it certainly on the "fun" side, but mostly we just hung together. We golfed, we drank, we discussed everything from crossword puzzles to politics, and yes, we sort of chased together, but never seriously. We just did a lot of flirting.

I don't need to elaborate, but it is widely known that Joe had a well-deserved reputation with the ladies, an animal magnetism that attracted women of all ages. He was often referred to as a "hot-blooded Latin lover." I guess you would have to say it was true. Joe did know a lot of women over the years, and frequently in the Biblical sense. Of Stella, Joe would frequently say to me, "One of these days, I'm going to make an honest woman of her." And of course, he did.

He always gave Stella credit for their good fortune. Stella eventually took over all of his business affairs, managed his money, and made some sense of his investments. One day, Joe said to me, "If it wasn't for Stella, I wouldn't have a dime." She not only put his financial affairs in order, but as Joe said, "She's made me solvent, and I'll be able to take care of her long after I'm gone."

Joe once said, "Stella re-established relationships with former friends I'd alienated over the years, and people talk to me again." I cannot say who those "people" were, because he never elaborated, but they would be on the east coast. Stella had a remarkable way with people and I don't think there is a person in the world who knew her who also didn't love her.

I must also add that Stella took a back seat to no one in the looks department, either. I don't recall that Joe's first wife, Uta Hagen, was any great beauty, but his second, Phyllis Hill, was most certainly a woman of uncommon looks, and his third, Rosemary Clooney, was absolutely a knockout when they married.

I cannot speak much to Joe's life in New York, Puerto Rico, and Florida, because I was not part of it. He always maintained an apartment in Manhattan, and for more than thirty years, a home in Ossining, New York. He eventually moved into a home in Coconut Grove, Florida, that was small by his definition, but primarily because there was no state income tax. He also lived in Santurce, Puerto Rico, for a time, using that as his "permanent" address because of taxes or something on an estate left to him by his mother. Eventually, he disposed of the penthouse in Puerto Rico and the "farm" in Ossining.

Joe's New York apartment, located just a half block from Carnegie Hall and almost directly across the street from the Russian Tea Room, featured a two-story living room with floor to ceiling windows. Over the years, the building was being slowly turned into offices, but because of rent control, Joe never wanted to move, although he eventually did, to an apartment on Central Park West. The new location was not as ideally situated as the old, which was within walking distance of the theater district.

A STORY THAT IS NOW FAMOUS

Joe called one night to tell me a story about an incident that occurred in the building that afternoon. I have heard other people relate this story about Joe, but they never get it quite right. I will tell it to you *exactly* as Joe told it to me.

First, I'll set the stage, so to speak. Joe was very well-known in the building, having lived there in his ninth-floor apartment for more than thirty years. One early evening, as the offices were emptying for the night, he decided to go downstairs for a newspaper. The rest of the story is his:

"The elevator was pretty full and everyone said hello, or 'Hi, Joe,' 'Good evening, José,' or 'Hello, Mr. Ferrer.' I acknowledged them all. Standing next to me was a forty-ish, fairly attractive woman, wearing glasses. When everyone else finished their greetings and the elevator was quiet, this person turned to me and said, in a voice loud enough to be heard back on the ninth floor, 'Mr. Ferrer, can I suck your cock?' In my usual brilliant way, I said something like, 'Uh, not right now, thanks,' and we rode the rest of the way down in silence.

"When we got to the ground floor, a friend stopped me, grabbing my arm, saying, 'Joe, don't you know who that was?' I had no idea and said so. 'That was Dustin Hoffman.'"

Hoffman was filming *Tootsie*, and was making the rounds, testing out his makeup. Joe said, "My God, I know Dusty so well, I couldn't believe I didn't recognize him." Hoffman told the story on *Jay Leno* in 2009, changing only one word, which was bleeped, anyway.

Anyway, almost every time someone brings up his name, someone in the group will say, "Let me tell you a story about Joe." Trust me, you have just heard it exactly as Joe related it to me.

I GET AROUND TO SOME MORE SERIOUS MANAGING

Even though Joe spent most of his life in the east or traveling, as I mentioned earlier, we were always in touch by telephone and letter. Mostly, our relationship was basically on a more important level than just business. We were friends. The "management" part of our lives was only incidental, although reasonably important since it soon brought his career back to life.

I finally put Joe with the agent, Velvet Amber, whom I've already mentioned. She did indeed pound the pavement and revitalized his career. Any number of casting directors, directors, and agents thought Joe was dead, literally, not figuratively. There were people who didn't want to take a chance on Joe because in the distant past he did have a habit of backing out of deals, but *never* after he signed a contract. He always claimed that when he decided against doing a project, it was always with the understanding of the producer or agent that he had not formally agreed to do the job; that they were just having discussions.

I should make it clear that as much as I loved Joe as a human being, he was not always the best client a person could have, as you will see. About a couple of years after Velvet started him back on the road to prominence, he suddenly began to turn down offers.

Those offers were not for small or unimportant roles. The money was excellent and the parts outstanding. He turned down four major projects in a row, and Stella and I spent hours on the telephone trying to figure out what we could do to get him to go back to work.

Joe was going through a more or less typical late mid-life crisis, doubting his abilities as an actor. He was often almost morbid about his future, saying things like, "I'm dead as an actor," and what's worse, saying it to interviewers so those comments found their way into print. It was a difficult fight to get him to once again believe in himself. I'm not sure I actually ever did. He may have just worked through it himself, or perhaps with Stella's help, or maybe he came to realize that the offers he was getting weren't out of pity.

The problem wasn't the quality of the offers or the money they were willing to pay, because Velvet was generating good parts in major productions. The problem was that he turned down roles that were excellent, and even though Joe refused to believe it, once the important people knew he was available, they *did* want him. That is not to say he turned down everything. It all depended on how much he wanted to come to California to see his kids.

Of course, he starred in *The Marcus-Nelson Murder Case*, from which *Kojak* spun off, making Telly Savalas a star. Joe portrayed an attorney and was exceptional. He co-starred with Peter Ustinov in *Gideon*, as the Angel of God, and with Henry Fonda in *Gideon's Trumpet*. Oddly, Joe and Henry never appeared in a scene together and met on the set one day just because they were old friends.

The point is that whenever there was a good script, Joe was terrific. When the scripts were ho-hum, he was better than average. It's not my intention to list all the television shows he did as a result of "Velvet's" work, but she did put him back in the public eye. However, there was one fairly minor role he took that I should mention. He was hired for a role in the television production of *Evita*, not a version of the stage play, but one of her early life. Joe portrayed the "Tango Singer" who took her virginity. The scene was on a train and called for Joe to "put his hand inside her blouse and massage her breasts.

The role of Evita was played by Faye Dunaway. The scene was shot on a closed set and Joe, being a method actor did exactly what the scene called for.

In going through my correspondence files, I realized that Joe turned down or ignored a great many offers with never an explanation. I accepted that because I was his friend, and not someone only interested in making money from his work. I suspect that he didn't want to work on the west coast because he felt unappreciated, or certainly *under*appreciated. I think there is considerable truth in that, but by then, Joe was very defensive about his relationships with Hollywood. It was a struggle to get him to work, and I remember saying to him, "Joe, if you won't work, you won't get work."

It's almost axiomatic in Hollywood that if you aren't working, not even necessarily on something good, people tend to forget, or even ignore you. Talent is not always a factor in casting. Consider the fact that in television, at least at that time, the industry first checked to see what your "TVQ" was. TVQ was some idiot's idea that unless you were instantly recognizable, by name, unless a certain sampling of the viewing audience knew who you were, you couldn't get a job. Who knows what that sampling consisted of, or what percentage of those people ever saw a play, read a book, or if they had any sense of the history of the industry? Jim Backus ran into the same TVQ problem, which was crazy!

Of course, looking at movies and television at the end of the 1990s and beyond, what we see is show after show, movie after movie, with names that no one knows and faces that all look alike. Everything is "white bread" regardless of their skin color or ethnicity. Talking with "older" actors—anyone over fifty—they tended to agree that there are very few real stars today. One or two who are instantly recognizable, but the Gables, Waynes, Grants, Stewarts, Coopers, and yes, even Ferrers are missing. There are Miguel Ferrer and Rafael Ferrer to carry on the name, and they're pretty good. Their father was proud of them, when they were breaking in, and he'd be even more proud today.

Actors have complained to me that they couldn't get roles because a part of the industry would go abroad to hire an English actor for a part that an American actor could have easily portrayed. The reason, they opined, was one of snob appeal, but not because the talent didn't exist in Hollywood or New York. I once asked Sheldon Leonard, a famous television producer and formerly a major motion picture and television actor, why he gave up working. His answer was that he couldn't stand working with the "morons who were now running the industry."

I TAKE A CHANCE TO SPOUT OFF

Leaving Joe for a moment, I'd like to express my personal feelings about certain aspects of "The Industry." It's my considered opinion that the moguls who run television and, to a great extent, the motion picture business, but not all, of course, have little concept of good and bad because they aren't sufficiently up on the history of their media. "History," to many of them, seems to go back only a dozen years. Since the glory days of the "studios" and their "star system," they have little more than a crop of largely mediocre actors to compare with even worse actors; mediocre writers to compare with incompetent writers, and what we, the viewing audience, settle for is too many actors, producers, directors, and writers capable only of re-writing mediocre product or making sequels of even worse product. An awful lot of the product is simply a rip-off of something else. Famous writer/directors steal blatantly from old pictures and are considered geniuses.

I have to wonder what has happened to the taste of our reviewers. There are very few intelligent, analytical critics anymore, although there certainly are some. Mostly they seem to be people who pander to producers so they continue to get free tickets. When I was in the publishing business, Steve Tolin and I did movie reviews. We weren't important enough to be invited to screenings, but did get free tickets from production companies—until we panned a picture. Then, the tickets stopped.

Our standards seem to have fallen so low that virtually anyone can be a star today, trash films can gross $100 million dollars, and maybe still lose money. I've always maintained that it's no great feat to spend money. The trick is to produce good product on smaller budgets.

That is not to say there are no good actors around. There is a handful, but there are too many inadequate actors masquerading as stars. I will relate a little story to point out one of things to which I refer: two of José's children were taking acting classes from a famous coach in Hollywood. Joe was asked to come to a session and critique student performances other than his own children. He listened to half a dozen or so, when the famous teacher stopped and asked him, "What do you think, so far?"

Joe answered, "What do I think of what? I didn't understand a word they said. Who are they talking to?"

The word "projection" seems to have no meaning any more. I won't even get into the music business and its fascination with pre-teen girls who have voices which wouldn't carry as far as the footlights without microphones and the backing of a half-dozen singers. Either that or they are screechers.

Go to the theater, not the movies, and you find that today virtually everyone has a microphone attached. Musical theater is a joke because singers have voices that can't be heard beyond the second row without electronic assistance. Of course, that may be a slight exaggeration, because I know some singers and actors fully capable of reaching the uppermost balcony without effort, but I remember going to the theater when I was young and being able to hear clearly every word from the back row, long before actors were electronically enhanced.

What all that has to do with Joe is only that I remember someone referring to his acting style as "bravura," more suited to the stage, and to an extent, there was some truth in that statement. However, most of today's actors go to the opposite extreme and underplay to the point of non-performing. Which was one of the reasons I tend to defend Joe so vigorously.

Over the years of our relationship, I turned down many, many scripts because I felt the quality was too inferior to even offer Joe. Obviously, he did take some work, and sometimes took work I wouldn't have recommended. But remember, I was working as his *friend*, not someone just looking to make a buck. If Joe wanted to do something, even if I disagreed, I was behind him all the way.

Although he always had reasons, I think largely he took that kind of work because it *didn't* require him to stretch as an actor. He once took a job so he could work with his son, Miguel. He took a job narrating "Peter and The Wolf" at some school back east as an excuse for not taking a major motion picture. When I met William Shatner, best known as Captain James Kirk of the *Star Trek* Starship Enterprise, he told me, "I'm getting rich taking parts that Joe's turning down."

Eventually, I started getting mad with his reluctance to work, his signing with New York agents, his not signing contracts with an agent in Los Angeles, his ignoring offers from legitimate producers and directors, and I must say, the more he did it, the harder it was for Velvet to get him work. The word was out that Joe was being difficult, and I wrote and told him so.

The end result was that after several years, we agreed to end our *official* business relationship, in favor of our even more official friendship. I continued to represent him more or less until his death. He still came to me for advice and I still got him offers, some of which he took, but I mailed back every commission check he sent me. One day, he wrote to say that I was getting a VCR and to try to send *that* back.

WE WILL GO TO ALMOST ANY EXTREME

I have talked about our work trying to get *Cyrano* back on the boards, and there was almost nothing he wouldn't do to raise money. Had he been able to sell his body, in the figurative sense, he would have done it. In fact, he once came close.

Joe heard about a woman who lived at the Beverly Hills Hotel, reportedly as rich as Croesus, who might be interested in backing the show. He made a date for lunch at the hotel, but told me to be sure to call at a certain hour. He would tell me how things were going.

At the appointed time, I called, and he said, "Get over here right now. I've saved you a half bottle of wine." From that, I deduced that things weren't going well and that he needed help. I raced to the hotel and into the dining room, where there was indeed a half bottle of wine waiting, which I immediately consumed.

The lady appeared to be in her sixties and rather worn out; she was far from attractive, but neither was she a dog. We consumed another bottle of wine and ordered a couple more bottles to go. If he was to do anything to or with that woman, he would have to be a long way from sober. I also immediately called Frank Sorel and said, "Get your ass to Joe's. He needs your help." Frank arrived within minutes of our arrival at the home Joe was leasing on Benedict Canyon, but no amount of drink could get any of us to a state where we could service the lady in any way she might have wanted.

Finally, she said, "I have three daughters. How would you like me to have them come over and we can have an orgy?" She produced pictures of her daughters and they were all very pretty, but unfortunately, none of the three daughters were home.

"Shall I call my ex-daughter-in-law? She can join us for dinner." Seeing no way to get rid of her, we agreed, and were met at a restaurant by exactly the type of woman I have always disliked: "Eastern Finishing School." She was tall, lanky, slouchy, but honestly, in that instance, very attractive.

WE ALL MAKE A NEW FRIEND

Carole, the ex-daughter-in-law, was not feeling well, but thought that company would do her some good. She was a terrific dinner guest, bright, well read, possessed good communications skills, and was easy to be with—to the point that we completely forgot her ex-mother-in-law. After dinner, everyone except the mother-in-law exchanged telephone numbers and we all went our merry way.

Joe was the first to call me and say, "I'm going to call Carole. I want to take her out." He did, and subsequently took her to dinner a few times and lunch several times. One day, I got a call from Carole.

"Jack," she said, "do me a favor and call Joe for me. Tell him I love having lunch with him and I love hearing the stories he has to tell, but tell him I don't want to fuck him." Just like that.

I said, "Okay," and then called Joe, who said that it was okay with him. A couple days later, Frank called and told me now that José (as he always called him) wasn't seeing Carole, but he was going to call her. I said that was okay with me; that I had no opinion one way or the other.

A few weeks passed and the telephone rang. It was Carole. "Jack," she said, "I really enjoy having lunch with Frank and I love the stories he tells me, but do me a favor . . . call him and tell him I won't fuck him, either."

Finally, I decided that I ought to ask her out to dinner, which I did. We returned to her house and stood in the kitchen, talking for about an hour. Since I had no intention of being the third one to get the message from Carole, we decided we should become good friends, and did. She was employed by Universal Studios, and I even went to a screening of a film with her, her stepfather, and her mother. Her stepfather wasn't fond of the idea that Carole was "dating" a married man, but her mother took a liking to me.

Oh, yes! It turned out that Carole's ex-mother-in-law didn't have any money of her own. Her ex-husband paid all her bills.

I have mentioned *The Marcus-Nelson Murders*. The script was by Abby Mann, who was known for his adaptation of and the scripting of the Nuremberg trials after the Second World War. Abby was, and probably still is, king of the adaptations. Joe also worked in a couple other projects he wrote, but the following deals with the shooting of Marcus and Nelson.

I dropped by the studio one morning and met Joe in his trailer. "There's a couple of good-looking women extras on this show," he said. "I think one of them has the hots for me. She's coming to my trailer at lunch time. Who knows, maybe she'll take care of us both."

"Which ones?" I asked.

"I can't remember her name, but she's a brunette, sitting with a girl friend, a blonde. You can have the blonde. Go introduce yourself to them."

So, I dutifully went over to a blonde and a brunette, who were sitting together, and struck up a conversation. The brunette was indeed beautiful and the blonde was good-looking in a "tired" sort of way. Being Joe's manager, and because I always did what he asked, I made friends.

At lunch time, the brunette did indeed show up at his trailer, but with a deck of cards in her hand. She proceeded to give us both a card reading. The lady was a psychic of sorts—really. She'd been studied at Duke University, and did Tarot and regular card readings both for fun and profit. In our case, it was for fun. It turned out that she was also some kind of minister, so you can see that Joe was not *always* perceptive when it came to women. The brunette eventually came to be a very close friend and later worked for me as a secretary.

I came to dislike Telly Savalas on that show. Twice, he held up production, once because his personal tailor was coming to fit him for a suit, and once because someone was sending over a hooker. I was in his trailer when the call came about the hooker, so I know it's true. Later, I came to dislike him even more when I started producing celebrity golf tournaments for charity and he would accept and then not show up, or send one of his brothers.

JOE WILL DO MOST ANYTHING IF IT HELPS HIS KIDS

Joe was offered a part in a movie filming in Lexington, Kentucky. Joe's son, Miguel, had been hired for a small part in a racehorse epic called *And They're Off*, and Miguel asked the director how he would like his father for the picture. Obviously, the guy went bananas for the idea and called Joe, who took the part, not so much for the money, but so he could be in a movie with his son. Then, he got his youngest son, Rafi, a part in the movie, too.

The story was as hackneyed as ever was made. It involved a poor but honest jockey in love with a rich but wonderful girl whose father owned race horses. There was also a has-been horse trainer (Joe), who owns a horse that no one ever gave a chance to win anything. He ends up with his horse in the Kentucky Derby running against the horse owned by the rich but cruel father of the young girl in love with the poor but honest jockey who is riding the has-been trainer's horse.

The producer, in an interview, described this picture as "Academy Award" quality. Joe said it was a stinker, "but they paid my price."

I found a note from him in which he says, "I'm supposed to be a down-at-the-heels horse trainer. So far, he's bought me seven sports jackets." He also bought and gave Joe a full-length leather coat. We should all be so "down-at-the-heels."

The picture never actually saw the light of day, and as far as I know, remains uncut in a bank vault. A banker who funded the picture, and who was going to fund two more pictures for the same producer/director, had embezzled the money from his bank and had the misfortune to get caught.

While Joe was in Lexington, he wasn't needed every day, and so the producer told him to go play golf whenever he wanted to and "just charge whatever you need to the company." So, he charged a set of golf clubs.

As it happened, a charity tournament was to be played at Greenbriar Golf and Country Club in Lexington and they asked Joe to play. They loved him and asked if he could bring a few celebrities the next year. He told them, "You have to talk to my manager."

They did, and that's how I came to be involved with that tournament for some fourteen years. The Children's Charities of the Bluegrass tournament committee (boy that's a mouthful) called me early the next year and asked me to bring five or six celebrities. Other than Joe, Leslie Nielsen, and Alex Trebek, I don't exactly recall who the others were. That is more a tribute to the loss of my memory than to their lack of celebrity.

Truthfully, over the ensuing years, I brought so many celebrities to Lexington, I can't keep them all straight, but the list included people like Hal Linden, Robert Morse, and Donald O'Connor, all of whom appeared on a show I produced for the tournament.

Robert Morse spent an afternoon playing with the children and an evening dancing with wives of tournament committeemen. Dale Robertson spent an afternoon in the hotel lobby playing the piano, and Leslie Nielsen entertained the ladies with his party specialty (a device which generated a sound exactly like the expulsion of gas) at a cocktail gathering in the office of Valvoline, one of the early sponsors. There were many, many more famous, near famous, and not so famous, but all did their part in making the tournament a huge financial success. I figure that during my fourteen years with the event, we raised at least a couple million dollars.

Chapter 12
The (Bing) Crosby Clambake

One year, Joe was invited by Kathy Crosby, Bing's widow, to play in the Crosby Clambake Golf Tournament at Pebble Beach, California, back before it became the AT&T Something Or Other, and obviously before Kathy moved the event to North Carolina. Generally, everyone, including celebrities, paid their own way into the tournament, but she invited Joe as her guest. He and Bing had been good friends. Besides, Joe told her he couldn't possibly afford it. Joe asked me to go with him.

Joe and I were billeted in the weekend home of Marcy and Stan Hyman, a wealthy couple, who lived just off the golf course at Quail Valley Lodge in Carmel Valley. We were shown into a huge bedroom with two queen-size beds and told, "You're on your own here. Breakfast stuff will be on the table in the morning if you want, but otherwise just pretend we're not around."

As soon as we settled into the room, Joe asked me, "Do you have any laundry?"

"We just got here," I said. "What could be dirty?" Joe brought dirty laundry with him and he went directly to the washing machine in the house and did a load.

Our hosts took an almost immediate liking to Joe and rather than being aloof, spent all their free time with us. Before the tournament, Marcy took us to play the golf course at Quail Valley and, of course, picked up the tab. One night, Joe took them to dinner. Each afternoon following tournament play, they were waiting for us in their immense living room with a couple of bottles of wine, which was hardly what I would call ignoring us. In fact, more than once, Stan cracked a "special" bottle from a vineyard in which he was a part owner.

No one had bothered explaining to Joe the way things were done at the Crosby Clambake Golf Tournament, so he was surprised to learn he had to hire his own caddie. Obviously, we had no idea where to get a caddie, but the Hymans or someone on the committee came up with a name. Normally, they told us, the caddies were paid $200 a day during the Crosby Clambake Golf Tournament, but Joe's caddie came marked down. He was only $100. Of course, he was half in the bag all the time, couldn't be counted on to arrive on time (although he would arrive at the last minute), and could rarely suggest the right club, but he did show up and he managed to carry the bag all three days without falling down once.

The weather at the Clambake was frequently and historically miserable. It had been played in rain, cold, and wind, but no one, as far as I knew, who ever played in the Crosby Clambake Golf Tournament dropped out. That year, the first thing I had to do each morning was scrape the ice off the windshield before we drove to the driving range.

Practice balls at the range cost $2 a bucket and even the pros paid. When they handed him a large bucket of brand new Titleists golf balls, I said, "Don't be a schmuck. Let's put the bucket in the car and then you can buy another bucket." He didn't think that was a good idea. Actually, he thought we couldn't get away with it.

Part of the tradition of the Crosby Clambake Golf Tournament was the Clambake, a dinner the night before the tournament to which only golfers were invited. As I was not a player, I wasn't allowed to attend, at least theoretically. However, Joe's oldest daughter, Maria, was dating Harry Crosby, the older of the two boys from Bing's marriage to Kathy, and he invited me as his guest.

Women were not allowed at the party, except for Rosemary Clooney, who entertained. She and Bing were very close, and from time to time, rumored to be involved romantically with one another. I am not in a position to say. I only know the rumors, and who am I to repeat rumors?

At that particular time, Joe and Rosemary were more or less congenial, so we went backstage immediately after the show to congratulate her on her performance. Wandering around as we waited for Rosemary, I ran into Alan Jardine of The Beach Boys. He was living in Big Sur, raising Angora goats and horses. His wife, Linda, was very much into horses and was a rider long before they got rich enough to move to Big Sur and raise them. Alan was surprised to see me there, and even more surprised that I was with Joe. I imagine he thought there was no life for me after The Beach Boys.

Jack Lemmon, who played in the tournament every year he wasn't working, called the Hyman's to ask Joe to join him at The Lodge for dinner, but Joe declined. It was a period of time when Joe was rather reclusive compared to most other celebrities, and another reason why his personal reputation in Hollywood suffered. Joe never was a member of the Hollywood party crowd, although he and Rosemary entertained all the time at their home in Beverly Hills when they were married. Joe said, "If we go there, we'll have to sit and drink (not that he was against drinking), and I'll have to buy a round every time he does, and it'll cost a fortune for dinner, and besides, I find him pretty boring. So, we went to dinner with the Hymans.

Although Joe was never a really good golfer, he never lacked for confidence and played rather well each of the first three days of the pro-am competition. Two things come to mind about the tournament: on one par four hole, he flew the green on his third shot, and the ball came to rest in a trap about seven feet deep. He walked down into the trap and lined up for his shot. Just as he was in mid-downswing, a voice called out from the gallery, "I bet you don't make it!"

Joe managed to stop his swing, stepped back from the ball, realigned himself, swung, and sent a high-arcing shot out of the trap to within a few feet of the pin. He turned to the crowd, removed his hat and took a deep, sweeping bow, to considerable applause.

The second was an incident Joe asked me not to repeat, but I'm sure he'll forgive me, at least until I show up wherever he is in the next life, should there happen to be one. Besides, it really wasn't horrible. There was a beautifully picturesque par three with the tee facing the emerald green ocean directly behind the green. Joe put his drive two inches from the cup and sunk the putt for a gross two. With his stoke handicap on the hole, he had a net one. His pro and teammates were ecstatic.

As we were walking down the fairway, he whispered to me, "Don't ever tell anyone this, but I aimed at the wrong green. I thought it was the green over to the left."

Although it was strictly against the rules, I walked the course with him every day. All spectators, including friends, were supposed to stay outside the ropes that protected the fairways. I walked with him, and after one marshal suggested I go behind the barrier, I said, "That's okay, I'm with Mr. Ferrer." For some reason, that seemed to satisfy him and I never had any trouble again.

There was no chance that Joe and his pro partner would make the cut for the fourth day. Jack Lemmon had been trying for years and hadn't ever made it, and Jack was almost as fanatical about the game as Joe. So, we packed up our gear after play the third day, said our farewells to our hosts, promising that one day we would all get together again, loaded my car, and headed back to Los Angeles, listening to a new Rosemary Clooney tape I purchased just for the trip. Joe's marriage to Rosemary had been full of problems, but he always loved her voice, and said several times on the drive, "She still has the pipes." We let it run and replay for the entire six hour drive.

THERE'S ALWAYS SOMETHING ELSE

Joe was a great talker, and I was a great listener, so we often found ourselves sharing a bottle or two, particularly on nights when we sat around his suite in Los Angeles, or when we were off in Lexington, Kentucky, for a golf tournament. One night, I asked him what happened between him and Rosemary, with whom he had five children. I said that it was surprising they broke up because he loved his kids and certainly had nothing against marriage, having done it three times.

When Rosemary kicked him out after several years of marriage and five kids, he was surprised. "Why are you doing this?" he asked.

Paraphrasing Joe, paraphrasing Rosemary, she said, "You cheat on me all the time."

He replied, "What made you think I'd change just because we got married?"

One of the things that bothered him most about the divorce was that Rosemary tried, he thought, to ruin his relationship with their children after the divorce, although he had no real proof. When I met the kids, they seemed to respect him, although I never saw a lot of affection on their part. I saw him as a concerned father, who tried to earn their respect if nothing else.

I spent a little time with Miguel and Maria Ferrer, when Jim Backus and I were in Vancouver, British Columbia, for a charity event, and came to know them pretty well. By that time, I believe they had begun to understand their father and to forgive him for not being around as they were growing up, although at a party after Jim's appearance in Vancouver, Maria introduced me to someone in a way that shocked me. She said, "This is Jack Lloyd, he's the father I can talk to." I don't think Joe ever tried to buy their love or respect, at least I never saw any evidence of it. He did, however, keep making deposits into bank accounts he had set up for them.

When I was still with Far Out Productions, I took Maria and Miguel and my kids to The Troubadour, one of the "hot" clubs around town then, to see and hear Eric Burdon, who was without The Animals, but with War, his new band. From that time on, I practically considered them my second family. Rafi was still too young, but Maria, Miguel, Gabri, Monsita, and I seemed to get along well.

While Joe was out on the west coast to do a television show, the Motion Picture Academy called to say they were doing retrospectives that honored actors, and that they hoped he would come to a special showing of *Cyrano de Bergerac* at the Academy Theater. He called me and my wife, and we joined him, all the kids, and even Rosemary for the showing. They sat in the back row, and Phyllis and I in the row in front of them. Sometime into the picture, I realized that Joe wasn't in the theater. I cornered him after the movie and asked why he left.

"I never watch myself in pictures," he said. "Besides, I lived the part for twenty-nine years. I don't need to see it on the screen." Only once do I remember him asking what I thought of his performance in the television production of *Gideon's Trumpet* in which he co-starred with, but never actually worked with, Henry Fonda. I thought he was brilliant, but then, as I've said, I'm prejudiced. I admit that I didn't always think his television performances were brilliant, but that one certainly was.

JOE IS IN THE ROSE PARADE ON NEW YEAR'S DAY

I don't remember the year, but Joe was asked to ride and be the star on the Puerto Rico float in the New Year's Day Rose Parade before the Rose Bowl football game. He had to be there at six-thirty in the morning and hang around on or near the float. It was one of those cold January mornings, the temperature hovering around the low 40s, and he was to be without a coat because there would be no place to store it while he was on board. He was freezing, and he complained to me that they didn't have anything hot to drink, and there were no toilets in the shed where the float was stored. By the time I picked him up, he was desperate for coffee and a toilet.

He and a couple of former Miss Puerto Rico winners were on the float, which I saw only partially finished and never on television, so I had no idea what it really looked like. Someone asked me what the float was, and I said, "I think it was two guys mugging an old lady pushing a shopping cart." I categorically deny any prejudice, and Joe thought it was funny. He laughed, even though I lost the telephone numbers of the two girls with whom he shared the float. I picked him up in Pasadena right after the parade and took him to the home of Sandy Robin, a friend from my high school back in Chicago, where he thawed out while we all watched the Bowl games.

JOE THE LOVER

Speaking of his renowned prowess with women (okay I *wasn't* speaking of it, but I am now), Joe related a story about Lana Turner, for whom he always had a fantasy. I don't think Stella will mind me telling it. Joe said that while he always lusted after Lana, she was dating the actor, Turhan Bey, who, according to Joe, had a reputation as a very rough character indeed, and so he never made a move toward her even though the opportunity had presented itself once or twice.

He and Stella were somewhere, staying in a hotel. The hour was late, and they were already in bed when the telephone rang. It was Lana Turner. She said that she was all alone in bed in her suite in the same hotel, was lonely, and thought it would be nice if Joe came down and joined her. When he told Stella who it was, he remembered, "My stock went up in her eyes."

Sometime after the non-incident in the hotel, he ran into Turhan Bey. After exchanging a few pleasantries, Turhan said to Joe, "Do you remember how it was when we were fucking Lana?"

Joe answered, "You wouldn't have cared if I had fucked her?"

"Hell, no," answered Turhan, "I always thought you were doing her."

Joe told me it was one affair he always regretted not having. I said, "Jeez, Joe, you can't win them all."

There are just too many stories to tell, and there are obviously things that shouldn't be repeated because, after all, we're all entitled to our little secrets. But Joe was Puerto Rican and the epitome of the hot-blooded Latin lover. Okay, that was his excuse, anyway. He very likely deserved his reputation, even though some of the stories about him were mere speculation and had little or no bearing on the truth.

Here's how things can get misinterpreted: someone spotted him in San Francisco having lunch with an old friend, Anne Brake. The next day, Herb Caen reported in his column that "José Ferrer is going to marry a waitress."

Gossip reporter Rona Barrett picked up the item and I was tipped that she was going to use it on her radio show. I called her and explained that there was no truth to the story at all.

Rona said, "It was in Herb Caen's column, so it must be true."

I told her that Caen was absolutely wrong. I explained that using the story could possibly hurt another lady, one he *was* in love with and was very likely to eventually marry. She used the item anyway, with the very mild, and at that time, inaccurate disclaimer that "His manager says he's actually going to marry someone else."

Another example: Joe was in Los Angeles for another *Columbo* television show that starred Peter Falk. He and Rosemary were on good terms at the time, and because she wasn't feeling particularly well, he was staying at her (formerly their) home at 1019 Roxbury Drive, in Beverly Hills. After several days, he wanted desperately to get away somewhere for a weekend.

A lady friend (they were everywhere it seemed), who appeared with him in the "Doctor Sketch" in a production of *The Sunshine*

Boys in Florida, offered her apartment for the weekend when she was off to New York to visit her fiancé. Joe asked me to come over and spend the weekend with him. The plan was for us to lay in a supply of beer, cook our own meals, and watch football.

When I arrived at the apartment, Joe was lying on the bed with his blonde friend and her brunette sister. He said, "It's too bad you didn't get here an hour earlier, you could have joined us." I said, "Some friend . . . you couldn't wait?"

Joe and I spent the weekend like two bums, doing what we had planned: drinking beer, making our own meals, and watching television.

Later, some people brought up the weekend, asking about the women who were with us, and naming names, a couple of whom neither of us actually knew. I knew only one other person who knew about the weekend, and he denied spreading the rumors, but I didn't believe him. So much for good friends.

Because we spent so much time together, we were frequently tarred by the same brush, even though either or both of us might have been completely innocent.

HOW TO BE READY FOR WHATEVER COMES

Joe almost always had a set of golf clubs wherever he was, either a set he brought from New York, or one he had taken to leaving at my house. He also stored things with me so he wouldn't have to travel with anything more than a couple of carry-on bags. There were three large suitcases full of clothes in our home, mostly things like socks and underwear, but lots of golf shirts and cotton pants. He would either take the dirty stuff home with him, or Phyllis would wash, dry, fold, and store.

When Joe was in town working, we'd get together either in the afternoons or evening for conversation or food, sometimes drink, and frequently spend time chipping golf balls to one-another in his hotel suite. No whiffle balls for us. We left more than one dent in hotel room walls.

One night, after chipping balls for an hour and then contemplating going across the street to Greenblatt's Deli on Sunset Boulevard for sandwiches to bring back, the telephone rang. Joe Sirola, one-time king of the commercial voice-overs in New York, was calling from Spago, one of Los Angeles' hot restaurants. He had a table and wanted us to join him—really only Joe—but since I happened to be there, he included me in the invitation.

Now, Joe was not the kind who would ever go places to be seen. In fact, he went out of his way to avoid being in the public eye. He once took his real estate agent to dinner, and the next day, the gossip columns reported he was engaged.

Anyway, about going to dinner at Spago, Joe tried to beg out, but finally turned to me and said, "Do you want to go?"

"I don't care," I replied. "Greenblatt's is okay with me." Finally, Sirola won out.

You have to understand that Joe preferred to lay about the hotel in a pair of chino pants and a golf shirt, and whenever we went out, he'd just add a baseball jacket or a sweater. He was a casual kind of a guy, except when the occasion called for something fancier. He did own six tuxedos and was prepared for anything. So, that night, we weren't about to make an "appearance" when we showed up at the restaurant.

Joe, who was never ostentatious, would lease a small, foreign car when he arrived in town. His own personal car for years was an old Volkswagen square-back station wagon he garaged about four blocks from his New York apartment. When he and Stella traveled, they frequently loaded the car with pots and pans and stayed in places with a kitchen, just so they wouldn't have to go out to eat. He finally got a Volvo when he moved to Florida.

We arrived at Spago in his rented Toyota Corolla, and we were immediately ushered out of sight and away from the Rolls Royces, Mercedes Benz sedans, and Cadillacs. Of course, none of the paparazzi who always hung around Spago recognized Joe, and the people watchers outside never gave him a second look.

However, inside, Wolfgang Puck, the owner, came running up and made a big fuss as he escorted us to Sirola's table. Puck immediately sent over a couple of his special pizzas and we did our best to be inconspicuous, although it wasn't easy as Sirola had secured a table close to the front door.

I looked around the room and saw Red Buttons and Don Rickles at two tables as far away from the front door as possible. I mentioned it to Joe, and he said, "Oh, God, now I'll have to go over and talk to them." I suggested that he not do anything at all until and if they noticed him. Well, of course, someone told them that Joe was there, and they waved at him and signaled for him to join them.

A BIT ABOUT ME

I had taken to driving to Santa Barbara a couple of times a month to a writers' luncheon where I usually sat next to Barnaby Conrad. You might not recognize the name, but "Barney" was a celebrity in his own right. He was famous for being an American bullfighter, more correctly, a "matador" or killer of bulls. He was also an author, filmmaker, and artist, and as it turned out, an old friend of Joe's. He had made a film, *The Death of Manolete*, owned a restaurant in San Francisco, The Matador, and wrote books. Barney frequently took a bus to the luncheon unless he could get someone to drive him. The problem was that he no longer had a California Driver License as a result of a few drunken driving convictions. After my first time at the luncheon, I offered to drive him home on the way back to Los Angeles. One of the first things that caught my eye was a painting he had done of Joe Ferrer. There was also a painting of Manolete, and a chair he had painted to resemble Toulouse-Lautrec. Barney's wife, Mary, like her cousin Julia Child, was a gourmet chef.

Barney worked in a separate building that served as his studio and workshop. He kept a parrot there for company. When I started to reach for the bird, he warned me that the bird was given to biting, so I withdrew my hand. About ten minutes later, I was in the kitchen talking with Mary, when I heard the "click, click, click" of talons on the concrete walk between the studio and the house. The bird had decided to visit the kitchen. It came into the house and I reached down, whereupon the parrot immediately jumped on my hand. I said to Mary, "Barney told me he bites."

Mary replied, "Only Barney."

CHAPTER 13
Some Odds and Ends

I have tried to reconstruct most every event in my life with José Ferrer, but have found it a virtually impossible job. Even with the aid of a hypnotist to regress me, I don't think I could recall everything we did together. Then, I believe you won't do something under hypnosis you wouldn't do otherwise. And it's true that there are some things I wouldn't talk about even with a gun to my head. So, I've fallen back on that old saw, "When all else fails, look it up," in an effort to fill in more than a few gaps in my memory, and I'll still leave a lot out—some accidentally and some on purpose.

Looking through my files, I find pictures, sketches he had a habit of drawing on paper place mats, linen napkins, and occasionally on table cloths, but they never let us out of the restaurant with a tablecloth. We tried more than once, but restaurants are funny that way. Who knows, they may be hanging in some restaurant offices today.

Those sketches depicted all sorts of things, from something sexually suggestive to something scatological, or simply something he saw at the moment that inspired him. They weren't always good, but even Picasso had his bad days. On my wall, there is a large, color pencil rendition of *The Real Cyrano*, standing before a commode with the famous Cyrano nose for a penis and a penis for his nose. He always intended to replace it with a painting, but never got around to it.

I DO MY PART FOR CHARITIES, ETC.

It was through Joe that my involvement with charity golf started. Shortly after, or perhaps even before our business arrangement began,

Joe was invited to play in a charity event in Riverside, California, hosted by former L.A. Dodgers catcher, Steve Yeager. There was a practice round on Friday, and I drove down with Joe and Stella to play with them. Joe asked Don Willis, the head pro at Indian Hills Country Club, if his "manager" (me) could play in the tournament too, and Don said yes.

I don't know which came next, but I think it was a Billy Barty event benefiting dwarfism research at Via Verde Country Club. Joe was invited as a celebrity, and I was invited, I suppose, as an afterthought. I still got the full celebrity treatment, even when Joe had to cancel a week before the event.

Returning again to Joe (rather than me), little things keep popping into my head. For instance, long before he married Stella, my telephone rang about eleven o'clock one evening, Pacific Time. "Hi, it's Joe."

"Where the hell are you?"

"Cleveland. In a strip joint."

"What are you doing in Cleveland? What are you being punished for?"

"I'm here to do something with the Cleveland Symphony."

"So, okay, what's up?"

"I just wanted you to know that I'm sitting at the bar with my left arm around a black stripper and my right arm around a white stripper and they both want to go back to my room with me."

"You called just to make me feel bad, right?"

"Right. Talk to you later."

Joe frequently did things like that to me. One night, he called to say, "I just wanted you to know that I'm having lunch with (actress) Kathleen Turner and you're not." We both had the fantasy hots for her, only he figured out a way to meet her. He would talk about casting her in a play down in Coconut Grove, Florida, where he was the dollar-a-year Artistic Director of the Playhouse.

Another evening, he called to tell me that a friend had been accosted by a very creative panhandler on the streets of Manhattan. The fellow approached his friend and said, "Pardon me sir, but could you spare one dollar? I am attempting to amass the wherewithal to purchase the Chrysler Building." His friend could hardly refuse.

I mentioned that Joe loved jazz musicians. One day, as he was walking down 57th Street in Manhattan, Louis Bellson, the great jazz drummer, stopped him and said, "Joe, come with me, I need you."

"Where are we going?" asked Joe.

"Pearlie Mae and me are getting married and I need a best man." That's how Joe came to officiate at the wedding of Pearl Bailey and Louis Belson.

When John "Dizzy" Gillespie changed to his now famous trumpet with the horn pointing skyward, he gave his old trumpet to Joe for his youngest son, Rafi. I stored it at my home for five or six years because Joe decided Rafi was too young to appreciate it. Joe had come across it while rummaging around the garage one afternoon at Rosemary Clooney's home.

Joe and famed jazz bassist Chubby Jackson, kept up a correspondence that seemed almost daily. I have a copy of a long letter he wrote to Joe, a few lines of which I will quote because it's too long to copy it all. It will give you a taste of the regard in which Joe was held by all jazz musicians and a taste of Chubby:

" . . . imagine 43 some odd (very odd) years ago we began a friendship—some politicians would remark that 'it's lasted all these years 'cause we jes couldn't do each other any good.' "Bosh," I'd counter—I was taken by the fact that you loved jazz; played piano; owned a sense 'o' humor that I thought only musicians had; you were the classy Duke Ellington of the theater; you never saw what made Vincent Price tick; the affection that existed between you 'n mom; my everlasting respect for your abilities; the Wash. D.C. Sun. at a theater where you sang 'I Love Paris' . . . 'n I played for youse; the rehearsals for your act with Duffy 'n I (Ossining 'n N.Y.C. where Red Buttons came in to listen (my note: Duffy is Chubby's son, now considered one of the better drummers in the US of A); your walk-on-stage stride that captivated audiences, performers on stage 'n critics alike."

Chubby had just finished teaching a six-week community college course in "Scatsmanship," and included with the letter a piece of lesson material from his class that was titled, "Phonetic Sounds to Scat Sing." The sub-heading reads: "Use these words to build possible phrases." The list is as follows:

"BOO-DAY, BOO-WHEE, BOO-DEE, BOW-WOW-ZZZ-BOW/WOW/ZZZ, BAH, BOODLE, DIGGADA-DO, DOO-DLAH, BEE, DOOTIN-BOO, DOO-DOW, DLEE-DLEE, BOO-DLEE, BEE-DLEE, BOO 'N BOO, WHEE, TOO-DLEE, BOO-DLAH, YAH, BEE-DEE, DEE-DEE, WEE-BEE, BOO, BOO 'N DOO, and AH."

Joe said in his note accompanying the above, "Memorize these and we can go on the road together."

Joe would send anything he considered idiotic, wonderful, strange, or just pieces of mail he received, sometimes from people he had never met. Frequently, these came without comment, like the letter he received from Senator Jesse Helms asking him to attend a "reception victory dinner" sponsored by his reelection committee. The letter is signed simply, "Jesse." Joe sent it to me because he thought it was so funny. He was a dedicated Democrat and hated Jesse Helms.

Or a note that accompanied a check, reading only, "Dear Jack. Here you be. Enjoy! **PLUS** an extra $1.00 bonus!" followed, each on it's own line, by "Pie In The Sky! Balm in Gilead! Loose shoos! Tight pussy! A warm place to shit! Yrs. in Christ." Followed by his caricature signature.

Two post cards come up. One is his handwriting reading, "Air, Hair, Lair!" with the following explanation, "Upper class British pronunciation for OH, HELLO!" The second was a card he received from La Gorce Country Club, his golf club in Florida. It reads in part: "Notice—Shrimp Peel Rescheduled." He thought it would be of considerable interest to me.

There are menus from all sorts of restaurants and dinners, a solicitation from Southern Delite Co. asking for an investment for "as little as $12,500." His financial contribution would be to help fund the company, which needed only $25,000 to manufacture a food supplement "which gives a man of 60 or 70 or 80 or even 90 years of age the desire, strength, and ABILITY TO GET AN ERECTION! (their caps) And he can keep it erect until his wife or partner climaxes! It is called *Klimax Delite-Kum Again*." Joe's comment added to the top of the letter is, "Dear Jack, won't you be my first customer?"

There are post cards from everywhere, some utterly ludicrous, but all revealing his delicious sense of comedy, irony, satire, and more.

I just ran across a post card from Fiji showing a group of Fiji Islanders playing musical instruments and apparently singing. The message was, "Dear Jack—The Beach Boys say they miss you. They're waiting for you to come back. Always."

In the file, there is a tract on condoms, with a note stating, "the sort of thing I find in my local drug store."

That reminds me of a story Joe related concerning his college days. There was a local girl, who many of his fellow "Princetonians" used for casual and frequent sex. Joe said, and this is pretty close to an exact quote:

"I was getting horny, and so I called her and told her I was coming right over. She was not very attractive, but she was fine for an occasional blow job, which was what I had in mind when I got there. She was always agreeable, so there was no romancing involved, but this night she said, 'Why won't any of you guys fuck me? I get tired of just giving head.' Well, nothing brilliant came to mind, so I said, 'I would, but I don't have any protection with me.' She said, 'That's okay, I do,' whereupon she opened a drawer and withdrew a condom. I was stuck, and like a gentleman, I did my duty. Having finished, I was about to toss it in the commode when she grabbed it out of my hand. I had no idea what she planned to do, so I watched . . . as she washed it out, powdered it, rolled it up and tossed it back in the drawer."

Portrait Gallery #1
JOSÉ FERRER

Painting of José Ferrer by Barnaby Conrad.

Barnaby Conrad, American Matador, author of more than 15 books, artist, and writer/producer of *The Death of Manolete*.

A chair, painted as José Ferrer appeared as Toulouse Lautrec in *Moulin Rouge* on the porch at Barnaby Conrad's home.

Mary Conrad with Barnaby's parrot who bit only Barnaby.

José Ferrer and Ricardo Montalban at rehearsal for the Nosotros benefit at the world-famous Hollywood Bowl.

José Ferrer publicity shot for the film *Cyrano*, for which he was supposed to be paid $50,000. He never got the second $25,000.

José and actor/singer Francesco Sorianello visiting on the set of *The Return of Captain Nemo*, a TV mini-series.

José with co-star Horst Buchholtz in *Nemo*.

José's other co-star, Burgess Meredith.

Actor Mel Ferrer (no relation) visiting on the set of *Nemo*.

A small party for José's 75th birthday in his Los Angeles hotel suite.

Meredith McRae, host of the television show *Mid-Day, LA*, where José was a guest on our way to a day of golfing.

José and actor Fred Holliday, co-host for the day on *Mid-Day, LA*.

José dressed casually for a day of golf at *Mid-Day, LA*.

José with Stella Ferrer (his fourth wife) and singer Herb Jeffries.

José playing for Herb Jeffries at a small San Fernando Valley club.

José and me at the tournament in Lexington; the last time we were together, I didn't recognize his weight loss as a sign of his illness.

Chapter 14
Jim Backus Calls Me

Sometime in the early 1970s, I got a telephone call from Jim Backus. Now, for those of you who are too young—or way too old—to know who Jim was, I'll give you a brief, crash course. Jim's career, incidentally, is well-chronicled in books written by Jim and his wife, Henny. That's why this is going to be brief. For more details, read their books. Jim began his entertainment life in radio, first as a disc jockey in Cleveland, Ohio, and later as a radio actor in New York. His first venture in the "Big Apple" proved fruitless, and he returned to Cleveland and more disc jockey work.

When he put together enough money, he went back, and that time, he connected. At his peak, he was doing forty radio broadcasts a week, running from station to station. Although people always thought he did a great many voices, he really only did two. One was based on his father, which eventually evolved into Mr. Magoo, and the other, an all-purpose voice that he used for everything from a gruff policeman to the desk clerk at a seedy hotel. He probably first came to prominence as a character named Hubert Updyke, III on the Alan Young radio show. When the show moved to California in 1946, Jim and Henny went with it. The character was reborn on television in *Gilligan's Island* for you youngsters, now renamed Thurston Howell, III. Maybe even more people knew him as Mr. Magoo, the little fellow who stumbled nearsighted through life. A bit of trivia: Magoo's first name was Quincy.

Jim had trouble living down those characters because people refused to think of him as the serious dramatic actor he actually was. I refer you to the motion pictures, *Rebel Without a Cause* and *Ice Palace*, in which he co-starred with James Dean and Richard

Burton, to name just two. Jim played the part of "friend of the hero" in more movies than I would care to name, and of course, he earned even more fame on a half-dozen or so television shows, including *I Married Joan*, starring Joan Davis (who Jim considered the funniest woman in show business), and *The Jim Backus Show*. But, as I said, I'm not getting into a biography here.

Jim called one day and introduced himself. He wanted to meet with Joe, who was in town for a couple of weeks. I saw no earthly reason why they shouldn't get together, particularly as they were hardly strangers to one another. Jim's wife, Henny, acted in *The Great Man*, a film in which Joe starred and directed. Even though they had long ago been friends socially, Jim did the right thing by going through me.

Joe was staying at the Beverly Hills Hotel in one of their small suites. As a rule, that was his hotel of choice in Los Angeles until someone entered his room one night while he was sleeping and made off with his credit cards, cash, and jewelry.

Jim showed up with a writer named Jerry Devine. They had a play in tow, which Jerry had written, based on *School for Wives*, and which Jerry had retitled *The Amorous Flea*. They wanted to produce it as a musical, wanted Joe to direct, and had in mind Sammy Davis, Jr. for the lead. The primary difference in Jerry's version, other than music, was that it would take place in Haiti, where they copied the French styles, manners, customs, and clothing of that era. It was to be an all-Black production, so Sammy would have been perfect.

I met Jim and Jerry in the lobby and took them to Joe's room, where I left them to discuss business, promising to return in an hour because Joe and I were going to dinner somewhere. I'm not sure whether we actually had a dinner date, or it was just an excuse to hold the meeting to an hour.

When I returned, Jim and Jerry were already in the hall saying goodbye to Joe. Jim stopped me and said, "Joe told me what you did to get his career back on track. Would you consider doing the same thing for me?"

Needless to say, I was surprised and did the intelligent thing by saying, "I'm flattered Jim, but why do you need a manager?"

"Because, I can't get work anywhere and I don't know why. I can't even get on Merv Griffin's show, and he's one of my best friends."

Rather than jumping in with both feet I said, "Why don't I call you and we can talk it over?"

He agreed, and gave me a telephone number—with the admonition not to give it to anyone else, which was something I hardly had to be told, but Jim had a bit of paranoia in him. I promised to call him the next day.

Joe and I discussed the play idea and agreed that it might be fun it—the giant Hollywood "if"—Jim and Jerry could raise the money to produce it. They had already raised money to produce a "movie" called *Mooch*, and thought they could do the same for the play. I'll talk about *Mooch* a little later, because mostly, this is still about Joe, but right about here is where I found myself managing two people, both of whom I greatly admired.

I agreed to contact Sammy Davis, Jr. about the project, and did so. Actually, I spoke with his personal manager because Sammy never discussed business himself. The story goes that Sammy once sold 110 percent of himself, which is why he needed a manager. His manager loved the idea and said Sammy would, too, but he didn't think Jim and Jerry could afford him.

"How much?" I asked.

His manager gave it to me quick. "Let me put it this way: his nut is fifteen thou a week in town and twenty-five thou a week on the road. Sammy can't afford to do a play or anything else for less. That's why he works Vegas all the time."

After that, Jim and Jerry went about doing rewrites and Joe put the idea on the back burner. Besides, Joe was getting more offers for television work now—some good, some mediocre, but none bad.

He worked in an Abby Mann, short-lived series called *Medical Story*, played Spiros Skouros in the mini-series adaptation of Harold Robbins' *Dream Merchants*, portrayed a Walter Winchell-type reporter in *Banyon*, and a whole bunch more.

Hoyt Bowers, who was head of casting at Paramount at the time, loved Joe's work, and after one show with him, wanted to cast him in anything and everything in which he was involved. Hoyt became a good friend and would always grant a reading to anyone with whom I worked. Most of the time, I sent him gorgeous women with whom I worked either as a manager or on a consulting basis. The reason I sent them to Hoyt was because those young ladies were generally naive about directors, producers, casting directors, and casting couches, but Hoyt was only interested in them as talent.

A VERY HOLLYWOOD STORY

Which reminds me of a story that has nothing to do with Joe or Jim, but which does involve my agent friend, Velvet Amber and a gorgeous redhead with considerable acting talent. I decided to work with her and turned her over to "Velvet," who almost immediately was able to get her a few minor parts, an excellent beginning for a total unknown. Velvet and I could see many dollars on the horizon because she was a great type. One day, Velvet called to tell me that—let's call her "Ginger"—informed her that she was going to read for the lead in a movie. Now, we all know that unknowns almost never get to read for the lead in anything other than what we used to call "stag films."

I called "Ginger" and asked for details. She met a self-proclaimed producer, who told her she was perfect for the lead in his new film. Since he actually had a script, she was certain he was for real. They were supposed to meet at his office at nine o'clock that night.

I explained to her that legitimate producers do not ordinarily conduct auditions at nine o'clock in the evening, but she was positive this guy was straight arrow even though neither Velvet nor I had ever heard of him.

I said, "Okay, you can go to your reading, but Velvet and I are going with you."

"Fine," she said. "I'm sure he won't mind."

"He'd better not," I said.

At the appointed hour, we arrived at the producer's office, a cubicle in a trailer that was normally used as a small dressing room in a honey wagon on the General Studios lot. I knocked on the door, which opened about half-way.

The producer stuck his head out and said, "Yeah, who are you and whaddya want?" Obviously a class guy. Through the door, I could see a pair of very shapely legs, her skirt hiked up considerably above mid-thigh. I thought, *Very talented legs, I wonder what she's auditioning for.*

I told him who we were, and he said, "Well, I'm not going to talk to her right now. My associate, my comptroller, is taking care of that tonight."

"Can your comptroller say yea or nay if she does a good reading, or do you have to see her, too?"

"That depends," he said. "If things go well, I'll read her tomorrow night."

"Uh-huh," I said. "Just where *is* your comptroller? It's obvious there's no room for him in there."

"He should be here any minute. Why don't you wait in the parking lot?"

"Ginger," I asked, "does this look like a big-time operation to you?" I could tell from her look that she was already having second thoughts.

After a few minutes, a new Lincoln Continental pulled up right where we were standing. I went up to the car and asked, "Are you the comptroller?" He was.

"Are you going to read my client tonight?"

"Well, first I thought we'd go to dinner, and then go back to my place, where it would be more comfortable."

"That's a great idea," I said. "Where are you taking us?"

"Whaddya mean?" he asked.

"Well, you weren't planning to take my client somewhere to discuss business without her manager and agent, were you? So where are you taking us to dinner?"

"I didn't plan to discuss business until after dinner."

"Ginger doesn't discuss business," I said. "We do."

He mumbled something about not planning on having three people for dinner, and I said, "When you want to audition my client during the daytime in an office, you can call Velvet." Of course, they never called her or "Velvet." They had no intention of making movies, just starlets.

JOE CONDUCTS BUSINESS WITHOUT ME

More thoughts about Joe: one day, he called to ask if I had been following news items about Luchino Visconti's plans to film Thomas Mann's *Death In Venice*. I said I had, but wondered how he could do it. "Don't I remember your telling me that you had the film rights?"

"That's right," he said.

"So, what's going to happen?"

"Oh, well, I took care of that already. I called Lucino and told him, 'I wouldn't start filming if I were you.' He asked me why not, and I just said, 'Because I own it.'"

"What did he say to that?"

"Luchino said, 'What am I going to do? I'm ready to start shooting tomorrow. I've spent a fortune already.' I told him that all he had to do was send me a check," and he mentioned a very healthy number. Visconti sent a certified check the next day.

WE DECIDE NOT TO DRINK THIS TRIP

Joe made a film in Greece, and shortly thereafter, returned to Los Angeles for another television show. As was our custom, I picked him up at the airport and headed for the Sunset Marquis, where he was staying since the incident at the Beverly-Wilshire Hotel. I asked if we should stop by the liquor store and lay in the usual supply.

Joe said, "I'm not drinking any more."

"Okay," I said, "I won't drink either. Do you want to get a couple of bottles of wine for guests? He did, and we stopped by the liquor store on Sunset Boulevard, just up the street from the hotel. As I wandered around, picking out some nosh to have on hand, Joe said, "See if you can find Ouzo."

"I thought we weren't drinking this trip."

"That's right, only Ouzo."

While he was roaming around Greece, Joe discovered Ouzo, and for some reason didn't consider that drinking. I had never tasted Ouzo, but knew it had a licorice or anise base, not my favorite flavors, but I never let Joe drink alone.

Once in the hotel with everything hung up or laid out, we repaired to the living room where we cracked open the first Ouzo bottle of the week. Joe said, "We'll drink it like the Greeks do, half-and-half with water." That sounded like a very good idea to me because I figured I might be able to handle it diluted. I had heard stories about the potency of Ouzo.

Well, Ouzo is a taste that grows on you. We sat across from one-another at the glass coffee table, close enough to hand the bottle back and forth and pour water from the pitcher between us. Half a bottle later, we decided it was time to get something to eat, only I discovered that I no longer had legs that wanted to cooperate. After pounding a little feeling into them, we somehow managed to get to the small restaurant in the hotel. On his next trip to Los Angeles, we switched back to Vodka and Sprite. Lower in calories, Joe reasoned.

SOMETHING DIFFERENT

I thought I would wind up this chapter with a couple of poems Joe wrote. Joe was a great limerick writer, and during the late 1930s, was quoted by all the New York columnists. He once wrote a song about Viveca Lindfors, an actress of whom he was not fond. He would sing it to me, but never wrote it down; a great loss. One day, the mail brought these two poems, which I think belong to history, or at the very least, they deserve to be memorialized right here and now:

OLD FRIENDS

Actors are wonderful people,
they're charming and talented, too.
Their law is the law of the jungle,
they really belong in a zoo.
Actors are simply delightful,
they give all they have to their art.
Don't say they are vicious and spiteful,
they're really just children at heart.
Actors are given to whoring,
it says in a book I once read.
But what makes them really so boring,
is they tell you about it in bed.

Actors have voices like thunder,
and oceans and oceans of gall.
Right now I'm beginning to wonder
if actors are people at all.
This song that I'm trying to sing you
is one that I've worked on for years.
I've doted on one or two Actors,
our dalliance ended in tears.
And after each arduous rapture,
I'd work on a verse in distress.
Each time I'd endeavor to capture
the quality Actors possess.
Actors make terrible lovers.
They're faithless, perverse and no good.
And would I be caught in their spotlight?
You can bet you left titty I would.

REFLECTIONS ON READING
DR. MARIE STOPES BOOK ON BIRTH CONTROL

The portions of a woman that arouse a man's depravity
are fashioned with considerable care,
for what appears to us a simple little cavity
is really an elaborate affair.
No, the doctors who have bothered to examine
the abdomena of numbers of
experimental dames,
have classified and listed all these various phenomina
and given them delightful Latin names.
There's the vulva, the vagina, the labia, the perineum,
and the hymen in the case
of several brides,
and other little gadgets thereabouts like the urineum,
and God knows what besides.
What a pity then it is that when we vulgar people
chatter of the mysteries to
which I have referred,
we use for such a delicate and complicated matter
such a short and unattractive little word.

Chapter 15
Backus Becomes a Full-Time Client

Jim Backus was now a part of my life. We had our meeting, and I confessed that I had no idea whether I could do for him what I had done for Joe, but that under the circumstances, I would be willing to try. I was being perfectly honest, because the truth of the matter is that being a successful personal manager has a lot to do with luck. When Ken Kragen, an extremely successful personal manager himself, decided to write a book on how to become one, people were smart enough to know that it was one profession you didn't learn from a book.

After it was published, I said to anyone who asked my opinion, "There's only one way I know of to learn how to become a personal manager. First, you have to find someone who doesn't resent you destroying their career, and then you go from there." Obviously, that's an exaggeration, but there is a bit of truth in it. Besides, that's more or less how I started, but I didn't really destroy anyone's career. I'll explain:

YOU SOMETIMES HURT THE ONE YOU LIKE

Back when I was still in the concert business with Irving Granz, we had an answering service with a *Yenta* for an owner. Rita, the Yenta, kept telling me that I should become a personal manager and that she had just the client for me. That "client" was also on her service, and Rita kept telling *her* that she should have a personal manager and that she knew just the person.

The other person in question was a young, beautiful actress named

Marj Dusay. She was comparatively new to the area, having lived in northern California while she was putting her husband through school. They had two children together, and he went on to become a reasonably well-known and successful psychologist. He also decided that he no longer needed her. Marj had worked as a model and actress up north, and she moved to Los Angeles to pursue her career.

We eventually met, more to appease Rita than anything else, and I told her that I would be happy to work as her manager. I believe we even signed contracts, but I never considered management contracts worth the paper they were written on even back then. If two people cannot agree to work together with a handshake, how can you possibly be happy holding one or the other to a written agreement?

Anyway, I made calls for her, negotiated a couple of deals, and helped put on a "Young Hollywood" party for her. A group of young actors of at least both sexes decided to have this huge party and they wanted me to help get some more celebrity types to attend and to arrange some press coverage.

I managed to talk the editor of *Vogue* magazine into coming to the party and she covered it in the publication. There were a few other newspaper types and the party was well-reported. The gimmick of the party was that everyone had to come dressed entirely in white and the only lighting in the house, other than bathrooms and the kitchen, would be black, so that everyone glowed in the dark.

I guess the party was fun, but I was already older than everyone in the place and was getting a little bored, so I wandered into the kitchen where I came upon Harlan Ellison, the mostly science-fiction writer, holding forth on his own genius. While I was leaning against a sideboard, I was approached by a very attractive woman, who said to me, "Hi, my name is JoAnne Worley."

I said, "I know who you are. How could I not."

She was with a girl friend, and they were getting bored, too.

"Why don't we split this place?" she asked.

I said, "I'd love to, but I'm one of the hosts."

With that, she handed me her card and said, "Call me sometime."

"Okay, I'll bring the wine; you bring the bread and cheese."

Not too long after that, having done little or nothing to improve Marj's career, she moved eastward and got married, so you see, thanks to my ineptitude, Marj was able to re-marry, but unfortunately not live happily-ever-after. That, however, is her story.

INVESTIGATING JIM'S PROBLEMS

What I told Jim was that I would check around and see if I could find out why he wasn't getting any work, what the resistance was, and if I could correct it, I would.

"However," I said, "If the reason turns out to be something you don't like, you have to accept it and do what I tell you. Otherwise, I can't work with you. I can only work with someone I like and where there is mutual trust and respect."

I offered Jim the same deal I offered Joe, and he agreed. At the time, I thought I would only have to deal with Jim and his wife, Henny. I didn't know yet about Charles Goldring, his business manager.

In those days, I seemed to know a lot of people in the industry, mostly because I stayed active during and after my tenure with The Beach Boys and Music Tours/The Visual Thing/Far Out Productions. I still had some connections with the talent bookers on a number of local television shows. I knew some casting directors and a couple of television and radio hosts.

I had met Jim's friend, Merv Griffin, on three or four occasions, and while we certainly weren't buddies, I could sometimes speak to him directly when I called, and always with one of his talent coordinators. (Merv Griffin was later to become a sort of in-law when his first cousin, Sarah Folger, married my son, Robert). Anyway, I did my homework, found the problems, and as I promised, started to correct them. I told Jim what he would have to do in order to get back in everyone's good graces, and he agreed to go along.

One "problem" was Jim's wife, Henny. It seemed that whenever Jim had or was offered a job, he always tried to get Henny involved. On television, she would always tell the director how she was to be shot, what lighting to use, how Jim was to be made up, and other things that just got directors upset. They just didn't want her, so they stopped booking Jim.

Of course, that didn't mean I could get him bookings right away because even talk shows hosted by friends didn't need him if he didn't have anything to talk about. And he, like Joe, hadn't had a job in some years. He did have *Mooch*, the film he made with Jerry Devine, but at that point in his career, there was no way to use that as an entree.

Here's where luck came in. Because Joe wasn't working all the time and turning down work besides, I picked up employment here and there for extra income.

My late friend, Joe Price, a writer and music columnist for *Daily Variety*, the show business "Bible," had gotten himself involved with a new record company, Oak Records, officially based in Hollywood at the 6430 Sunset Boulevard building, but financed out of Texas. Ray Ruff, the head of the label, a former singer himself, was producing an album to be called *The Truth of Truths*, a rock and roll version of the Old and New Testaments, with one LP for each.

He had recruited for his cast some well-known, some slightly known, and some unknown, singers for the various roles, wrote some of the songs himself and some with a few of the singers. Artistically, it didn't turn out too bad, but then there was more than a little competition from *Jesus Christ Superstar* and *Godspell*. I started hanging around Oak Records and did a little promo work for them, mostly with Joe Price. Ray was looking for someone to portray the voice of God on the record, and I suggested Backus. Everyone thought I was crazy, but I persisted.

"He's got this great, deep baritone voice, and besides, think of the publicity tie-in: 'From Magoo to God.'"

They asked if he would audition on tape and I assured them he would. It took about five minutes in the recording studio to convince everyone that Jim was the man for the job.

I had asked for a very modest $100 for doing the audition tape, and $500 for recording the actual material. If it looked like the album was going to be a bust, Jim's name wouldn't appear in the credits.

BREAKS START COMING OUR WAY

Now, that doesn't seem like much of a start, but it was an opening to get Jim on talk shows. We booked the Merv Griffin and Virginia Graham shows locally, on which they played portions of the album.

Merv and Virginia were very kind to the album and got a kick out of the Magoo to God promotion.

Then, I suggested that the record company send us around the country to promote the record on every available talk show. When they agreed, I asked for a small, 1 percent of sales, and then an advance against future royalties when we actually went on the road. They agreed to that, too.

They turned their in-house promotion people loose and contacted independent publicists in places like Atlanta, Chicago, Minneapolis, and Philadelphia. Interviews were set up across the country. One thing I was sure of: there's nothing like a cross-country tour of talk shows to revive one's TVQ.

We actually made two trips for Oak Records and got advances against royalties each time. Of course, they paid all our expenses, first class air fares and hotels, reimbursed us for out-of-pocket expenses, and had people meet us most everywhere we went. I honestly believe that Jim made more money with his advances than the record company did on sales.

WE EXPAND OUR HORIZONS

We decided to pick up a "casual" on the way to the first city of the first tour. A "casual" is really a fancy way of saying "One night stand," often just a date one does on the way to somewhere else, although much of the time those are local gigs you do just to pick up some quick cash. Telethons and celebrity roasts are casuals, too, and they paid well.

I found a booker, who got Jim a date in El Paso, Texas, at some private club. A friend told Jim that we should stay at a Sheraton Hotel a little outside of town because it was pretty new. The management of the club and our booker said we had to stay at the Ritz Hotel downtown because the suite had already been reserved and paid for. We were going to stay in "The Presidential Suite." How could we turn that down? Besides, as long as there was nothing we could do about it, we said, okay, we'd stay there.

Arriving in El Paso, we neared the hotel and began to get an uneasy feeling we might have made a mistake. We were driving through what appeared to be El Paso's red light district. The hotel was imposing, but old, and the porno movie houses in the neighborhood did little to allay our misgivings. A musty smell greeted us as we entered the lobby.

The hotel manager ushered us up to the seventeenth floor. A left turn out of the elevator led us to a glass door, enclosing a short hallway. On the wall adjacent to the door was a brass plaque that read, "Presidential Suite." Still, there was something uncomfortable, something that seemed not quite right.

We walked about thirty feet down the corridor to another locked door. Inside was the largest hotel room I'd ever seen. The living room alone had three television sets and half a dozen columns supported the ceiling.

I left the door open to see what if anything was going on in our corridor and farther down the hallway. There were three other doors in our little hallway which no one bothered to explain.

While Jim was testing the furniture in the living room, I checked out the two bedrooms. The room with the double, not queen or king-size bed, would be Jim's. The second bedroom had twin beds.

I checked the bathrooms. We each had one, and found the towels to be small and thin. I figured I would have some bath towels sent up while we were at the club for dinner.

Jim always liked to get wherever we were going a day early so he could get a good night's rest and rehearse the act before he had to work. First, however, we decided to explore this seedy part of town for half an hour before showering and dressing for dinner.

While Jim was unpacking, I happened to look out the door to our suite and noticed a middle-aged woman with a clip board in her hand. Assuming that she must be a supervisor of some sort, I walked out across the center hall where the elevators were located and to where she was busy checking something. I excused myself and asked if she might possibly arrange to have some bath towels sent to our suite.

She replied, "Go ask someone in the hotel."

I said, "I thought I was in the hotel."

"And stay away from my girls," she shot back at me, as she walked away. Puzzled, I returned to the room, told Jim what happened, and called down to the Housekeeping Department. I asked for four bath towels, which they promised to deliver. A few moments later, as I passed our open door, I noticed a young woman wearing only a slip, standing at a pay telephone back where I had spoken to the lady with the clipboard, and I wondered again just what we had gotten ourselves into.

We took our little walk and returned to the hotel to await our ride to dinner. On my bed were four towels, exactly the same as those I thought were hand towels. It was apparent that those *were* their bath towels, but with about six each, we could probably dry our entire bodies after a shower.

The booking agent arrived around seven o'clock, and she drove us to the club to meet the manager and for me to check the sound system, the stage, and the layout. Our deal called for one show on Friday and two on Saturday, but the club manager informed us that there would be have to be two shows on Friday, as well, because Jim had completely sold out. With the agent there, I insisted on more money for the extra show, which they came up with after a little haggling and my complaints about the room we were forced to take instead of nice, new rooms at the Sheraton.

Then, the club manager said, "You have to do two different shows each night. You can't repeat, because our members always stay for both shows."

Naturally, we hadn't planned on that because the booker failed to mention it.

Back at the hotel, Jim preceded me to the room and I stopped to talk to the hotel manager who had accompanied us to dinner. First he confirmed that there were no other bath towels, and then I asked, "Who are all those other people on our floor?"

"Oh," he said, "didn't they tell you? That's the YWCA."

I walked into the suite and said, "Jim, I just wanted you to know were staying in the YWCA. And we've been warned not to touch."

We spent the next few hours going over material, splitting it into two shows by adding some gags from his joke file and from material I started accumulating when we decided to do casuals until television and/or movies opened up again for him.

I wrote out the two acts on four by six index cards, which I made a habit of carrying from the time I first went on the road for Irving Granz. We spent two hours rehearsing and hit the sack. The next afternoon, we took another walk and stopped to see the better part of a semi-porno film called *The Stewardess*, or something akin to that.

WE GET INTO ROUTINES

After Jim took his afternoon nap, while I memorized the act, we were driven out to the club. It was on that very first trip that we began our dinner routine on show nights. Dinner consisted of soup, iced tea, and a dish of vanilla ice cream. If everything went well, we'd have a light bite before bed. If it went very well, we'd have a light bite and share a bottle of red wine. More about Jim's alleged drinking habits a little later.

We finished the two nights in El Paso and headed out for Atlanta, Georgia, where the promotional tour began.

Even after our two promotion tours for Oak Records, I wasn't quite through with *Truth of Truths*. Ray Ruff asked me to go along to a meeting with executives at NBC-TV in New York to talk about a television version of the album. With the success of *Godspell* and *Jesus Christ Superstar* networks were looking for anything that tied rock music and religion. I met with the executives, who agreed to fund our production. I called Ray Ruff and told him that all he needed to do was prepare a synopsis of what the proposed show would look like. By the time I got back to Los Angeles, they were already auditioning singers and dancers. The only problem was that no one bothered to do a synopsis for NBC.

Chapter 16
We Begin to Tour and Build a TVQ

Jim Backus and I left El Paso, flew to Atlanta, Georgia. As airplanes generally have a habit of doing, ours finally arrived, and we took a cab to our hotel.

Now, one of Jim's little foibles—and there were many—was a fear of heights. Actually, I'm not sure whether it was heights, the fear of being up high in case of fire, or whether it was his idea, or whether it was one planted in his mind by Henny, who, among *her* foibles, was absolutely afraid of being high up in buildings. Whatever the reason, we always tried to book rooms no higher than the fourth floor.

What may have been the first Hyatt Regency Hotel had just opened in Atlanta, and naturally, to impress Jim, the promotional people booked us . . . on the twenty-third floor. After all, that's where the view was.

When the desk clerk handed me our room keys, I said, "Tell me that just because the room number starts with twenty-three, it doesn't mean it's on the twenty-third floor."

"That's what it means," beamed the hotel manager. "Nothing but the best for Mr. Backus."

Jim said, "Please, can't we have rooms on the second or third floor, or even just one room for me?"

The smiling desk clerk said, "I'm sorry, Mr. Backus, we thought you'd want to be up high, away from the lobby noise. We're completely booked."

"C'mon, Jim," I pleaded, "let's give it a try, we're only here for a couple of days. You can handle it."

With no other option than to try to find another hotel, he agreed, but on the ride to our floor in the glass-enclosed elevator, he never once looked down towards the lobby.

Reaching our floor, Jim stayed close to the wall because all the corridors were open and looked down to the ground floor. The sight was spectacular, and I kept saying things like, "Jim, you really ought to take a look at this," and he kept answering, "Why don't you just tell me about it."

As soon as we were settled in, I suggested a drink in the lobby bar, which was just fine with Jim—anything to get off the twenty-third floor even if he had to face the glass elevator again. For the return trip, he could at least be a little fortified.

As was our custom, we arrived on Sunday. Like most towns in the Bible Belt and the south, there was nothing much doing on Sunday in Atlanta, and drinking the night away was not an option, so we decided to go somewhere nice for dinner. We didn't want to eat in the hotel because even the Hyatt Regency had "hotel" food and we were looking for something better. The hotel manager suggested The General Apartment Towne Club, which had a private restaurant in the upscale, exclusive apartment complex. We thought that sounded good, and the manager called ahead to make arrangements and get us a cab.

The food was excellent as was the ambiance. Although very crowded, it was quiet, which always made for good dining, and neither of us liked noisy or brightly lit restaurants. To top it off, when we went to settle the bill, we found that it had already been paid by one of the diners. The waiter explained, "The man said it was to thank Mr. Backus for the hours of enjoyment you've given him on television and in the movies."

A BAD REP DEBUNKED

Right here might be a good place to talk about Jim's drinking. When I first began to work with him, friends cautioned me not to let him drink too much because he was "an alcoholic." When I met the wonderful actor/singer/dancer, Donald O'Connor, one of Jim's oldest and best friends, he took me aside and suggested that I get him out of town and into a hospital where he could kick his habit.

Donald told me how he had done it for himself, and suggested the same plan of action for Jim.

Donald, who had a long-standing drinking problem, told me that one day he woke up in a hotel and had no idea where he was, how he got there, or even why he was there. For years, he had managed to make appearances while drunk and get away with it, but that time, he was scared. He *did* check into a hospital and went cold turkey. He said he had gone through several million dollars and had no idea where it went.

I tried explaining to Donald that I had never seen any evidence of alcoholism in Jim, and I thought I had a pretty good idea what an alcoholic looked like because my father was one.

The most Jim and I ever had to drink together was when we would share a bottle of red wine before bed, and that amounted to two glasses each. When we found a good Chinese restaurant, if they served it, we'd each have a Mai Tai. Other than that, the most we ever had to drink was when Henny met us at the door on the return from a trip with a carafe of white wine for each of us. I never saw Jim take a drink in the morning, and mostly not even after that. There were, however, a very few occasions when he might have had a little too much to drink and I packed him off to bed.

Once, at Kiawah Island, for *Business Week*, they were so enamored of him that everyone wanted to buy him a drink, and he was so enamored of them, he took them. I sent him to bed and I went swimming. It wasn't even twelve o'clock yet.

Anyway, getting back to Atlanta: the next morning, I rented a car at the hotel so we could do a bit of sight-seeing on our way to WSB-TV for Jim's interview on *Today in Georgia*. The hosts, Ruth Kent and Billie Williams, made a big fuss over Jim, which gave him a needed shot in the ego. "See," I said, "people really haven't forgotten you. We just have to remind some of them that you're around."

As a result of the broadcast, Atlanta newspapers picked up the theme of "Magoo to God." That promotional gimmick got him nationwide recognition. In fact, we received so much publicity that copies of articles filled four huge scrapbooks back at Oak Records. When we returned to Los Angeles, I called UPI and AP news services and they put the story on their wires.

From Atlanta, we flew into New York, where a few telephone calls from Los Angeles had resulted in bookings on *What's My Line*, where he was the special guest with a secret that he was playing God. There were also interviews on ABC-TV's *Midday*; there were interviews with famed deejay Barry Gray on WMCA radio; and finally, there was an appearance on *The Tonight Show*.

INTERVIEWS GO NATIONAL

Jim Backus had a reputation as a story teller, to which I can attest. We sent a lot of time talking, when we went out for a walk or a drive, or when we were seat mates on planes somewhere. It was during those one-on-one times that Jim wasn't "on," and that was when I came to know him well. I learned that Jim was a youngster at Kentucky Military Institute (KMI), where he got to know and become best friends with future motion picture star, Victor Mature. They played on the KMI football team together and often got into trouble together. Jim and Victor spent more time having fun than they did becoming military men. Once, the two of them were called into their Commanding Officer's office and read the riot act. Among the many things the officer said to them was that they were incorrigible and that they would, with their attitudes, never amount to anything, nor be successful in life.

Moving forward a few years, Victor became a major star, and Jim, while not a major star, always worked as a character actor. They happened to be working at the same studio and were on their way somewhere when they came across a "hot set," a fancy office set that was kept ready all the time. They immediately went to the Wardrobe Department; outfitted themselves with a couple of thousand dollar suits, corralled a half dozen or so starlets and a studio photographer, and had themselves photographed with the starlets draped all over and around them. They had the picture made into an oversized print, which they signed with the message: "And how are all the 'successful' people making out?" They sent the print off to their former Commanding Officer."

Jim had once told another story on Johnny Carson's *The Tonight Show* about him and Victor. In 1953, they were both appearing in a picture called *Androcles and the Lion*, much of which was being filmed near the town of Bakersfield, a desert community about a hundred miles north of Hollywood. Their roles called for them to wear Roman Centurion costumes, which while the description might have been slightly inaccurate, certainly painted the appropriate picture. Their wardrobe/makeup call was early since it involved donning heavy leather, metal outfits, and body makeup to give them a manly, healthy glow. It took so long to get them ready that they stayed in costume all day, even on breaks for lunch. Victor owned a chain of television retail stores, and one day, he had to go into town to, as Jim claimed, ". . . sign for a load of hot Philcos" being delivered." They drove into Los Angeles together, did what had to be done, and headed back to the desert. Since they still had some free time, Victor, who had a well-earned reputation as a drinker, suggested they stop for a belt or two. Jim later remembered the moment they stepped from the bright sunlight into the bar's dark interior. "The lone bartender was standing there polishing glasses and arranging the olives in numerical order, when he looked up and saw two hulking Centurions blocking the doorway. He stood there for a few moments without moving, not quite sure what he was seeing, when Victor broke the silence, saying, 'What's the matter . . . don't you serve members of the armed forces?'"

Johnny Carson was the regular host of *The Tonight Show*, but unfortunately for us, Joan Rivers replaced him on another night when Jim was to appear. I say unfortunately, because a mention by Carson was always good for a huge boost in book or record sales. Joan Rivers wanted to do shtick with Jim, and the record got only a passing mention as Jim entered the set and only a brief show of the record jacket as he left. The rest of the time she urged him to tell show-biz stories which of course, he did.

She also screwed up the evening because her first guests were a singing group she liked and she carried them over into the second segment. As far as time was concerned, Jim got his seven minutes, but author William Peter Blatty was sitting with me in the Green Room and he was furious. Blatty had written *The Exorcist*, the hottest book in the country, and it was already or soon to become a block-buster movie. Blatty was getting more agitated by the second, as the time grew later and it looked as though he wouldn't get on at all. He was ready to walk out, but I took it on myself to talk about his anger to whoever seemed to be in charge, and then I assured the author that he would get his time. He calmed down, but only a little. Bill Blatty, as he asked to be called, ended up with about three minutes, finally appearing at one o'clock in the morning.

From New York, we took a two-hour limousine ride to Philadelphia and checked into a fairly new hotel near the studio the night before appearing on *The Mike Douglas Show*.

By the time we were checked in, Jim wanted only a sandwich for dinner, and we were directed to a hamburger joint and beer bar at the below ground railroad station. The only interesting features of the place were the peanuts. There were barrels of peanuts in several places, peanuts on the bar, and peanut shells completely covering the floor. We had one drink and a bunch of nuts, but the kitchen was closed and hamburgers or any other kind of food were out.

One of the owners of the bar suggested a private club in town and made a call to get us in. The "club" was an intimate little bar called The Drake. They issued a membership card to each of us, just in case we ever wanted to come back. We sat at the bar, although there were some booths, and talked with the woman who ran the place. She was even able to scrounge up some food for us.

"Is your friend interested in a woman for the night?" the manager asked me.

"A hooker?" I asked.

"Very high class," she answered. "Not your average street walker. A call girl. She's really okay, and very discreet."

"How come she's here?"

"Sunday's are usually pretty slow, and we're friends, so she drops in. If she gets a job, her service calls her here. If you or your friend are interested, I could introduce you."

"That's very nice of you, but I don't think either of us is up for it. Besides, Jim has to call home as soon as we get back to our rooms."

"Maybe you'd like to meet her anyway, just in case. You never know."

She turned and motioned to a very attractive woman, who seemed to be about thirty-five, sitting on the opposite side of the square-shaped bar. In the dimness of the room, neither of us had noticed her, which was very unusual because one of us always could spot a pretty woman. After all, what trouble could we get into just by talking or looking?

The young (thirty-five was young to us) woman seated herself between us as I moved to the next stool. She handed us each a business card, which read: *Erection and Demolition Service—Day and Evening Service, T. Diamond, Contractor* and a telephone number. I still have the card.

She turned out to be a very bright, charming woman, very well-educated, and seemingly pretty intelligent about the money she was earning. She didn't believe in pimps or agents and had stashed away a goodly sum. She already owned a couple of businesses that were in the black. Her real name was Pat M., but "Tiffany Diamond" was a name to remember. I told her about my friend, "Velvet Amber," who used that name for the same reason. Well, not exactly the same reason, but so she would be remembered.

Jim had been friends for years with Mike Douglas, the host of the show that we were there to do, and they had even vacationed together with their wives, so they worked well on camera. Off-camera was another matter altogether, because all Mike wanted to talk about was Mike. During the show, I cornered Mike Krauss, the show's producer, and convinced him to book Jim later for a week as co-host.

Chapter 17
We Hit the Road Again

Oak Records sent us out on a second tour to cover some major markets we missed the first time around. We had television and radio bookings in New Orleans, Miami, Minneapolis, Cincinnati, and Chicago. We wanted to do Miami primarily because La-Z-Boy was having their annual sales convention at the Doral Hotel, which would give Jim a chance to score a few points with his one big commercial client.

New Orleans holds no memories except that Peggy Lee was appearing at the Roosevelt and we caught her act. We spent a two or three days in Miami, one whole day with La-Z-Boy, and two days doing talk shows like *Miami Magazine* on WPLG, and *The Larry King Show* on WTVJ. We even went out on a "date" in Miami. Jim had an old flame still living in Miami Beach, and we dropped by to see her.

BEING SOCIAL ISN'T ALWAYS FUN

Jim's old flame insisted we all go to dinner, and while I really didn't want to go, she persisted, saying she would have a date for me. Now, this lady was older than I, and if I was going to dinner with someone, I preferred it be *anyone* closer to my age. She said, "Oh, don't worry, I know a nice young girl for you. She works where I bank." I agreed, reluctantly.

Mostly, I agreed so Jim wouldn't have to drive from our hotel to her place, then to The Luau, a Hawaiian-style restaurant on Miami Beach, and then back again to our hotel. On the other hand, if Jim was going to spend the night with his lady friend, I would need the car, and then I would pick him up in the morning.

That evening, when we arrived at his friend's apartment, she said, "I'm really sorry, Jack, but the girl I wanted you to go with is busy tonight, but don't worry, I've fixed you up with a girlfriend of mine."

Her "girl" friend, was even older than she and looked older than that. In fact, she looked older than dirt, but not quite as attractive. She was dressed in a silver lame' jump suit, ideal for a teen-ager with a great figure, but this lady had lumps and bulges where other women have curves and angles. To complete the picture, she had a face exactly like an English Bulldog, jowls and all.

The lady was obviously loaded, and not just with money. She had converted three apartments into one even though she lived alone. I can't imagine anyone wanting, of his or her own volition, to live with her. She gave us a tour of her place, which elicited the mandatory compliments from Jim and me. When we returned to the living room, I took a seat on the couch while she made drinks.

I said, "I don't think I've ever seen so many telephones in one place."

"Yes," she said, "I have twelve, so no matter where I am, there's a telephone next to me."

"You'd better not sit here, then," I said. "There's none over here," I said, pointing to the end table next to the couch where I was sitting. "In fact, it's got to be almost fifteen feet to the nearest telephone."

She immediately wrote a note to herself to order *two* telephones the next day, because one telephone would have given her thirteen and that would have been unlucky.

I was stuck with her for the night, and I figured we might as well get it over with. After we finished the drinks she made for us, I hustled everyone down to our car. At the restaurant, the two ladies sat next to one another on one side of the table, while I sat alone on the other side. Jim sat at the head. From that moment on, I don't think either one of them said two words to us. Rather than order food, they suggested we have a few drinks first. Jim and I had our usual one Mai Tai each and they stayed with Martinis—one after another.

The waitress asked if we wanted to order and although the ladies preferred to keep drinking, Jim and I ordered and they decided to have something, too, which, incidentally, they hardly touched. While they were busy drinking, I slouched on the table, resting on one arm. I was praying we could eat quickly and get the hell out of there.

The camera girl, Judy G., approached me to ask if it would be all right if she took a picture of our party. The restaurant owner had recognized Jim. Jim had no objection, although I don't know why not, so there is a picture hanging somewhere of two ladies getting sloshed, one guy looking miserable and practically lying on the table, and Jim raising a glass in salute to the owner.

A few minutes later, photo in hand, the camera girl came to show us her work and to ask Jim to autograph it. She could also see how miserable I was and asked, "Would you like my telephone number?" Well, she was gorgeous, and I was very unhappy, and I told her that I most certainly would like her number. She dropped it off a few moments later and I promised that I would call her the next night for dinner. Jim wanted to know where we were going and I replied that I had no idea what he was going to do, but that *I* was going to dinner with a good-looking girl and that he could call his lady friend to come get him if he wanted to go somewhere. I did and he did, and that's enough about that except that Jim stayed the night with his lady friend.

BEVERLY HILLS DOESN'T ALWAYS HAVE THE BEST

Even when he was wearing eyeglasses, Jim was not the greatest driver in the world, another reason I didn't want to leave the car with him. Jim was having severe headaches almost from the moment we left Los Angeles. By the time we arrived in Miami Beach, his eyes were giving him trouble and he was having serious headaches. The pain was severe enough that he had stopped wearing his glasses altogether. I had to do something or he would be miserable for the entire tour. So, I placed a call to Joe Ferrer, who was in New York, even though Florida was then his legal residence at the time, and asked him if he knew an eye doctor Jim could get to see on short notice. He suggested Doctor David Sime, who was kind enough to squeeze Jim in for an eye examination.

In case you don't recall the name, David Sime (pronounced *S-I'm*; rhymes with slime) was a track star, who ran the 100 and 200 meter dashes in the Olympics and was an NCAA champion in those events.

When we arrived at Doctor Sime's office, I was struck by the fact that the waiting room was full of women—not a man in sight. He had about six assistants, all gorgeous young girls. When he came out to meet Jim, it was immediately obvious why. Doctor David was an inch or two over six feet, in the same physical trim he was when he ran in the Olympics, and to put it mildly, he was a hunk. The women, according to Joe Ferrer, drooled over him because he was a very eligible bachelor.

Jim had only recently undergone a thorough eye exam and been fitted for glasses by someone he described as "The most expensive eye man in Beverly Hills." The frames he selected were heavy, gold, and a style I referred to as "Hollywood Hoodlum." Doctor Sime's examination revealed that the lenses were the wrong prescription, the focal point was in the wrong place, there was no correction for astigmatism, and a couple other small errors, not to mention the weight of the frames. All those factors added up to pains. Fortunately, Jim had an old pair of glasses with him that felt "comfortable," and Doctor Sime was able to get new lenses ground and fit into the frames by the next day. That was long before you could get glasses made in an hour, because the lenses had to be ground from scratch.

IT'S GREAT GETTING POPULAR AGAIN

While we were still in Miami Beach, a booking agent called to see if Jim would be interested in a "casual" for Motorola, down in San Diego. The money was exceptional and we hated to turn it down. The date was actually open, coming during a hiatus between Minneapolis and Chicago. Minneapolis was going to be a quick stop, with an appearance at a record store and a couple of early morning radio shows after which we were going to fly into Chicago and spend three or four days there.

I asked the agent to see if Motorola would be willing to fly us first class from Minneapolis to San Diego and then back to Chicago, and while he was at it, to see if they would fly Henny and Phyllis down from Los Angeles to meet us there. They not only agreed, they asked if there was any Motorola product Jim might like in addition to his fee.

He wanted a stereo with a tape deck, and also a television set for Henny's bedroom. I wanted three small television sets, one for each of my children and one for my office at home. They agreed to everything, and after his Minneapolis gig, we flew to San Diego, where they had put us up at the Westgate Hotel (later the Westgate Little America), which was the newest, most posh place in town.

There is a semi-interesting story of how the hotel came into being. When General Dwight Eisenhower was in San Diego campaigning for President, they booked him into the U.S. Grant Hotel, really the only decent hotel in town then. Ike, speaking of the Grant, said to his friend, C. Arnholt Smith, who later went to jail for some heinous crime, "Is this the best you people can do?"

Smith spent the next two years combing Europe with his wife, buying art works and furniture, and then built the Westgate. There was what was purported to be a genuine Velasquez painting hanging in the lobby and a desk reputed to have come from the palace at Versailles. The bathtubs, enclosed by drapes, were really designed for two people.

Henny and Phyllis were there ahead of us, having flown down in the early afternoon. San Diego was only about twenty minutes away once you were in the air. The Motorola people had a limousine waiting when they arrived and then waiting for us a couple of hours later.

Henny, who was terrified of flying, had a ritual she would go through whenever she had to fly anywhere, even for a twenty-minute flight. When Phyllis picked her up at their home in Bel Air, Henny had already knocked back about three double Bloody Marys. They left about two hours before flight time because Henny liked to get to the airport early enough to have a couple more belts before boarding. Once settled in her seat, she would focus on a broach she wore, as a trigger that would induce a sort of hypnotic state. She stayed semi-conscious until they landed.

Jim did his thing for Motorola's guests, and we flew back to Chicago for appearances on the *Sig Sakowitz Show, Kennedy and Company*, and the top talk show in Chicago, hosted by Irv Kupcinet. Irv, the #1 show-biz columnist in town and the Chicago version of New York's Earl Wilson, was an old friend of Jim's, going back, I believe, to radio days. He flew Bob Denver (Gilligan) in for the show as a surprise.

Jim hadn't seen Bobby since *Gilligan's Island* was canceled and had no idea what he'd been doing or where he was living. Since they last spoke, Bob had married a girl named Dreama, and they were living, he said, in a school bus with a couple of Jaguars or Leopards or something and a chimpanzee or two.

Kup gave *Truth of Truths* and Jim another boost with a wonderful piece in his daily column.

Our last stop on the tour was Cincinnati, where Jim was set for an appearance on the *50-50 Club*, a syndicated talk show hosted by one of the best I've ever encountered. Bob Braun had become the announcer/host, when the long-time female host quit the show, and he stepped in and took over. It was then the most popular show in a five-state area, and the audience was packed with women. Bob was very handsome and women swooned over him.

Our hotel in Cincinnati was the Netherlands Plaza, an ultimate class hotel that had been a favorite of mine from the time I was old enough to travel to Cincinnati alone, from about the age of six. Not that I stayed there, but they had a wonderful restaurant, with an ice show at lunch, and when I got old enough, a fantastic arcade of shops under the street level, where I spent a couple of hours every time I came to town.

There was only one problem with the hotel: the rooms were unbearably hot, and there was no air conditioning. I called down to the desk to complain and was told that since it was October, the air conditioning had been turned off and the heat turned on.

"But it's eighty eight degrees outside," I complained, "and about a hundred in here."

"Sorry," he said, "that's just the way it is."

My cousin, Neil Bortz, one of the most successful builders in Ohio, hosted a party for us at one of his buildings, attended by all the local radio, television, and newspaper people, so *Truth of Truths* and "Magoo to God" got extensive coverage, and, of course, the more coverage we got, the more valuable Jim became as a personality.

THE WORK STARTS ROLLING IN

The end result of all our traveling and promotion was that Jim was back on the talk shows, there were offers for television and a couple of pictures, and he began to feel good about himself and his future.

Offers began coming in for casual bookings, one-nighters, including trips to Kiawah Island, South Carolina for *Business Week* magazine, the Cal Neva Lodge in Tahoe for a group of four hundred hunters (which paid very well and allowed for a little raunchier material), and a few days in Vancouver, British Columbia, for a charity. *That* was one of the more interesting events.

"*Schmockey*," in Vancouver, Canada, was their major charity blow-out of the year, benefiting a number of British Columbia charities. The event consisted of a concert, a hockey game between politicians, and several members of the news media, which turned out to be a real donnybrook because of the natural enmity between the politicians and the political writers. I guess every Canadian is born with skates on his or her feet and learns to play hockey before they can feed themselves; it was apparent there was very little love lost between the two sides. What's more, they played surprisingly good hockey.

There were "chariot races" on ice with the "chariots" pulled by members of a local club, a pee-wee hockey game or two, a girls soccer game on ice, and a "broom ball" game between strippers (maybe they were cheerleaders for the football team, but I was told they were strippers) and wrestlers that ended when the wrestlers jumped the girls in the middle of the ice rink, something completely unexpected, according to the show producer with whom I was talking.

All this led up to Jim's appearance standing on a plywood plank laid down over the ice at one end of the rink.

Looking at the souvenir program, I see the broom ball game was supposed to be between members of the B.C. Lions (football) and the wrestlers. All I know is that there were a bunch of gorgeous girls out there, and if there were any football players, they were on the same side as the wrestlers.

The Vancouver trip also presented some interesting side lights. Rosemary Clooney was appearing at Isy's, one of two clubs owned by the Walters brothers. The Cave, their other club, was less formal, but Isy's was a Las Vegas-style club, where over the years, many of the top acts appeared. Jim and I dropped in unannounced the evening we arrived in town. I was a little tentative when we walked into the dressing room where Rosie was giving some instructions to her son, Miguel Ferrer, who was playing drums for her. Because of her relationship with Joe Ferrer, which was often very difficult, I never knew if she was going to be mad because I worked with Joe, or in a good mood, because her life was going well.

Her back was to me when I said gruffly, "Okay, what's going on here? Why aren't you on stage?" She turned towards me, obviously thinking I was someone from the club, ready to read her the riot act, when she saw it was just me. Right then, I found that Rosey was still talking to me, and certainly talking to Jim. In addition to Miguel, Rosemary had brought along her oldest daughter, Maria Ferrer—just for company.

THINGS HAVE A WAY OF GETTING ODD

The next night, I guess Isy's was dark because I asked Miguel to go to dinner with me and Jim. We were going to some local coffee shop, and having nothing better to do, he came along. When we hit the lobby, I saw a very pretty young woman at the desk in conversation with the manager. I had noticed her outside the hotel, when we returned from rehearsal earlier that afternoon.

I asked casually, "How's business?"

She said, "It's been a slow night."

Jim asked me what I meant, and I explained that the lady was a "working girl," but that she hadn't had any customers. So, I asked if she had eaten, and if not, did she care to join us. Because she had nothing better to do, she said, "Why not." The doorman hailed a cab, and Miguel, Jim, and the lady piled in the back seat and I in front with the driver. I could hear Jim whispering in the back asking if she was indeed a hooker, because he was interested. Now, don't get the wrong idea, even if Jim had ideas, he never had any cash and I don't think she would have taken a credit card. I always carried "mad money," three $100 bills, in my bag, which was still in the hotel. Jim asked me if I had any cash and I told him where to find it, but to take no more than one of the bills. By the time we reached the restaurant, Jim had negotiated a deal and he and the hooker returned to the hotel. Miguel and I stayed and ate.

Besides, Miguel wanted to look around in some of the clubs, hoping he might find a couple of girls. The manager of the restaurant pointed out a few nearby clubs and a burlesque house. We were just about finished eating when two of the ugliest (not "most unattractive") women I have ever seen came in and took the booth next to us. Miguel said, "I'm going to talk to them."

I said, "Miguel, don't even think about picking them up."

Both women were tall, nearly six feet. They wore theatrical makeup and way too much of it, especially the black around the eyes. I assumed they were strippers at one of the nearby joints. It had to be a "joint" because no club or burlesque theater of any class at all would hire two such ugly people.

I have no idea what Miguel said to them, but he returned after two minutes and said, "They're going to drive us back to the hotel. Do you have any booze in your room?"

"I have a bottle of wine you can have, but count me out if you want to share it with those people. I don't even want to be seen with them, especially in the lobby of our hotel. Do what you want, but leave me out of it." I mean, *they were beasts!*

As we left the restaurant, a car pulled up and an even less attractive woman, taller than six feet, with even more garish make up emerged. I definitely would not have wanted to meet her in a dark alley. She turned out to be a friend and co-worker of the other two, and Miguel asked her to go with us.

Back at the hotel, we stopped by Jim's room and found that the lady of the evening and Jim were more than half way through a pint of vodka the cab driver scrounged up and sold to him for too much money. I guess he must have had *some* cash with him.

Miguel and his ladies stayed in Jim's room, while I excused myself as quickly as I could and went to my room, praying that those strange women would somehow just go away. I was to learn later that the hooker took Miguel aside and said, thinking she might get some money out of him when she finished with Jim, "Don't you know that they aren't women? They're guys in drag."

Miguel apparently didn't say anything just then, but when the four of them arrived in my room, looking for my bottle, he whispered to me, "I've got to ask you something."

He relayed the information from the hooker and said, "I've got to find out."

I said, "Miguel, don't ask."

"I've got to know," he said. I repeated myself, and so did he.

"The lady in Jim's room says you're guys. Is it true?"

They were kind enough not to hit Miguel, but they got up, pulled him off my bed where he and I were sitting, and said, "Come with us."

I gave him my bottle of wine and said, "Whatever happens, don't come back here."

The next morning, Miguel told me what happened. They went back to Jim's room and the ladies confronted the hooker. One of them said, "Let's just see whether we're women or not."

With that, they took off their clothes and forced the hooker lady to fellate all three of them. They were indeed women, even though, as I have said, they were the most unappealing people of the female persuasion I have ever encountered. Miguel was fortunate to escape them and locked himself in his room.

A FUN TRIP AND COMMERCIAL SHOOT

One trip took us to Washington, DC, where Jim was to make a six-minute film and several Public Service television spots for the American Pharmaceutical Association. As usual, we flew east on a Sunday and immediately set up quarters at the Georgetown Inn.

The film involved Jim as a harried businessman, someone who took too many pills. The character took uppers, downers, anti-histamines, pro-histamines, sleeping pills, waking pills, whatever. What they didn't know that Jim was the world's champion hypochondriac and that we carried a make-up case full of pills and potions.

The film was shot on a few locations including a Georgetown restaurant that didn't open until noon, so we were there working by nine o'clock in the morning. I say "we" because the actor they hired to play the scene with Jim canceled at the last minute, and I was rushed in as a replacement. Well, not exactly *rushed* in, I knew about it the night before.

I had one line: "What's the matter, Ollie?" which I spoke as Jim entered the restaurant and approached the booth where I was already seated. What you saw of me was the back of my head and a little bit of the side of my face and left ear as they shot more or less over my shoulder.

Jim said a line or two and we were joined by a waiter—a real waiter—whose dialog consisted of, "May I take your order?" Simple enough, but twice he turned to the camera and smiled; two or three more times, he ad-libbed another line like, "Can I freshen your drink, sir," speaking to me, and several times he simply screwed it up. It went on like that for about ten or twelve takes.

Before we started shooting, the waiter brought me a glass of Jack Daniels and water. What the hell, as long as I wasn't getting paid, I might as well have the real stuff, I figured.

Every couple of takes, I finished one drink and started another. By the time the film was "in the can," so was I.

The written dialog just didn't sound right; there was some spark missing. So, Jim and I ad-libbed something based on an old joke, and it turned out fine. Over the next day or two, Jim did several one and two minute public service spots at locations in and around Georgetown and Arlington, Virginia.

The night after shooting the film in the restaurant, I had a date to meet some friends, who had moved to Washington from Columbus, Ohio a year or so earlier. Before, however, Jim and I went to dinner at a terrific Georgetown restaurant with George Griffenhagen of the APA. I left early and took a cab to a jazz club on Capitol Hill.

During dinner, we were approached by a young man named Jasper Graham Hall, Jr. Jasper was a freelance promotion man, who offered his services to Jim if he needed someone to show him the town. We thanked him, but Jim begged off, saying he probably would return to the hotel right after dinner.

Jasper had an apartment about half a block from the restaurant. I don't think he actually lived there all the time, using it mostly for visitors and partying. He wrote out the address for Jim and me, saying, "There's always something going on there, twenty-four hours a day. If you've got nothing better to do, drop in. The door's always open."

Chapter 18
Jim Gets Desired

I left Jim with George Griffenhagen (you remember him from a page back) assuming that George would take care of him. I grabbed a cab and drove off to meet my friends, spent a few hours listening to some pretty good jazz, and returned to the hotel to look for Jim. He was nowhere to be found.

Well, Jimmy was my responsibility and I worried about him. He could get lost walking down the hallway to his room from the elevator. There was no telling where he might have wandered off to, even though I left him only a block or so from the hotel. However, as there were no really strange people at the restaurant when I left, other than Jasper Graham Hall, Jr., I wasn't concerned that he'd been kidnapped, or that some dastardly deed had been done him.

So, I decided to check Jasper's party apartment. True to his word, the door was unlocked. While there wasn't exactly a party under way, there were perhaps eight or ten people sitting or lying around—all clothed. What was normally a living room held two large beds, one in use by two men and two women in their late twenties or early thirties, who obviously knew each other before arriving at the bed. They were engaged in casual conversation when I entered, and they barely gave me a second glance. There were a few people in the diminutive kitchen area and one couple sitting on the floor of the living room, even though the second bed was unoccupied. I supposed they didn't know one another well enough yet.

"Has anyone here seen Jim Backus?"

"He's behind the curtain," someone answered.

The "curtain" was an old blanket strung on a rope, enclosing an open arch into what once had been a dining room and was then a bedroom because it was a room and had a bed in it.

I was just about to go inside when I was stopped by a young, extremely attractive female, who asked, "I wonder if you could help me for a second?"

"Sure," I said, "what do you need?"

"Well," she said, "I want to go to the bathroom, but there's someone sleeping in the tub. Could you help me get her out of there?"

Being the perfect gentleman, I agreed, and sure enough, there was indeed a young woman sound asleep in the bathtub, using a folded towel for a pillow.

I will not tell you who she was, but she was a well-known Hollywood actress, spending some off time in Washington during the filming of *All The President's Men*, which starred Dustin Hoffman and Robert Redford (in alphabetical order because I take no sides in billing). With the help of the young lady in need of the facility, I hefted the dozing beauty out of the tub and carried her to the unoccupied bed in the front room. You can tell what kind of an apartment *this* was. And then I went looking for Jim.

Supine on the bed behind the curtain was James Gilmore Backus, fully clothed. Sitting—not lying—next to him was a very attractive young lady in her mid-twenties I would guess, and she was fully unclothed, doing her best to get Jim to do something to or with her, and having no success whatever. I sat down on the other side of the bed, while the lady continued trying to talk him into having sex with her, and paying no attention to me at all.

"If he isn't interested, how about me?" I suggested. She ignored me. I might as well not have been there. It was obvious she wanted a star to add to her collection.

There was no chance Jim was going to do anything, but he obviously didn't know how to escape either, particularly as that young lady was holding him down, her hand planted firmly in the middle of his chest. I didn't want to get forceful, because for all I knew, Jim was enjoying himself, and besides, it's never a good idea to get pushy in a strange city.

"Jim," I said in my best managerial voice, "we have to get out of here because you have a very early call tomorrow."

To the young lady I said, "Miss, I really hate to drag Jim away, but after all, he is an actor and needs his rest because he has a hard day ahead of him. Maybe tomorrow night."

Actually, we *were* shooting the next day, but not early. Not being a late sleeper, I got up and wandered into a gift shop that was on our floor. The owner, a woman, I would guess (I seem to do a lot of age guessing) in her middle to late forties, was the only person in the store and we struck up a conversation. She was definitely foreign, with an intriguing accent. I seem to recall thinking she might have been Russian. What she was for sure was very attractive, and I made a date for Jim to take her to dinner.

I have no recollection what my plans were, but I must have done something because I was at the hotel later when Jim called. They were at a nearby restaurant and had a date for me. As they had yet to order dinner, I agreed to meet them.

After dinner I offered to walk the young lady who was my dinner date back to her apartment. She offered to walk me to my hotel room.

Jim's call was for early evening in a pharmacy in Arlington, Virginia, where the women we had spent the previous evening with were going to join us after work. The production company had to wait until the store closed for the day, which meant that Jimmy would have a chance to sleep in, one of his favorite things to do.

However, I didn't get the same opportunity. At six o'clock in the morning, there was an insistent knock on my door. It was Jasper.

"What the hell do you want?" I shouted from bed. It's only six. Go away."

"Get up," he insisted, "we're having breakfast with Dustin and Bob."

"Not even if they come here," I yelled back. "I'm busy. Call me if they want to have lunch." He didn't call.

We finished our work in DC. I was offered an application to join the Screen Actors Guild, which I declined with, "Are you crazy? It's tough enough being a manager." We flew on home for some rest and to prepare for another trip back east where Jim was going to co-host *The Mike Douglas Show*.

WE RETURN TO PHILLY FOR A WEEK

Co-hosting meant an entire week in Philadelphia, and once again, we arrived on Sunday, that time staying at the Warwick Hotel, which was where all Mike Douglas Show co-hosts and many of the guests were usually housed. It was an older hotel, but still charming. The next morning, we walked the two blocks to the television station and met with one of the talent coordinators to work out Mike's interview.

Mike Douglas was one of those people who, as Jim so succinctly put it, "couldn't ad-lib a belch at a Hungarian picnic." Every question in the exact order Mike asked was written on several sets of cue cards so no matter which way he turned, he could read them. If anyone inadvertently answered the next question before Mike asked it, he plowed relentlessly ahead and asked it anyway.

We finally were called into Mike's office, whereupon he began regaling us—really Jim—I just happened to be in the room—with stories of his success in Las Vegas.

"I was a smash," he said. "Even though I had 'Vegas throat' the first couple of days and just did stand-up."

"I didn't know you did comedy," I said as any good straight man would.

"Yeah, I killed them. Full house every night."

Jim and I were properly impressed, and massaged his ego, which hardly needed any help from us. During the show, his producer told me, "Mike was a bomb in Vegas. Played to half houses."

I mentioned earlier that Jim and Mike were old friends, their wives were old friends, and they had vacationed together, but when the week was over Jim said to me, "I was really disappointed. He kept telling me how great his house in King of Prussia was, and he never once asked me if I wanted to come over for dinner or just to see the place."

Standing in the wings the second day of shooting, I saw an interesting and very attractive young lady. What made her interesting was that she held a large sketch pad and was doing quick drawings of the set and celebrities. What made her attractive, in addition to her good looks and sensational figure, was that she wore clothes so tight everything fit like second skin.

I automatically presumed she was part of the staff because she seemed to have total freedom to wander the set, but learned later that day that she was an art student who just had permission to come in and do sketches. She told me about her work and wondered if Jim would like to see some of it. As an after-thought, she suggested that I might like to see some, too.

The next day, she brought several pieces to our hotel and Jim and I figured it was just a ploy on her part to get close to him and/or me, and that the very sexy young lady might have the hots for one or both of us. I really don't know where I got those silly ideas. I had pegged her age at about twenty-five, but she turned out to be seventeen, naïve, and actually just wanted to sell a picture or two.

Jim did buy a piece, which somehow never showed up, even though the Mike Douglas people claimed they sent it, along with the home movie footage Jim brought along. Her artwork was intriguing and different enough to have been added to their art collection had it ever arrived. I have occasionally wondered what happened to her and her art career.

JIM GREETS A LONG LIST OF FRIENDS

On the first show of the week, Jim showed the home movies of Mike, his wife, Jim, and Henny romping on a beach in Florida, but other than that brief bit, the shows were taken with guests, a couple of whom Jim had asked for, including Natalie Schafer, who played Lovie on *Gilligan's Island*. We had dinner with her at the hotel the night she arrived, and just as Jim warned, she was as flighty in person as she was on television.

Some of the other guests who appeared that week were Vikki Carr, who was on Kup's show in Chicago with Jim when we were there promoting *Truth of Truths*; Billie Jean King, the tennis great, who introduced a line of tennis clothing under her name, singer Kay Stevens, actress Molly Picon, actress Gale Storm, comedian Victor Borge, actor Billy de Wolfe, Amy Vanderbilt, and the great clarinetist Artie Shaw.

Amy Vanderbilt, of course, talked about etiquette and manners. When she got around to the etiquette of marriage, she turned to Artie, who had been married, I think, seven times, and said, "Now, Artie, we know all about you and your weddings, so you don't talk."

That's all she had to say to Artie, who from then on, wouldn't leave her alone. She got to talking about children, grandchildren, and ex-spouses, when Artie said, "Wait a minute, this sounds like you've been through it more than once. How many times have *you* been married?"

She tried ignoring the question, and finally Jim took it up, too. In exasperation, she turned to Artie and said, "Four times, are you satisfied?"

The entire audience and everyone on the set broke up.

We made one more trip to Philadelphia, staying out on City Line Avenue in a motel I'm sure was a Marriott. It was so big, and our rooms were so far away from the lobby that Jim hired someone to lead him back to the room when I had to leave him in the restaurant for some reason.

Jim was booked into the Downingtown Inn for a one-nighter, but I can't recall why we were back in Philadelphia, unless it was just because it may have been the closest major city to Downingtown. The Downingtown Inn is a family-type resort near Valley Forge, Pennsylvania, not all that far from The City of Brotherly Love.

Before we left Philadelphia, Jim and I checked the night life because we didn't want to spend the night in our rooms, and found that Buddy Greco was appearing at Palumbo's, a famous club reportedly owned by the mob. I called and made a reservation under Jim's name, which was guaranteed to get us a good table.

We were seated at the second table back from the stage, directly behind a group of perhaps sixteen people. Eight men sat on one side of the table and eight black-clad, somber ladies on the other.

The maitre d' informed someone at the front table that Jim was sitting right behind them and they invited us to join them. It was, I suppose, an honor. We declined the invitation because, we said, we didn't want Buddy to be distracted by Jim's presence. In any case, there was no check at the end of the evening.

After the show, we went back stage to see Buddy, another old friend of Jim's, who took Jimmy aside and said, "Jim, you're a good friend of Danny's (his wife who had recently left him for a famous actor). Tell her she has to come back to me. Tell her how much I love her."

Jim said he would, but that he didn't know what he could do about their situation.

There was a gorgeous girl stretched out on a bed in the dressing room with Buddy, just listening to Jim and Buddy. I said, "Why don't you introduce us to the young lady?"

Buddy mumbled a name and said, "She's my secretary."

I said, "Yeah, how come she's not taking notes?"

A very tough-looking gentleman came into the room and introduced himself to me, saying that he was Buddy's manager. He didn't seem the type. He gave me his business card with a very Italian name and a company name indicating something like a button and thread company. Whatever it was, it certainly was a most unusual management company.

DOWNINGTOWN IS DIFFERENT

We hired a limousine for the trip to Downingtown, really the easiest way to get there. The resort was ostensibly owned by Mickey Rooney (and for all I know, may have been), and was a haven for honeymooners from Pennsylvania and New York.

Jim decided that he would like the services of a hooker for the night, but the odds of finding one in Downingtown didn't seem very favorable. He telephoned one of the Rockefellers in New York, who gave him a number to call. Of course, I had to make the call, get a price, and arrange for her to get to Downingtown from New York. The lady's price was $150 for the night, which was okay with Jim. I told her to take a train from New York and that I would have a car pick her up at the Downingtown station.

About an hour later, she called to say that Hurricane Irma had washed out the train tracks and that it would be impossible for her to get to us. I suggested she fly into Philadelphia, where I would have a limousine waiting for her, and she agreed. An attorney friend of Jim's decided he would drive up with his girl friend, so I had to be Jim's "beard" for the evening.

The young lady arrived in time for dinner, so I ate with Bernie F., his girlfriend and *my* date for the evening. Bernie's girlfriend and the hooker, who was very beautiful, were about the same age and they found things to talk about, so I was mercifully left out of the conversation.

I should point out that by then, Jim was being treated for Parkinson's Disease with L-Dopa. While I still am not positive he actually had the disease, he did have the medication. The effect was that he always felt as though he was about to orgasm. The irritation (if that's the correct word) at the end of his penis would drive him crazy, and the only relief was an actual orgasm. The relief, unfortunately, was only short term.

Later the next morning, Jim told me that he had purchased a room for the lady, since he finished quickly and one blow job was enough for him. I kidded him by cursing him out for not sending her to my room since I had, after all, paid her for the entire night.

JIM LAYS AN EGG, BUT IS SAVED

Whoever booked Jim at that gig thought he would be an ideal act for their kind of audience, and basically that might have been correct, except that, as I've said, Jim was not technically a stand-up comic. He was a story-teller, and worked best in an intimate setting with 300-400 people maximum. When we saw the room, we knew he was in deep *merde*.

First of all, the room held something like 1,500 people. Second, it was flat and covered an enormous area, so that people in the back could hardly see the stage, and third, the sound system was made more for a singer or a band. Jim didn't work "loud," and with the added distraction of a sound man who never physically checked the sound in various parts of the room, resulted in a situation where he couldn't be heard very well. There were repeated calls of "louder" from the back while he was working.

The show was pretty much a disaster. Jim did the best he could, but because only the people up close were paying any attention, the noise level from the audience was terrible. I wanted him to cut the show short and get off the stage, but Jim kept plugging away.

Over in nearby Valley Forge, there was a tent theater, and starring in something was John Raitt, the great baritone, and a friend of Jim's. He had finished his performance and stopped in to catch the show. Someone had directed him to me, and we were standing together, since Jim was on stage, dying a slow death.

Raitt turned to me and asked, "Would you mind if I go up and give him a hand?"

"Mind?" I said, "You'll save his life. Please, go."

With that, he jumped up on the stage and began a dialog with Jim, who was thrilled to see his friend. Raitt asked Jim if it would be okay for him to sing a song, and Jim, relieved, accepted, gave John a terrific introduction and then got off the stage.

"When John is through," I said, "go back up there and thank everyone for being an understanding audience and let's get the hell out of here."

Which he did. Jim turned in early, because he had his date from New York. I went into the "rock" club they had in the hotel, only because Mickey Rooney, Jr. was headlining, and I wanted to meet him. I knew his dad a little, and in fact, called him in Florida for Jim while we were there.

I made the mistake of asking Mickey, Sr. how he was feeling, and he told me. For thirty minutes, I heard how he was so much better now that he had found (re-found?) god and how he had changed the life of one of his sons (not Mickey, Jr.). Then, I heard all about the string of theaters he was planning to open—and never did. By the time he finished, I had forgotten why I called in the first place.

Mickey, Jr. and I hit if off immediately and decided we'd go out to a bar he knew somewhere down the road. He didn't like drinking at the hotel because he had no privacy there. At that bar, he was just another customer.

We had a few drinks and thought we'd catch a cab back to the hotel, but discovered that the edge of Hurricane Irma was inundating the roads and that no cabs would come out in the storm. So, we waited until closing when the kindly bartender drove us back to the hotel. The highway was ankle deep in water when we arrived and we had to wade to our rooms.

I've only spoken to Mickey, Jr. once since then, when he called me at home around three o'clock one morning, wondering if I knew where he could score some "coke."

The only other memory we took home with us from Downingtown was crabs, not the edible kind, but apparently from the bed linen. We know it was from there because Jim's attorney friend and his girlfriend both ended up with the same affliction. As they didn't sleep with either of us, so it had to be from the beds. What a place to go for a honeymoon!

Chapter 19
Backus Becomes My Main Client

Things had been going very well for Jim, but as I have already mentioned, my other client, Joe Ferrer, was in the midst of a mid-life crisis, turning down work for senseless reasons or no reason at all. As a result, which I have also mentioned, I pretty much withdrew as his "official" manager, although I continued to represent him in California because we were first and foremost friends, and that's the sort of thing friends do. However, I soon began working less with Joe, which gave me more time with Jim.

Offers for casuals were now coming in pretty regularly for Jim and for the most part, we were accepting them. There was a time when "name" actors wouldn't work casuals, considering them demeaning, but that stigma was beginning to wear off and the biggest stars were looking for one or two-nighters.

By now, the casual of choice seemed to have become a week or two on a cruise ship. A celebrity and his wife (or whomever) might be offered up to a month at sea with the best accommodations, by a major cruise line.

In addition to being treated as a first class passenger, they are often paid very handsomely, although more often than not, the trip was without financial remuneration; just no expense to them. Frequently, all that is asked of a celebrity is that they be seen, sign a few autographs, do a little sight-seeing if they wish, and be treated to a very pleasant vacation.

Singers and comedians love this kind of booking because it generally entails only one or two nights a week, and as I said, the pay is good. We never did a cruise, although Henny would have loved it.

The same thing is more or less true of television commercials. There was a time in the not too distant past when no self-respecting star would do so much as a voice-over. The entertainment world has changed, there is so much competition for work, and on-camera commercials can pay such enormous amounts of money, agents and managers are busily seeking work for top names.

Back in the 1970s, when Jim was doing casuals, cruise ship gigs for non-performing celebrities were a rarity. One reason we tried to book those "one-nighters" was that they generally paid the same money he commanded for a full week. What's more, our contracts always called for first class air fare and hotel accommodations for us both. Quick gigs worked out well for Henny, who didn't like being left alone very long, and who hated traveling even more, except by train.

She told me a story about when they were both filming, *If It's Tuesday, It Must Be Belgium*. I said she hated to fly, and that trip entailed a flight from Los Angeles to Europe. She was, at best, a "white knuckle" flyer, but she managed to get there and back with her self-hypnosis trick. However, she was not happy with something on the flight and wrote a personal letter to the president of the airline. A response came back with a check for $100 for whatever inconvenience she suffered. Not satisfied with that, she wrote back and inquired why they just didn't give her a free flight to Europe, even though the thought of flying anywhere was terrifying to her.

SOMETHNG ABOUT HENNY

I have mentioned Jim's wife, Henny a few times and perhaps this is a good time and place to say a few words about her. As Jim became better-known, first on radio, then television, and later in motion pictures, Henny took more and more of a back seat to Jim. She was, however, a star in her own right. In biographies about her, they talk about the fact that she was a child actor on Broadway. Mostly, they forget to mention that she was a member of Orson Welles Mercury Theater. You weren't chopped liver if you worked with Welles, and she even worked with him on Broadway.

When she was only seventeen, she was a well-known photographers' model. What doesn't always appear in bios was that she was the youngest showgirl on Broadway in *George White's Scandals*. She told me that she was still in high school and occasionally would still be doing her homework inside the giant clam shell in which she sat nude. George White apparently looked after her (he was gay), to make sure no one took advantage of her. I once asked her if there was any truth to stories about "Stage Door Johnnies," men who waited at the stage door after a performance ready to ply showgirls with gifts. She said it was absolutely true, and when I asked if any ever gave her jewelry she said, "absolutely" and that she usually "hocked it."

Jim had been married to Betty Kean (of the Kean sisters), but separated, when he was going with Henny. They both lived in the Royalton Hotel in New York, an early home base for a good many future stars. Henny, who worked regularly, often cooked for out of work or at liberty actors. She actually rented two units, one as a studio where she worked as a sculptress. She was so good that much of her work was on commission and included such stars as Katherine Cornell, Greta Garbo, Bette Davis, and Katharine Hepburn.

Jim told me that his father was a terrible bigot and at first objected to his marrying Henny, who was Jewish, but relented when he decided that Jewish women were good with money. Jim also told me that his father made off with all the nude photos Jim had of Henny. They were a perfect compliment to one another, wrote books and scripts together, and when his Parkinson's got the better of him, she was there for him all the time.

Henny wrote a book about living with Parkinson's in which she described the difficulty of sex, to which I can attest. One morning, I got a call from Jim asking that I come to their home to help him with something. Since I was used to spending free time with him, walking, driving, just talking about things, I went right over.

Jim and Henny had separate bedroom, but as Jim explained as I went upstairs with him, the previous night he was "feeling a little frisky" and joined Henny in her bed. He managed to perform adequately, but found that because of Parkinson's he was unable to "get off her," and could I demonstrate for them how he could do it—without Henny, of course. We should have filmed it.

WHAT IN THE WORLD IS TROY?

One of casual trips took us to a place called Troy, Ohio. What made Troy interesting was that what passed for "downtown" was right out of the 1930s. Except for parking meters, there was nothing to suggest that the town had ever left that decade. The main street ended in a cul de sac at the Town Hall. A river ran behind the town hall, completing the perfect picture of "small town America."

The only "sour note" was one empty lot among the commercial buildings on the cul de sac. When I asked "How come?" I was told that a retail business once erected a very modern edifice on that site, which a short time later mysteriously burned to the ground. I think people in Troy liked things just as they were.

Jim had written a movie script several years earlier that was called *In The Rough*. Naturally, it dealt with golf, but it took place in a small town that could easily have been Troy. The entire plot is unimportant, but the two antagonists in the story were owners of competing stove works.

The nearest town to Troy was Piqua, which coincidentally was the home of a then idle stove works, and Piqua was just as antique as Troy. There was a picturesque nine-hole golf course in Troy that could have been a championship layout if they ever added the other nine holes, but which would have been ideal just as it was for *In The Rough*. We thought we had found the perfect location, if only we could get the financing.

Why were we in Troy, Ohio, a place no one would likely seek of their own volition? Good question. Jim was there to do another casual for Hobart Industries, manufacturers of commercial and residential kitchen equipment, largely under the brand name of Kitchen Aid. He was hired to headline the annual show, which the company produced as part of a week-long celebration for Hobart's top employees. There was close to a thousand people in the local high school auditorium that night.

The best hotel in Troy was a privately owned Holiday Inn, which tells you a lot about Troy, Ohio. There was a golf driving range that was adjacent to the hotel, but it was closed for the season. Since the Holiday Inn owned it, they offered to open it for us. We accepted gratefully because, among other reasons, there just wasn't much to do in Troy during the day, unless, of course, you had a day job.

GOLF IS MORE THAN A GAME

Jim hadn't played much golf over the past few years. Now, except for chipping "wiffle balls" with me over the pool in his back yard, golf was limited to an occasional day on the pitch and putt course at Comstock Park, a quiet retreat near his home. Although the course was barely noticeable, threaded through the park were eighteen holes we could play for a dollar each, not for each hole, but for each of us. Of course, people were always wandering in and around what passed for the fairway because, after all, it was a park, and the "course" wasn't very clearly defined.

We'd play a hole or two, or cross over to another out of order, but it didn't matter much because we were usually the only people on the course and we did it mostly to be out in the fresh air. Mark Twain was wrong when he said golf was a good walk spoiled. Incidentally, in the Bel Air-Westwood Village area, Jim always claimed there was an ordinance requiring the air to be "fresh."

He used to tell a story in his act concerning a spinster living in Bel Air, and in describing the area, he would say that "Bel Air was very clean. In fact, there is a law that says pigeons passing over Bel Air must fly upside-down."

We rarely got out on a regular golf course together, but we did play in one tournament for the Los Angeles Police Department. Every year, there was a celebrity–police event at Rancho Park, which at one time was the home of the Los Angeles Open, so you know it's tough. Jim didn't feel up to playing the entire round, so he asked the police if I could play every other hole for him; we'd be, as they say in horse racing, an entry.

By the time we'd finished the first nine holes, he was having so much fun he forgot he wasn't feeling well and decided to play the remaining nine, which he did and so did I, flashing moments of the form that made him a Junior Champion back when he was a kid in Ohio. The only trophy he ever kept was a small silver loving cup he won at the Junior Amateur State Championship.

Now, there in Troy, a few years and a few hundred hypochondriac incidents later, he was banging out straight-as-an-arrow 250-yard drives. Jim's physical/mental condition could swing from great to bad for no apparent reason. He was, in fact, feeling pretty good in general that week, except for the usual pre-performance jitters.

Everyone in town seemed to know that Jim was there. I suspect that very few major celebrities ever made their way to Troy except to perform at the yearly Hobart event, and most of them were not nearly as recognizable as Jim. Wherever he went, people stopped to say hello and thank him for coming. He held interviews with the local newspaper, television, and radio stations in our hotel rooms, where incidentally, I took the photograph he used as his publicity shot the rest of his life. We were invited out to dinner at the country club, primarily to look over the layout in the event we ever raised the money to make *In The Rough*.

Several people in Troy thought the money might be raised right there in the community and offered to give it a try. What's more, the country club boasted the absolute best restaurant in town. The next best was the Holiday Inn, and that, too, tells you a lot about Troy.

Like Joe Ferrer, Jim began experiencing a "somewhat past mid-life crisis." It wasn't that his health deteriorated yet, but he was having the standard doubts about himself mostly because there were no offers for good motion picture parts or series since *Gilligan's Island* was off the air. There were days when his attitude could best be described as depressed, and it was my job to pull him out of it.

IT'S A DIFFERENT HOLLYWOOD NOW

Jim had been a pampered actor, when success was coming easily. He lived the life of a Hollywood star, having breakfast in bed every morning and, except for times when he was working in films, not getting started until noon. When work slowed down, he used the bed as his crutch instead of going out to meet people or going to his office to do something creative. I had to virtually drag him out of the house, if only for a walk.

The world's greatest "straight man," George Burns, told him, "Jim, don't get married to your bed." George was up and out around nine every morning. He would go to his office, work on new material, or rehearse old material, then go to lunch at the Hillcrest Country Club. He'd have his two daytime martinis, play a little bridge and often end the day at dinner with some attractive young woman. He always said, "I liked eighteen-year-old girls when I was young; why shouldn't I like them now?" That, of course, was a joke, but the women he did go out with were certainly younger than he.

Jim hung around the house every day until I finally convinced him we should meet at his office—he had a one-room office at an independent sound stage in Los Angeles—by ten o'clock in the morning. We worked on projects, wrote material, and had lunch. *Then*, he'd go home and do nothing, but at least he was getting out. As I said, Jim had permanent possession of the U.S.A. championship cup in freestyle hypochondria.

One of the problems I had with getting work for him was that Jim, like José, wouldn't settle on a full-time agent. Most of the top agents don't want to work for someone without an exclusive agency agreement, even if only short term. I asked—no, I *begged* Jim not to sign with anyone until I spoke with them first, but he'd do it anyway, and then call and ask me to get him out of the contract.

One day, he informed me he was thinking of signing with the Kurt Frings Agency. I asked why he would do a thing like that, and he replied, "Because Kurt represents Elizabeth Taylor and Richard Burton."

"So," I said, "what's that got to do with you?"

"Well, he's very big-time and commands a lot of money for his clients."

"That's true enough, but Frings lives in England or Europe somewhere, and just how is *he* going to get you bookings here? Besides, he doesn't have to sell Taylor and Burton. He just sits at home and waits for the telephone to ring. Then he says 'no' to whatever the offer is until they raise the price. He's not going to do that for you."

Of course, Frings never did anything for him, and about two months later, Jim did ask me to break the contract. That was not easy because it was a valid, SAG-approved contract and the agency could have held Jim to the entire term, which I think was only a year, had they wanted to. Two hours of cajoling resulted in their agreeing to tear up the contract. I wouldn't swear that Kurt Frings ever knew Jim was signed with the agency.

Chapter 19: Backus Becomes My Main Client

Shifting my mental gears back to Troy, I remember how we dressed early and went down to the hotel dining room for our usual pre-show meal: soup, iced tea, and vanilla ice cream. We also developed a standard traveling breakfast: an English muffin, a side of crisp bacon, and hot tea, or, if the weather was a bit nippy, we might add a bowl of hot oatmeal.

Anyway, just as we sat down, an extremely pretty young, I would guess (there I go again) under thirty woman walked by us and took a nearby booth. She nodded a hello, and I turned to Jim, saying, "She's got to be from out of town, because she's far and away the prettiest woman we've seen since we got here."

Jim said, "Go ask if she'll be here when we get back, or see if she'd like to go to the show with us."

She thanked me for the invitation, but since she was already committed to dinner, she couldn't go. She added that she would be more than happy to have a drink later if she happened to be there when we returned.

Our driver was already waiting by the time we finished our "meal." It was about an hour after the curtain "went up" (there was no actual curtain), when we arrived at the auditorium. We figured we'd be more comfortable at the hotel than sitting around somewhere until Jim was actually due on stage. There were several acts and some speeches scheduled ahead of Jim who was, naturally, the headliner. Jack Lescoulie, the well-known radio and television announcer, who every year served as emcee, agreed that the best place to be was anywhere but at the auditorium. Jim was on next to closing, the best position in a long show, going back to vaudeville days and probably long before that.

We had contracted for a forty-five minute show, which is a long time for any comic to be on stage, especially one who doesn't do free-association comedy, and even longer for someone like Jim.

About forty minutes into the act, I signaled "five minutes" by holding up five fingers, but he was being received with such enthusiasm, he kept right on going, dredging up material from some deep recess in his brain. At just short of an hour, I gave up trying to get his attention with the traditional "cut" signal of drawing an index finger across my throat. Either he couldn't see it, or was ignoring me. Finally, I yelled at him from the wings, "Get the hell off the stage."

He looked at me like I was crazy. I pointed to my watch and he looked at his, surprised to see how long he was on. He did another five minutes and then walked off to a standing ovation. He was so juiced, he wanted to return immediately to the hotel for a full meal, and to celebrate with a Mai Tai or maybe even two.

Back at the hotel, there was a party mood in the dining room. The very attractive girl we saw earlier was dancing with a man I presumed to be her dinner date, and they were dancing to a combo playing 1940s music.

The richest man in Troy, the town's only undertaker, had four or five girls in a booth with him and invited us to join him, but we declined saying we wanted to have dinner first.

I GO SOCIAL

I went to the bar to get a couple of drinks and found myself standing next to the young lady who was seated on a stool next to the young man with whom she'd been dancing.

I said hello, told her I thought she was a good dancer and that I was surprised anyone as young as she knew how to dance to that kind of music. She said something in response, and just as the bartender handed me the drinks, she said, "Would you do me a favor?"

"If I can," I replied.

"Would you kiss me?"

"Gladly," I said, "but what about your boyfriend?"

"He's not my boyfriend," she said. "I was just dancing with him. So, how about it, will you kiss me?"

"My pleasure. Is there any particular reason?"

"I've never kissed a man with a beard before."

Well, that seemed a good enough reason to me, so I did my utmost to uphold the honor of bearded kissers. When we unclenched, I said, "That was very nice. By the way, my name is Jack Lloyd."

She said, "Glad to meet you, Jack Lloyd. My name is Holly, and here's my room key."

Naturally, I asked if she would you like to join Jim and me for dinner. She reminded me that she already had dinner, but agreed to join us while we ate.

"Would you like to dance?" she asked.

"I most certainly would," I said. "Jim can wait a couple of minutes for his drink."

While we were busy on the dance floor, Jim joined the undertaker and his group and had our food sent there. I finished my dinner, and was deep in conversation with Holly when Jim announced that he, the undertaker, and several others in the party were going to drive the thirty-five miles to Dayton and spend what remained of the evening at Sutmiller's, one of the best small night clubs in the mid-west.

I didn't much feel like going to Dayton, so stayed behind, dancing until midnight when the bar closed. No 2:00 a.m. closings in Troy. Apparently, Jim was a smash at Sutmiller's, getting up on stage and improvising for fifteen or twenty minutes. He must have been a hit because when we returned to Los Angeles, I got a call asking if Jim would like to do a week there. Unfortunately, they couldn't come close to his price.

Although I kept in touch with the owner of the hotel for a few months, no one was ever able to raise the money to make Jim's movie.

I have no idea what ever became of Holly, who, as I learned that night, was a traveling saleslady. I guess the old jokes about the traveling salesmen (and by extension, salesladies) had a ring of truth to them.

Right here I am reminded of a joke Jim used in his act:

"I loved to gamble," he would say. "Mostly I liked the slot machines—the old fashioned kind with the handle—the 'one-arm-bandits' as they were called back then. When I'd get going, I put everything I have into it. One night in Las Vegas, I was my usual, aggressive self when my hand slipped from the handle just as a beautiful young woman was passing. I hit her right in the breast. Turning to her, I said, 'Madam, I would like to apologize, but if your heart is as soft as your breast, I know you will forgive me.' And she replied, handing me her room key, 'If the rest of you is as hard as your elbow, I'm in room 319.'"

Another joke Jim used to tell was about an ultimately wealthy spinster, who lived high up in the Bel Air region of Los Angeles: "Bel Air, for those of you who are unfamiliar with Los Angeles, is an area of very expensive homes and extremely rich people. It is a very clean area. It is so clean that there is a sign reading 'pigeons flying over Bel Air must fly upside down. It's the law.'

"Anyway, this lady was a recluse who had never been married; never wanted to be married; lived her entire life among her fine furnishings and artwork. One day, as she approached the middle earlies of her life, she had a change of heart and decided it was time to take the step, only she wanted to marry someone who was a virgin, someone who had never known a woman, so they could start out on an equal footing, so to speak.

"She sends out searching parties throughout the world trying to find a man who fits her needs. One by one, they report back that they have had no luck; there just isn't any man of the appropriate age who has had no experience whatever. Finally, just as she is about to call off the search and resign herself to a life of spinsterhood, word comes back from the deepest recesses of the Australian Outback that they have found the perfect man. He has never even met a woman. His mother died in childbirth and he was raised by an uncle. They had no radio, no television, and no newspapers. He didn't even know what a woman looked like, and best of all, he was six feet four, gorgeous, a hunk, a Greek God. She cables the search team to crate him up, toss in six dozen oysters, and ship him directly to her home for the nuptials.

"He arrives and is taken directly to the garden where the minister and the bride-to-be, both dressed in basic black, are waiting with the license, and they are wed. Retiring to her boudoir for a night of connubing—of connubial bliss, she leaves him and repairs to her toilette where she prepares herself: a little Aqua Velva behind the ears, her best seersucker peignoir, and returns to the bedroom. To her shock and dismay, she finds all the furniture has been moved. The bed is standing on its side; everything has been moved against the walls. She turns to her groom and says, "What's going on?" And he replies, "Well, ma'am, I don't know anything about women, but if they're anything like kangaroos, we're gonna need all the room we can get."

Chapter 20
Jim's Hypochondria Gets Real

I've said that Jim was a hypochondriac, but later in our relationship, Jim's illness became real, when he was diagnosed as having Parkinson's or Parkinson's Syndrome. I guess there's not much to choose between them. I was talking with Jim's internist at Henny's birthday party, and he told me, "Jim does not have Parkinson's, but he's determined to keep trying doctors until one of them tells him he has it." Within a few months, Jim called to tell me that he found a physician who told him, "I'm pretty sure you have a touch of Parkinson's," whatever that meant.

Phyllis Diller, an old and dear friend of the Backuses, sent Jim a copy of Norman Cousins' book, *Anatomy of An Illness*, figuring that if he read how Cousins fought and beat a serious illness, it might help his attitude, if nothing else. Henny sent the book to me with instructions to underline the parts it was okay for Jim to read. If Jim were to read about Cousins' symptoms, he was certain to develop them.

A particular illustration of his hypochondria comes to mind. We were in Minneapolis/St. Paul, Minnesota for a two-week stand at a club/restaurant, Diamond Jim's. This was long after *Truth of Truths*, but actually came about because of the nationwide publicity, which went a long way towards reviving several aspects of his career. The agent had us booked into a hotel in St. Paul, but Jim didn't like it; it was "cold," and besides, it was too far away from any activity, not that I found much in Minneapolis, unless you were into rock and roll and the bar scene.

We canceled our reservations and drove into the downtown area of Minneapolis where we found a hotel we liked. The general manager came out to greet Jim and offered us a two-bedroom suite for the price of a single room. That was too good to refuse, especially since Jim was paying our expenses other than the first class air fares. So, Jim invited him to the show as his guest.

We were getting pretty hungry by the time we settled into the room and called on the hotel manager to suggest someplace we could get a bite and possibly a drink before bed-time. Terry Dunlay, the manager of the Hyatt Lodge, sent us to a hamburger restaurant nearby, which turned out to be more a bar than a restaurant. That would have been okay, but the kitchen was already closed by the time we got there and we wanted something other than a couple of drinks.

The restaurant manager recognized Jim and was more than happy to find us some place still open, where the food wouldn't kill us. After a couple of calls, he spoke with the manager of the dining room at the North Star Inn, a fine hotel we missed in our search for a new place, and it was not too far away. They agreed to keep their kitchen open until we got there.

Hang in there, I'm getting to the part of his hypochondria, but I have to set the stage first. I'm pretty nearly there.

We arrived at the North Star within a matter of minutes and were shown to a rear booth, where we would be undisturbed by any of the diners still there. The waitress took our order and we sat back each with a glass of red wine. When I looked up, one of the most beautiful women I had ever seen was walking towards us.

"Don't turn around," I said, "but there is a gorgeous creature headed our way. Maybe she's coming to meet you." When she got close to me, it was obvious she had no intention of stopping, so I did something I had never done or even contemplated doing before. I reached out and grabbed her arm. Naturally, she tried to pull away, but I said, "Only if you promise to come back here later."

"I can't" she said. "I work here and I'm not allowed to sit with customers."

I said, "Okay, then I won't let go."

As I wasn't letting loose, she agreed that she would return as soon as she finished whatever job she had to do.

I tell you this as a preface because I had an occasion to ask for her help the next morning. The young hostess I accosted, Gail, did come back to our booth, and the three of us talked for more than an hour, mostly about her broken love affair that had ended just the night before. Her then-ex was a musician, who used to whack her around every so often. She told us that she went to his apartment every day to clean and cook for him before she went to work as a hostess at the North Star.

She had given up thoughts of having a real singing career herself—she sang regularly as part of an act that performed in a well-known restaurant somewhere along the river in Minneapolis—before taking that job full-time in the evenings at the North Star Inn. She worked as an evening hostess in order to take care of her boyfriend during the day, while he worked nights as a drummer in a rock and roll club. Because he was crippled in some way, she needed the daytime to tend to his needs. That way, she could also pick him up at night when he finished work.

We commiserated appropriately and asked if she would like to come back to our hotel and share a bottle of champagne the stewardess handed me as we left the airplane. She thought that would be very nice and showed up a few minutes after we got into our suite. Sometime around one o'clock in the morning, she decided it was time to leave, and Jim said he would walk her to the car. If Jim wanted to take a shot at her, I, being only the manager, would certainly defer to him. He was gone for about forty-five minutes, and by then, I figured *something* happened. I mean, that girl was certainly no virgin. However, when he walked back in the door he said, "All she wanted to do was talk some more about her ex-boyfriend and how unhappy she was. She needs a shrink, not a shtup."

"Oh, shit," he added. "I invited her to the show."

"Don't worry; I'll sit her with Terry Dunlay and his friends. I'll take care of it."

In the morning, Jim and I met in the center living room and I casually asked how he was feeling. I should have known better. He replied, "I don't know. I'm feeling kinda shnotzy" (his word, not mine).

I suggested it was probably just due to a change in the weather, and that he'd be fine after breakfast.

Here's where the hypochondria came in.

I don't think I can go on," he said. "I'm not one of those guys who believe 'the show must go on.' If I have to cancel, I will."

I dug out Gail's telephone number, which I managed to get just in case I needed to call her for something—like a date for dinner. I asked if she knew of a good nose and throat doctor, one who treated opera singers with a sore throat or runny nose. She did.

I said, "Do me a favor and call him. Tell him that Jim Backus is in town and has a little problem we'd like checked out. And tell him that if Jim has anything short of Bubonic Plague, to say he's fine and that he can work.

The weather was more than a little warm for that time of year, but Jim bundled up for the Arctic. In addition to a wool turtleneck sweater, he put on a corduroy jacket that zipped up to his neck. When the doctor finished giving Jim a thorough going over, we sat in his office to hear the verdict.

"Jim," he said, "you're in excellent health. The only thing I can find is a slightly elevated temperature of 98.8°."

"That mean's I can't go on, right?"

I said, "Jim, that's two tenths of a degree. You've got enough clothes on to raise it that high".

The doctor assured him that his temperature would not cause him to miss even a single night's work. He wrote a prescription for what I thought I recognized as a placebo (I was a Hospital Corpsman in the Navy), and sent us on our way. Whatever it was worked just fine, and Jim ended up having a terrific two-week run.

BACK WORKING IN CLUBS

Diamond Jim's was Jim's first night club job since an appearance at the Fremont Hotel in Las Vegas a few years before we got together. (Later in our relationship, he worked the Hacienda). Needless to say, even with the "medication" he was pretty nervous. We had gone through his files and resurrected some of the material he used at the Fremont, modifying it to work there. We decided to keep it simple.

Diamond Jim's was a "private club." I put that in quotation marks because there were 20,000 members, making it not quite exclusive, although it *was* private, each of whom paid $20 a year for the privilege of eating a $3.95 buffet dinner and paying 99¢ for "well" drinks. They also served a fancy drink something like a Brandy Alexander for $1.99 that was made with vanilla ice cream. The membership fees covered their entire entertainment budget for the year and then some. Jim was getting the top of their weekly budget.

He did two shows a night, with three on Saturday. The club was dark on Sunday and Monday, which meant we could fly back to Los Angeles on the second Sunday. Not a bad gig. The club had a very good house band that provided more than music; they were also the opening act. Jim wanted to sing in his portion of the show, and we rehearsed a couple of numbers with the band, settling on a tune from the play, *Mack and Mabel*, called "I Won't Send Roses," which he could practically talk-sing.

As I said, we arrived in Minneapolis on Sunday, went to the doctor on Monday, and rehearsed Tuesday afternoon. After acquainting me with the club, the stage, and lighting, as usual, we had lunch at the club's expense in another restaurant they owned on the same property. It was still early enough to return to the hotel and for Jim to take a nap before we dressed for the show.

While he was asleep, I took a walk around downtown and noticed there were no real showrooms anywhere, certainly not within walking distance of our hotel. Minneapolis, before the days of regular coast-to-coast air travel, was a mid-week stop for acts going from one coast to the other by train.

The Radisson Hotel housed the once-famous Flame Room, then just a lounge with an occasional trio. It had been, years back, a great club where all the top acts played. Because it was a mid-week job, they were able to book major acts at very good prices.

I began to have thoughts about trying to get the place for a club that we would call Big Jim's, or Jimbo's, or something like that. Jim could front the club and appear perhaps three or four times a year. As it was, Diamond Jim's was practically the only place for entertainment other than rock and roll or disco. There was no place for adults with money.

Minneapolis, at least in the 1970s, was pretty much dead in the winter. Football was played in an open-air stadium in Bloomington, where the baseball team played in the summer. They did not yet have major league basketball. The favorite pastimes of the populace, seemingly for all social groups beyond the age of eighteen, appeared to be drinking and sex. The drinking part was obvious.

The sex, for us at least, was limited almost entirely to rumor and innuendo (I'll get to that in a bit), although as it happened, one lady did have the hots for Jim. I don't know for certain that anything came of it, although not for lack of trying on her part. I could have been wrong because I wasn't with him all the time.

That situation came about because Jim knew some people in Minneapolis, some kind of manufacturer he and Henny met somewhere in their travels. They made reservations for six people and asked Bernie Dahlberg, the club manager, to tell Jim they were coming. When they arrived at the club, Jim greeted them, and his friend asked, "What do you guys do between shows?"

Our usual routine was to leave the club immediately after the first show and drive back to our hotel about fifteen minutes away. That gave Jim about an hour to rest before we had to get back. His friend insisted that we join him, his wife, and the two other couples at his home between shows since it was only five or six minutes away.

We followed them to a magnificent two-story home somewhere in St. Paul, and headed straight for their lower-level bar. Jim sat with the men at a coffee table, while I joined the three women at the bar. I was drinking Jack Daniels in those days and asked for a "short one," because I still had a night's work ahead of me. Jim, of course, didn't drink at all.

Our hostess's idea of a "short" drink was about four fingers of Jack Daniels and a splash of water. I tried to let the ice melt a little before I drank it. During the time it took me to finish my one drink, each of the ladies put away three of the same size. Our hostess couldn't stop talking about Jim and how cute he was—no one mentioned how cute *I* was.

The next day, I got a telephone call from her. No calls were ever put through directly to Jim except from his wife. The lady from the past evening flat out told me that she wanted to meet him privately somewhere, preferably his hotel room, so I more or less arranged for them to meet.

On the second night, Gail, the young lady we met at the Northstar

Inn, came to the show and I sat her with Jim's other guests. When we first met her, she wore her blonde hair in a tight bun, but then, she wore it down and it reached well below her waist. I didn't even recognize her at first. Every so often, I would stop by the table, speak with Terry Dunlay and his guest and two others from the hotel, and Gail.

IT'S GOOD TO BE A STAR

Towards the end of the show, Gail stopped me and said, "I have two roommates who are pretty casual about sex. Should I invite them back to the hotel?"

"Are they as pretty as you are?" I asked gallantly.

She assured me that they were, and I told her to make the call. She came back a few minutes later to tell me that they would meet us at the suite. Jim and Terry (the hotel manager), Gail, and I returned to the suite and were joined a few minutes later by a gorgeous redhead and a very attractive brunette. I had ordered a couple bottles of wine to go at the club so we could have a few drinks.

Jim paired himself off with the redhead, Terry with the brunette, and I was left with the blonde, Gail. Jim, Terry, and the two girls got into deep and quiet conversation and I, already knowing that Gail seemed to be a losing cause, devoted myself to her, primarily to give the others a chance to get better acquainted. After perhaps thirty or forty minutes, Jim rose from his chair and announced that "we're going to bed." Terry immediately followed, saying that he and the brunette were leaving, and so Gail and I were left alone in the living room. As it was then about 3:30 in the morning, I was a gallant gentleman and offered her my bedroom for the night, which she accepted. I could use the couch in the living room. She ended up spending, off and on, the better part of two weeks with us.

I GET SERIOUS ABOUT HAVING OUR OWN CLUB

Over the next several days I spoke with Gail about my idea for The Flame Room. I asked her to find the name of the owner of the hotel and how I could reach him. She told me that the maitre d' at The North Star, her direct boss, was planning to open a restaurant/club and suggested that he and I talk, which we did on several occasions before Jim and I left for Los Angeles.

Gail secured all the information I wanted, and I called the owner to propose re-opening the room under Jim's name. He loved the idea and we set a meeting. However, before we could get together, he called me with a counter proposal. He would *give* me the main ballroom free of rent, every Friday and Saturday night, and split the net income from food and liquor sales. The offer was attractive, except the ballroom held perhaps a thousand people, and I wanted an intimate club.

The Flame Room with its 300 maximum capacity would have been perfect. The hotel owner and I talked five or six times before Jim and I left town, but he wouldn't change his mind, and so my grandiose plans for a club essentially for Jim and me went by the boards. It's too bad, because we could have made a go of it, particularly since the IRS shut down Diamond Jim's about a year later.

Interestingly, almost everyone I have met over the years believed that Jim was a master of voices. As I have mentioned, he did only two. The Magoo voice was a distillation of one of the voices he used on radio: the hotel desk clerk in a seedy hotel, or the tough cop, combined with the way his father spoke. His other voice was Hubert Updyke III—later to become Thurston Howell III—basically the same character with many of the same gags.

Wherever we went, people would ask him to do the Western Airline commercial—"The only way to fly!"—but no matter how he insisted that it wasn't his voice, they would persist until he did it. Actually, they had hired another actor to "do Jim."

Jim was more or less famous for another commercial for a California wine company. The "tag" had Jim saying the words, "That little old wine maker—me." The following year, they changed the commercial and had some singers warbling a jingle, ending in the words Jim had done the previous year. Jim then added one word as the tag: "Me." He claimed to be the highest paid commercial actor . . . by the word.

EVERYONE NEEDS A LITTLE HELP SOMETIME

Jim was one of the stars on the original pilot for *Hollywood Squares*, which was produced by the team of Merrill Heater and Bob Quigley. Frequently thereafter, he was a guest celebrity on the show. For some reason, Bob and his wife, Keith decided to have a surprise costume party for Jim's fifty-eighth birthday. Everyone, except Jim and Henny, of course, were required to come dressed in their favorite costume or uniform. I came in a navy uniform (I was a Hospital Corpsman, 3rd Class); NBC executive Perry Lafferty came in his Major's uniform . . . which still fit. Rose Marie came in her daughter's Confirmation dress, with ruffled panties to which was attached a sign reading "I was a child star." Among the guests were Esther Williams in a caftan, Fernando Lamas, Jack Carter, Tracy Keenan Wynn, author Harold Robbins and his wife, Grace, and Peter Marshall. Peter showed up wearing a "hard hat" with a major dent in it that came from his appearance in a Broadway show called *Skyscraper*. The dent resulted from when some scenery fell from above and hit him in the head; that hard hat saved his life.

At the party, Keith Quigley had employed the services of whichever caterer was the currently "hot" name among Hollywood caterers, and we were fed at long picnic-style tables on the covered patio. I don't remember what we ate and I can't tell you what was served as the main course, but most of us were surprised to find that we had already eaten it. Following what was obviously a dessert, we all adjourned to the living room, where comedian Jack Carter had volunteered to open the gag gifts. Jack, who is unquestionably one of the funniest men ever to grace night club stages (without ever getting to be the major star he should have become), began by doing ten minutes on the food, and not in a complimentary way. Needless to say, the Quigleys failed to laugh. As nearly as I can remember, Carter was never again hired for any Heater/Quigley show. Jim always said that Jack Carter was the funniest man ever in a living room.

Jim was almost never at a loss for a funny comment, and generally, lines just flowed out of him. Yet, whenever he appeared on *Hollywood Squares*, where he was a frequent guest, he had to have his meeting with producers where they gave him his ad-libs. Still, he always delivered his gags as though he just thought of them. I recall one time he whispered to me that he had to leave me because he was going to get his ad libs and gag answers, but that I shouldn't say anything. I told him that just about everyone on the show—that night at least—had already been to a meeting just like the one he was headed for.

That brings to mind a story about one particular appearance on *Hollywood Squares*. As most people know, all five shows were shot the same night, with a change of audience after the first three. Before the fourth and fifth shows, there was a break for dinner. If you stayed on the set, there was some wine, but no serious drinking. However, several of the "regulars" would go across the street to a restaurant where there was considerably more drinking—to the point where the next two shows were always looser and funnier.

That night, before the fourth show, everyone was waiting in the wings to be introduced by Peter Marshall, the great host of the program. Standing with them, I said, "Don't you ever get tired of doing the same old thing? This time, when he introduces Mickey Rooney, why don't you," I said, pointing to Tony Randall, "go out and do Mickey?" Then, I suggested to JoAnne Worley that she do Tony, right on through the entire cast. Peter caught on immediately and went along with the gag. Finally, Paul Lynde came out doing JoAnne. I don't know whether Peter or the audience liked it, but I did.

There was one time when Jim was at a complete loss for something to say. Well, he did say something. It happened up at Lake Tahoe, the resort community along the lake that borders both California and Nevada. Bill Harrah, the owner of Harrah's Hotel and Casino, invited Jim to his annual Comedians Golf Tournament, and Jim knew he would be expected to get up on stage at the dinner and do shtick. To prepare for that eventuality, he bought an act from a well-known gag writer.

Milton Berle, according to Jim's story, was on just ahead of him, and he did Jim's entire act. It seemed that Milton bought the same material from the same gag writer.

Anyway, Harrah called on Jim next. He got up on stage, looked out at his audience and said, "Milton just did my act," and sat down. They roared, thinking Jim was just being funny old Jim.

I take it back, there was other time he was temporarily stumped, in Seattle, but I'll get to that later.

Chapter 21
We Go on the Road Again

Not long after Jim's success in Minneapolis, we were offered two weeks in Seattle, Washington, at a club called The Trojan Horse, aptly titled since it was owned by Greeks. Henny, I guess, wasn't very happy about our taking the date (Jim would be gone for two weeks) because as we were walking through the Sea-Tac Airport, Jim heard himself paged. It was Henny. She wanted to know how the flight went and to remind him to call as soon as we settled in our hotel. Jim wanted to go check out a strip joint or two, but we had no choice but to go to the hotel and call her first.

Not only did Jim speak with her, but I stayed in his room so I could talk to her when they were finished. Henny was very bright about some things, particularly show business, having been in it since she was about sixteen or seventeen years old and the youngest showgirl in *George White's Scandals*. She gave me a few instructions on how things should be handled for Jimmy, Of course, I knew what she was going to say, but as she was right, and so I didn't make any fuss; I just agreed to do whatever it was she wanted. But Jim also had to call every night when we arrived at the club and then again as soon as we got back to the hotel following the show, which meant no hanky-panky—sort of.

On the way to the hotel, we asked the cab driver if he knew of a good strip joint not too far from where we were staying. He gave us the name of a place and then drove by it so we could take a look. After doing our thing with Henny, we grabbed another cab and went back. We took a table one level back from the stage and ordered a couple of glasses of wine. As usual, someone recognized Jim, and the club owner joined us within a few minutes.

Although Jim usually had me make inquiries for him, that time he was very up-front. "Do you suppose," he asked, "that one of your girls might like to pick up a quick fifty bucks?"

As it was obvious that Jim did not have in mind a dinner companion, the owner said he was certain he could find someone. He left the table and was back not five minutes later with a very pretty young lady in tow. She told Jim that she would *love* to go back to the hotel with us (him) as soon as she finished her next turn on stage. When she was up there, it was very apparent that the woman had talent.

As Jim never offered her another fifty for me—and I wouldn't have spent it on myself—Jim spent a couple of hours alone with her. I probably should say that Jim never asked much of ladies of the evening, normally settling for oral sex.

The Trojan Horse was a good club for a performer. The stage was considerably lower than the tiers of tables that extended both downward and upward from the street level entrance. The lighting and sound were good, and the owners cordial. At first, it looked to be an ideal date. It wasn't bad, but it certainly wasn't ideal. I'm not sure the owners quite knew what to expect from Jim, but if they were disappointed, they didn't show it, although we were. I bring this up because as good as the club was, it was not really for Jim.

It was located in what would not be considered the best area of town, and it catered more to a drinking crowd than dining and show group. The fact that it was Jim Backus appearing brought in some people, but not the regular heavy drinkers they were used to, which probably did disappoint the owners. We tried modifying the act to some extent by adding some semi-risqué material, and while it helped hold the interest of people already there, it didn't bring in a larger audience.

JIM SCORES—JUST NOT ON STAGE

On the other hand, Jim found a fan. I got a call one afternoon from a Sally Roberts (not her real name). She lived in Bellingham, Washington, and was crazy about him as an actor, and she wanted to know if I would reserve a very good table for that night. I was happy to do it because truthfully, we weren't playing to full houses during the week.

Sally arrived early that night, and I had a front row table for her. She wanted to know if I would introduce her, and I said I would immediately after the show, because I didn't want anything on his mind other than his material. We always arrived at the venue in time for Jim to change into his tuxedo and relax for half an hour before show time, which was what he was doing at that moment.

As she arrived early, I took her into the bar and asked what she'd like to drink, because I am nothing if not a gentleman.

"I'll have a Vodka Martini," she said, "with five onions. I prefer onions."

"And that way you won't have to eat dinner either after you've had a couple of those," I said. Sally was a very attractive woman about, I would guess, (there I go again, guessing) in her early to mid-forties. She was dressed expensively and in good taste, showing off what seemed to me a very good figure.

Backstage, I introduced her to Jim right after the show, and they talked for perhaps half an hour. She was a widow, left with a lot of money. She worked in Bellingham, I think, in a fancy boutique of some kind, but didn't need to. She told Jim, and later me, that she had a quarter million dollars in jewelry, which she generally took with her wherever she went because she was afraid to leave it at home or in the car.

When she left, I walked her to her car and noticed that a bar suspended between the rear windows held several items of clothing. It appeared that she expected to stay the night. Jim, unfortunately, either misread her signals or was too much of a gentleman to ask . . . that night, anyway.

She came back every night, making the drive to and from Bellingham, probably close to a hundred miles each way. Finally, I said, why don't you just take a room in town, which she did for the last three days of our stay—Jim's room.

SEATTLE IS DIFFERENT

My room at the Edgewater Inn faced Puget Sound. Jim didn't want to see emptiness below his room, so he stayed on the street side of the hotel. One afternoon, I found myself sitting in a chair in front of the large open picture window that faced the Sound. I had my feet on the sill, my chair tilted slightly back as I wrote a letter in which I began commenting on the beauty of the scene before me.

I spoke of how the sun sparkled on the water, like so many diamonds shimmering in the light chop. As I wrote, the scene changed and I found myself describing incoming clouds, then the driving rain, then the high winds that whipped the wavelets of the Sound into full-blown white caps and sent the curtains flapping into my room, then the sun breaking through the clouds, and finally, the sunlight reflecting on the quiet water again. Before I finished the letter, I watched the same scene repeated four more times. That's Seattle.

I don't know if it's still done, but back then, you could rent a fishing pole in the lobby and fish for mud sharks from your hotel window. There were dozens of photographs at the rental stand showing guests with their prized catches. I'm told that mud sharks don't attack humans (I had no desire to check it out) and that they made good eating, but I decided to take their word for it. I'm not a fisherman, even from a hotel window.

While we were in Seattle, Jim did several radio and television shows to build up the audience. It was at the first station that I ran into Jimmy Carl Black, Frank Zappa's former drummer with The Mothers of Invention. My young friend, Mike Zugsmith, and I had been close to managing Jimmy's new group several months earlier, but found it impossible to have an intelligent conversation with any member of the band because they always appeared to be stoned.

Jimmy stopped me and said, "I've got to talk to you."

I explained why I was there, and told them I'd be back home within the week and for him to call. Mike and I met with the band again, booked them into a club in Orange County, where I went to hear them play and met with them afterward. They were still impossible to have any sort of decent conversation with, and still seemed to be stoned, and that ended that.

Getting back to Jim Backus and Seattle . . . by the Friday night after Jim's radio appearance, the club was pretty much filled. By that time, I was collecting Jim's pay in cash each night. They were supposed to come up with half the fee in front and the balance at the end of the first week. Since they didn't seem to have it all at once, we just compromised. The crowd was also good on Saturday, and it looked as though, if we had been booked longer, that Jim might have built a following. Unfortunately, we left on Sunday.

Part of the reason he did not draw as well as I thought he should was because the owners did not, in my opinion, do a very good job of promoting Jim's appearance. However, it was on Thursday night that Jim was, as I mentioned earlier, almost at a total loss for words.

Jim did two shows a night, and it was during the second show with not too large an audience still in the house, that Jim noticed people paying him little or no heed. The seating in the club was a three-quarter circle, with seats, as I mentioned, rising several levels above the floor. Jim suddenly realized that a large part of the audience was looking up to the top row, into a dark corner behind him.

He turned his attention to the corner and watched—with the audience—while a young couple was busily . . . coupling. Jim said, "The heck with the show, let's watch that." Which he—and they—did for the next five minutes. "In my day," said Jim, "we did things like that where God intended us to—in the back seat of a Chevy."

Chapter 22
Charley Goldring

Jim, as I have mentioned, had a business manager with whom I had problems. Charley Goldring wanted to be Jim's "personal" manager as well, not so much because he had any idea what a personal manager did, but because, in my opinion, he had an enormous ego and wanted his name listed along with Jim's picture in the *Players Directory*, put out by the Screen Actors Guild. However, whenever anything actually needed to be done, the job fell to me. An actor/producer friend of mine, who was well-acquainted with Charley, hated him because my friend believed it was Charley's handling of his friend's finances that resulted in his suicide. However, that was not the primary reason I didn't much care for Charley.

Charley was an attorney, but whenever Jim needed some sort of legal advice, we had to go hire someone who understood show business. Perhaps Charley just couldn't be bothered doing the work. His nephew handled the accounting and bookkeeping for the clients, so I was never quite sure just what it was that Charley did to earn his money.

What Charley was best at, according to Jim, was having a hooker in his office just about every day at four-thirty. I never met anyone who actually liked Goldring, including his nephew. When Jim and I were in Downingtown, Pennsylvania, Jim got a call from Charley, who was in New York and looking for a hooker, and he wanted to know whether he knew of any. Now, I had nothing against Charley for indulging in hookers now and again, but I felt he paid more attention to them than he did to Jim. Of course, that's just my opinion.

How they came together is worth mentioning. Several years before Jim and I met, Charley had come to Jim's rescue, when a previous business manager left him almost penniless. Charley covered Jim's income tax payments in return for Jim becoming a client. I know Jim felt an allegiance to him, but while almost every other business manager in town was by then charging 5 percent, Charley took 10 percent of everything Jim made. That was legally okay, but morally, considering how little he actually did for Jim, unacceptable. At least, that's *my* opinion.

I once asked Jim why he kept him on if Charlie actually did so little himself, mostly sending monthly accounts of expenditures to Henny, and Jim said "I owe him." I wondered aloud how come Charley lived so much better than his clients, and Jim's reply was, "He has lots of clients."

I replied, "Yeah, but most of *them* aren't working at all."

Over and above my personal feelings that Charley was taking advantage of Jim, I encountered many people in the business who just didn't like or trust him. And it wasn't because Charley drove a hard bargain for Jim's services. In fact, antipathy towards Charley sometimes created a roadblock to getting deals for Jim.

I MEET WITH THE "OWNER" OF MR. MAGOO

Hank Saperstein, the owner of UPA Studios for which Jim made all the *Mr. Magoo* cartoons, decided to create a "new" cartoon from parts of the old ones. That meant Jim would have to be paid another fee. Hank was perfectly aware of that and was fully prepared to pay him. By the time I went to Hank's office for a meeting, Charley had already called.

Considering that we had never met before, Hank greeted me very warmly, offered a drink, and sat me in a very comfortable chair. "What do you think of Charley?" he asked as soon as I had settled down.

"I'm not crazy about him," I answered. "I don't think he's very smart about this business."

Saperstein had a lot more to say about Charley, none of which was very flattering. Over the past years, there had been some acrimonious negotiations between them. Hank, who I found very easy-going, didn't appreciate Charley's antagonistic attitude; Hank preferred friendly, face to face, open negotiations.

"I imagine you're here to talk about the new contract," he said.

"Well, sort of," I replied. "I had a figure in mind and I thought I'd just throw it at you."

He asked what I wanted and I suggested, "$10,000."

Hank sat back in his seat and laughed. I figured I had really pulled a rock on that one, but he said, "You know, that's exactly what I was going to offer Jim, and would have paid it gladly, but Charley has been calling me insisting he wouldn't take a penny less than $5,000, so that's what I'm going to pay him."

I said, "Well, now that you know I'm involved, how about jacking it back up to $10,000?"

"Oh, I'd give him the $10,000, but then Charley would think it was because of him, and I just don't like him. I'm sorry for Jim, but I'm 'giving in' and Charley is getting just what he asked for." "I'll bet you gave him a hard time over the $5,000, didn't you?" I asked.

"Sure . . . I made him work for it."

I let it go at that.

THINGS GET CONTENTIOUS

I tried to make it clear to both Charley and Jim that a personal manager was entitled to his percentage regardless of whether the manager was directly involved in an offer for work, just like Charley who had virtually nothing to do with Jim's ever getting work.

In fact, according to Jim, Charley did very little for him at all. Charley kept bragging that he put Jim into 20th Century Insurance Company stock when they opened in California, but Jim couldn't remember him getting him into any other real investments. Jim told me that when he found a house for sale in Bel Air, the area where he and Henny lived, Charley wouldn't let him buy it, saying that "Real estate is a very poor investment." Apparently, a year so later, the house sold for many times the original asking price.

Then there was the time Jim wanted something like $3,500 to get into an oil investment a friend had told him about. Charley turned him down again, and according to Jim, his friend was dragging down monthly checks of more than the original investment for years, well over twenty times the investment.

Anyway, my position was, as is the position of all the personal managers I know, that because I put him back in the market for the first time in years, it made no difference whether an agent developed the offer, or if I did, or if it came directly from some producer, or director. The renewed interest in Jim was because I had done some important work for him, work that no one else had done for years, especially his business manager. Not that I'm a genius, but I did recognize opportunity when it came along and I did get him agents that got him work.

Deals were frequently presented to personal managers instead of agents, often because producers hoped to make a better deal by working directly, ostensibly with the act, which was often the case. Agents, on the other hand, were sometimes so anxious to make a deal they might take whatever money was offered.

One reason personal managers often negotiated directly with production companies was that they were likely to get not only the proper money, but perks of other kinds. The agents still got their money, and still made the actual contract because in California, at least, a personal manager is not allowed to solicit work. That is the job of the agent. There is no such prohibition on a manager doing the negotiating, however.

Still, whoever ended up finalizing the contract, the personal manager always got his percentage. That's just the way the game was played, and while there were always exceptions, and while people in the business were always getting screwed by someone, mostly people played by the rules. Regardless, I still had my problems with Jim and Charley—with Jim because he was afraid to go against anything Charley wanted, of which I will speak more later.

In the management agreement used by Kragen and Fritz, one of the better management companies at that time, it was spelled out very clearly that they, as managers, were entitled to 15 percent of "any and all gross monies or other considerations . . . throughout the entertainment, amusement, music, recording, and literary and music publishing industries, including any and all sums resulting from the use of (the artist's) artistic talents and the results of the proceeds thereof. The manner upon which the (manager's) compensation shall be computed shall include any and all of (the artist's) activities in connection with the matters as follows: motion pictures, television, radio, music, literary, theatrical engagements, personal appearances in places of amusement and entertainment, records and recordings, publications, and the use of (the artist's) name, likeness and talents for the purposes of merchandising, commercial exploitation, advertising, and/or trade."

The agreement goes on to describe the term "gross monies to include any and all means of compensation, including any means not yet known or contemplated."

An example not involving Jim, but for Joe Ferrer's services, which Joe made directly with the producer, created some problems because of two talent agencies and because I was not directly involved from the onset. I ended up working to correct the situation and to assuage both talent agencies, each of which had been approached inadvertently by the producer's people. Although this is somewhat out of chronological order, it might be a good place to tell the story as it will lead to something which directly relates to Jim.

HOW THINGS CAN GET CONFUSED IN HOLLYWOOD

Joe was offered a major role in the *Hallmark Hall of Fame* production of *Gideon*. The producer, George Schaefer called me at home wanting to know if it was all right to discuss something with Joe directly. Even though I knew they were personal friends, I cleared it with Joe and gave his telephone number to Schaefer. That's where the troubles began.

A vice president of Schaefer's production company contacted CMA (agency) accidentally, thinking she was calling the William Morris Agency. Joe, at that time, was unsigned to anyone, although CMA did represent him—without contract—for Equity (stage) work in New York and the east coast. They did not, however, represent him with or without contract in any other aspect of the entertainment industry. Schaefer's V.P. asked for a specific agent by name, who actually worked for the William Morris Agency. She was told that this particular agent did not work for them, but that CMA represented him, which of course, was untrue.

When the production company moved to Los Angeles to work on the show, that same V.P. contacted the William Morris office in Beverly Hills, still unaware that she had already spoken with CMA. Are you still with me? Hang in there. The William Morris office then called me to ask if they could submit Joe for the project, to which I agreed, being totally unaware of the previous events.

A day later, WMA called back to ask how CMA got into the act, so I called the Schaefer office. As CMA had actually been involved in the opening negotiations, there was no question that they should have priority because Joe wasn't signed to anyone, even though their actions were still on the shady side. When I explained the situation to WMA, they backed off immediately, showing considerable character . . . certainly more than CMA.

CMA contacted me with the salary offer, which I considered unacceptable, but they dragged their feet when it came to making a counter offer to Schaefer, so I stepped in and negotiated directly with the production company until we reached an agreement that Joe would receive "top of the show," exactly what they were paying Peter Ustinov (who played Gideon), *three times* the amount CMA originally offered Joe.

Jim's story is slightly different, but also indicates the importance, for some actors, of having a personal manager. I would like to make it perfectly clear that not every actor needs or should have a personal manager. Mostly, when there are many choices to consider, lots of offers, and when the commission (15 percent or more) has no real effect on their net earnings because the manager's commission is tax deductible. Sometimes a *good* and personally involved agent (like Tom Korman became for Joe Ferrer) is equal to or better than a manager and won't cost the talent the additional expense.

Jim and I were on the road somewhere when a call came through from an agent in Los Angeles. As usual, the call was put through to me even though the caller asked for Jim. That particular agent did not represent Jim, although once—several years earlier—he had done some work for him.

That well-known agent, who shall remain nameless, said, "I've got this great deal for Jim."

"Okay," I said, "what's on your mind?"

"Well," he said, "I heard about a big show they're casting now, and I figured Jim was perfect for one of the parts."

"That's very nice," I answered, "but you don't represent Jim."

"I know," he said, "but Jim and I are old friends, and I did represent him once. I figured I might be able to do him some good."

"Okay," I said. "What's the deal?"

"They just started casting a television version of *Of Thee I Sing*, and Jim would be perfect for the part of the southern senator."

It immediately occurred to my suspicious mind that this agent was probably hanging around the casting office when someone said, "You know, Jim Backus would be a perfect fit for this part. Does anyone know who his agent is?" Of course, this is speculation, but as long as I'm speculating, I speculated that this agent said, "I am."

The part would have been good for Jim, so I asked what they were paying. He quoted a number that I felt was much too low for that particular role. I said, "Forget it. That's probably bottom of the show."

"How much do you want?"

"Double that, with a four-week guarantee," I said

"My god, they'll never go for that. That's what the leads are getting."

"Jim's a star," I answered. "Why don't you just go and ask them?"

We left town the next morning and didn't hear from the agent for a couple of days, when he finally caught up with us.

"Hi," he said, "I did what you asked. It was a tough fight; I really had to sell him, but they finally agreed." Of course, he would have gladly sold Jim for their initial offer.

Getting back to Charley (Jim's business manager, remember?), because this seems like a good place to bring it up. He was the cause of the only falling-out Jim and I ever had, and a temporary end to our personal relationship.

ALMOST THE BEGINNING OF AN END

Jim had been representing La-Z-Boy chairs for several years, when I agreed to work as his manager. It was a project with which I had no connection, at first. Through some connections, I had managed to line up several commercials for him, voice-overs on television and some radio spots. Naturally, as his manager, I filed "Member Reports" with AFTRA—the American Federation of Television and Radio Artists. It was required by the union to insure that payments to Jim were proper and that deductions had been made and paid to the union health and welfare plans.

Just what red-flagged the union and got them looking back over previous reports filed by Charley, I can't say, but they did. I got a call from an AFTRA rep informing me that Jim had signed an illegal contract with La-Z-Boy and that something would have to be done about it. Charley had negotiated the contract that called for, among other things, for Jim to record four thousand "dealer tags." A dealer tag is merely the addition of a line or two at the end of a commercial, in this case something like, "This is Jim Backus telling you to buy your La-Z-Boy chair at Jones Furniture," followed by an address. Charley had offered them a flat fee of $2,500, which they, naturally, accepted.

The only problem was that the union contract called for, as I recall, $14 for each tag, a not so trifling matter of $53,500 under union scale. I had a long talk with representatives of the union requesting them not to make too many waves because I couldn't be sure La-Z-Boy would hold still for a financial hit like that, and because his contract was up for renewal that year. They were very understanding and assured me they would come up with some compromise that would be satisfactory to the company and the union.

Jim wanted to avoid any fuss because that was his big-time client and he didn't want to lose them. He wanted the union to forget it, but they wouldn't. I tried to assure him that everything would be fine and that he wouldn't lose his client, but he insisted on talking to Charley about it before I went any farther. I told him that Charley had mucked it up in the first place and that he ought to let me handle the matter.

A day or two later, Jim called and said, "I don't want you to talk to AFTRA any more because Charley says he'll handle it and doesn't want you involved."

I said, "Jim, I'm already involved. I'm your manager and I've already set the wheels in motion. I think Charley should keep his nose out of it. He's the reason there's a problem in the first place."

Jim said, "But Charley wants to handle it, and I can't go against him. After all, he made the original deal."

"That's the problem," I said. "Just let me straighten it out."

Jim insisted, and I had no choice but to agree because, after all, a personal manager is just an employee of the talent. I let Jim know that this was not the way I wanted to work with him. Either he trusted me or he didn't.

While AFTRA and Charley were busy talking, I had occasion to be in Chicago. There was a furniture convention in full swing at the Furniture Mart and La-Z-Boy was exhibiting. I dropped in because I knew all their executives would be there and I had already come to know several of them through telephone conversations and our visit to Miami, Florida. They hadn't yet been contacted by AFTRA or Charley.

I went over the details of the original contract and explained the problem and that AFTRA would be in touch with them soon. At first, there was considerable consternation on their part, but I assured them they wouldn't get billed for the whole amount, that the union would work out something amicable. Before I left, I had a promise they would renew Jim's contract for the following year, with a raise, all of which I dutifully reported to Jim on my return.

Eventually, the matter was settled with Jim getting an additional $36,000, on which I fully expected some commission. As I have mentioned earlier, it doesn't make any difference who started anything or who completed a deal; that the personal manager gets paid regardless, just as the business manager gets paid regardless of what he did or did not do to create income for his client.

Charley told Jim that he wouldn't pay me because, "he wasn't involved in the original negotiations."

I told Jim, "You tell Charley that if I *had* been involved, this never would have happened in the first place. After all, it isn't difficult to look in the AFTRA pay scale manuals.

Anyway, I didn't get paid because Jim apparently was afraid to disagree with Charley.

I told Jim to take his job and shove it.

Chapter 23
I Start a New Phase of My Life

And so, I walked away from Jim Backus . . . for two years. Of course, I still had plenty to do with Joe, and from time to time, I picked up some money running insurance investigations or writing, either as a ghost, or on assignment for my friend Steve Tolin who was still into one form of publishing or another. I did a few concerts with my friend Jerry Fox, who had met some people from back east who were looking for someone to produce concerts with their money and who were willing to foot the bill for an office and secretary.

They found a two-bedroom apartment in West Hollywood we could use as an office and they could use for a place to stay when they were in town. Jerry and I agreed to hire my old secretary, Lori, mostly because she already knew how to chase down available venues, and because she would work for $100 a week. For our first venture, we decided to do concerts with the comedy team of Cheech and Chong, the first being two shows at the University of Akron (in Ohio, of course), followed by a show at Eastern Tennessee State in Cookville, Tennessee.

Our sponsors decided to do a "show" of their own in Ohio, arranging to stage a space ship "landing" in downtown Akron. They lowered a "ship" from the top of a building to a busy street, with "green men" emerging. They used laser light guns to simulate the invasion and made the local papers and television news. Between shows, they staged an attack in the theater where they had placed globes around the auditorium which they could explode with their laser guns. It was quite a performance and we sold out two shows.

Between shows in Akron, we all repaired to a nice "lounge" area, which somehow was infiltrated by several young girls. Tommy Chong immediately lit up a joint, which he gladly shared with anyone in the room. (Jerry and I did not participate. After all, we were *producers* and had to maintain our decorum. Besides, I wouldn't smoke anything). One of the young ladies lit a regular cigarette and was immediately chastised by Tommy Chong. Marijuana was okay he said, but not tobacco . . . which could kill you.

In Cookville, there were no tall buildings and only one show. The student entertainment committee backed the event, and it was also a sell-out. After meeting some members of the faculty advisory committee, Jerry and I were anxious to get away from the auditorium. The student group, in order to get the backing from the faculty, sold Cheech and Chong as "political commentators," who worked "clean."

Never having seen them work myself, I wandered into the auditorium to see and hear them. I thought they were reasonably funny, but every time they said "shit," the audience went crazy.

WE GO COUNTRY

We managed two more concerts for our sponsors; a country/western show in South Dakota, featuring the David Houston Band and singer Barbara Fairchild. We did shows in Rapid City and Watertown that did not do particularly well, although Watertown did somewhat better.

Jerry and I flew into Watertown first to do a little promotion work, having come from Bangor, Maine, where we had gone to check the possibility of doing a Ray Charles gig, and because I had connections there from The Beach Boys concert. We had made reservations at the one decent hotel in Watertown, but on arrival discovered they had given away our room to some truck driver because we hadn't arrived before six in the evening. I complained that they knew we'd be late because our flight was still in the air at that hour, the best they could do for us was to find a room "somewhere."

The "somewhere" turned out to be the second worst motel room I have ever seen. The room was so small that the distance from the foot of the one queen-size bed to the wall was less than a foot. I told Jerry that there was no way I was going to sleep in that room and the same bed with him sober, so we went back to the hotel where we were supposed to stay because they had a bar where we could drink ourselves into oblivion. Neither of us would shower in the morning because of the little "animals" crawling around the bathroom.

We drove across the state to promote the Rapid City date, which we had booked into the high school auditorium. The ticket sales were not going well, although the people we spoke to originally when we decided on the date assured us the show would be successful because they never had "name" entertainment there. We did all we could do to stimulate sales and drove back leisurely to Watertown, stopping at Mt. Rushmore to check out the monuments that neither of us had ever seen other than in movies or on television.

NOT ALL IS EVIDENT

What really ended our relationship with the sponsors had nothing to do with the shows we produced. Our sponsors had come into Los Angeles, basically on a vacation, and I was in some sort of meeting with one of them and his wife. He brought out some photographs of his wife performing oral sex on his partner's wife. While I found them intriguing, I didn't quite understand why he showed them to me and not to Jerry. It was because I was married and what they were interested in primarily was a six-way orgy where we would share one another's women and the women could "do" one another. When I explained that while their wives were very pretty and all, my wife and I couldn't consider the offer. They closed the office they rented month-to-month, and we never heard from them again.

During the time we were ensconced in their office, I got a telephone call from a friend, who had taken a job on "spec" as a publicist with a company planning on producing a string of concerts with a Peking Opera company out of Taiwan. He had arranged for me to handle the souvenir book sales if I wanted.

Chapter 24
Change Is the Only Constant

My friend, Hal Sloane, had somehow encountered a husband and wife team intent on bringing the Peking Opera to the U.S. and had sold himself to them as a sort of General Manager for the eventual tour. Peking Opera is a kind of misnomer in that their form of entertainment was not limited to Peking and it was not an exactly an "opera" as is generally thought of in the occidental world. It is a series of skits mostly with singing and acrobatics, although not necessarily in the same acts.

In Hal's past, he had been General Manager of something called the *Teen Age Fair*, which they produced all over the United States. It consisted of musical entertainment, exhibit booths, food, and a carnival. They had been successful wherever they went, and my connection to that was their attempt to buy The Beach Boys for a Los Angeles show at the Palladium back when I worked with them as head of their production company. We never got together since our price was too high, but Hal and I had become friends.

I met the people producing the Chinese spectacle and they asked me to shepherd a souvenir program book.

My background included book-selling starting back when I was in college and later when I was involved with concert producer Irving Granz. My book artist would create the book for the Peking Opera and I would split the profits with the promoters, all in all, not a bad deal since they paid the production costs, any travel I would have, and the artist.

The promoters had taken fairly expensive offices in Beverly Hills and assembled a group of people, all of whom had seemingly agreed to work on spec, which should have been a tip-off to me and would have been had I been privy to the inner workings of the company. One of their "employees" had been brought on board to book the venues for the planned tour. It turned out he had no previous experience, and his idea of a booked date was to find a bunch of locations with available dates.

As it turned out, they did not actually have any reserved dates anywhere other than San Francisco and the Greek Theater in Los Angeles. San Francisco was an obvious start because of their large Chinese population. That date was sure to be a winner.

The promoters somehow connected with Charles O'Curran, one of the top movie choreographers in Hollywood, whose credits included several movies with Elvis Presley. They bought O'Curran a one-way ticket to Taiwan to see Peking Opera and to make recommendations. He wired back that they should forget the "opera" parts and just bring the acrobats. However, the producer's wife loved the opera and insisted on having the entire show. Since O'Curran didn't have a return ticket and couldn't get one from—let's call them Bob and Nancy—he was basically stuck in Taiwan or would have to pay his own way back.

Bob and Nancy did come up with enough money to pay for the souvenir books (I presume) and put together a celebrity trip to San Francisco for the grand opening. Naturally, because I had to sell the books or have them sold, I went along as did Hal and my secretary, Lori. I can't recall all the celebrities who went along, although I do recall Johnny Carson's ex-wife, Joanne, her ex-boyfriend, Glenn Ford, Cesar Romero, Burgess Meredith and his wife, and several others. The show was well received although a few of the celebrities snuck out during the "opera" parts and idled around the lobby.

Following the performance, there was a reception back at the hotel at which Lori was approached by Glenn Ford with this exchange of dialog: Glenn: "Hi, my name is Glenn Ford. Would you like to go to my room and we could make love, or something?" Lori: "Of course I know who you are. And . . . no thanks."

I had the unsold souvenir books shipped down to the Greek Theater and did very well there. However, as I had pretty much predicted in a meeting in Beverly Hills, there was no place else to send them because they had not actually booked any other dates. I stored what was left of the books at the Greek, where they stayed for another month or so until they were burned as trash.

THE PEKING OPERA GIG IS SHORT-LIVED

Bob sent the troupe to a projected date somewhere in central California and abandoned them there. Someone contacted a rich Chinese, who came to their rescue and sent them home to Taiwan. Some time later, someone else brought the *acrobats* back to the U.S. where they cleaned up. Had Bob and Nancy listened to Charley O'Curran, they, too, would have cleaned up. A few days after the Greek Theater performance, I went to their office and discovered they had moved and taken most of the office furniture and equipment with them. I also learned that it had all been rented, unpaid for, and essentially stolen. I guess I was the only "employee" who made any money and not much, at that.

Chapter 25
Backus and I Re-Connect

Two years had passed since I quit working for Jim Backus, when I got a telephone call from Helen Miles, the woman who owned the soundstage where Jim had his office. She wondered if I would call Jim because he needed me for something. I told her that if Jim wanted to talk to me, *he* could call me. I explained that holding onto grudges was a waste of energy. The next day, there was a call from Jim. Neither of us mentioned the situation with Charles Goldring.

Jim had been offered a two week gig in Dallas, Texas, for a one-man show (he thought) at the Crystal Palace, a dinner theater, and would I come back and stage his performance? I agreed to meet with him and discuss it. He had already hired a dancer to teach him a simple routine he could perform while he sang a song. Jim had a pretty good baritone voice and as long as the song wasn't too complicated or required too much range, he would be fine. In a television production of *Damn Yankees*, he was required to sing "You Gotta Have Heart," and came off well. The song he chose was "I Won't Send Roses," which he had already done in Minneapolis. As I have mentioned, the song came from *Mack and Mabel*, a reasonably successful stage musical about famed director during the days of silent film, Mack Sennett, and actress Mabel Normand.

I met with Tybee Brascia, the dancer, who with her former husband had a successful career as night club dancers, and had her teach me the routine she worked out for Jim, so that I would be able to work with him on the very simple movement around the stage. The comedy part would not be a problem since it would just be an extended version of what he had been doing for previous casuals. I agreed to stage his act, and then accompany him to Dallas for a week, until

Henny would join him. I also agreed to once again serve as his manager, but only when he had a job of some kind. That way, he wouldn't call me every night at the end of Johnny Carson's *The Tonight Show*, which had become a habit before.

IT COULD HAVE BEEN GREAT

The people in Dallas had arranged a couple of rooms for us at a nearby hotel and an apartment adjacent to the Crystal Palace for Jim and Henny when I left. When we got to Dallas, we learned that Jim was expected to do what amounted to three shows a night, and that there would be an opening act prior to each show. The opening act consisted of an orchestra backing a group of several very talented young dancers.

I took all Jim's material and split it into three parts. The first would consist of Jim's "Magoo" material, during which he would also sing his song. We decided we would take a boy and girl dancer from the opening act and have them waltz to Jim's singing. In that way, he wouldn't have to "dance" himself and we could forget the dance steps he had trouble remembering. The other problem was that Jim wasn't aware the theater was "in the round," which would have entailed my re-working the dance anyway. The second part of the act would be material as the rich man from *Gilligan's Island*. He worked dressed in a Hawaiian shirt, a coconut straw hat, and shell beads. For the third act, he would be in a tuxedo doing "Hollywood" stories while seated on a stool. As the theater was in the round, he could swivel around on his stool. Amazingly enough, it all worked, and the reviews were all good.

As I had proposed a figure for my services, and as it was probably lower than it should have been, Jim agreed to everything. However, as the first weekend approached Jim tried to change the rules. He said: "I don't have to pay you for weekends, do I?" I laughed and told him that as long as I was here, I got paid.

Henny arrived maybe a couple of days earlier than expected and she set about arranging a dinner party at the theater at which I would have to serve as the extra man so that there would be a male to each female. Oil man, E. E. "Buddy" Fogelson, who had backed

Mooch, Jim's short film about a female dog who comes to Hollywood seeking fame and fortune, and his wife, actress Greer Garson, were among the guests. They were properly impressed by Jim.

Henny decided she didn't like the apartment accommodation because it had only one bathroom. She insisted upon—and got—two adjoining and connecting hotel rooms, while I used the apartment for a couple of days until my return to California. There was no sense in my staying any longer now that Henny was there to run him. Besides, if I had stayed, Jim would have to pay me. Jim's "frugality" dated back to his first days in Hollywood and his unfortunate encounter with his first business manager. Anyway, I packed up and flew home, leaving Jim in Henny's care. Everything should have been simple, but Henny—who incidentally, I actually cared a lot about and with whom I continued to be close after Jim died—was pretty good at creating problems, and she created a big one.

A couple of days after I left, the promo people for the Crystal Palace arranged for Jim to be interviewed at a local radio station. As he was getting into the car, Jim bumped his head and Henny insisted they take Jim to the emergency room of a nearby hospital, even though he insisted he was fine. The doctor diagnosed Jim as having suffered a minor concussion, but indicated that he would be fine, but Henny then insisted the rest of the job be canceled, and they returned home. A couple of weeks later, Jim called and told me what happened. He was too embarrassed to call me any sooner. I kept thinking about his "illness" in Minneapolis, where a placebo enabled him to work the whole two weeks just because I wouldn't let him be sick.

Chapter 26
A Florida "Vacation" for Jim and Me

In 1979, Jim got an offer to do a film in Florida for an English production company. The picture, titled *There Goes The Bride*, starred the former English model Twiggy (whose real name was Leslie Hornby) and Tommy Smothers, the funny one of the Smothers Brothers. Their American co-stars were Jim and Martin Balsam.

English actors of note in the film were Sylvia Syms, the fine dramatic actress, and comedic actors Hermoine Baddeley and Graham Stark. Graham is probably best-known for his portrayals of Peter Sellers suffering-in-silence side-kick in the *Pink Panther* movies. Graham, who was also a highly skilled professional photographer, spent most of his off-time taking pictures of the girl who played Jim's secretary, April Clough, a ravishing blonde of extraordinary proportions.

The picture had a rather silly premise: Tommy was a brassiere salesman about to get married, but who was having fantasies about a "dream" girl played by Twiggy. His inability to rid himself of the fantasy was responsible for his constant delaying of the wedding. In some dream sequences, Tommy had to dance with Twiggy, and he was taking daily tap lessons that continued all the time Jim and I were there. Twiggy was already a pretty good dancer.

Jim and I would be walking down a hallway in the hotel and run across Tommy, who would stop us and say something like, "Wait a minute. You've got to see this step I just learned." Then he'd do a little routine.

The rest of the movie plot is pretty inconsequential, certainly of less consequence than what I've already told you. The picture was very lightweight; something they still call "Summer Fare," easy to look at, pleasant fluff, which doesn't require the use of any brain matter by the audience.

The film was shot in Vero Beach, Florida, apparently because the backing came from three or four ladies who lived there. Jim, Tommy, the director, the producer, and the cast all had rooms in the newer section of the hotel. The crew was quartered at a nearby motel, and I had a second floor suite in the old section overlooking the pool.

I think they assigned me to that room because no one else would take it. The stairs to the second floor balcony wobbled and creaked. The balcony had a decided list to it, and it shuddered when I walked to the room. It seemed ready to topple if I walked too heavily, but the room was large and airy, and who was I to quibble, anyway?

Florida, among many *fine* things, is also known for things like "no-see-ums," pesky little flying insects that suddenly surround you from out of nowhere, and what they call "palm beetles," but which I call cockroaches. Palm beetles are gigantic and can fly. I should have suspected something, when I opened the medicine cabinet in the bathroom and found an aerosol can about nine inches high of insect spray. I *really* should have suspected something when I found a second can in a medicine chest in the bedroom/living room area.

The first night, on returning to my room after dinner and a leisurely hour or so poolside with Jim, I found one of the creatures ambling across the floor. I took a can of bug killer from the living room cabinet, and from a distance of about two inches, sprayed directly on the beast as it strolled casually across the carpet. I sprayed continuously as it covered six or seven feet, but it showed no ill effects whatever.

I think maybe it looked back at me a couple of times as if to say, "Just who do you think you're fooling with? We've been here millions of years and we'll be here long after you're dust." So I took the heel of my shoe to it. Four solid whacks later, it finally gave up the ghost. Two more of the creatures made their way from under my bed and suffered the same fate before I decided it was safe to go to sleep.

Jim was having such a good time on *There Goes The Bride* that, once again, he forgot to feel ill; something that happened often when he was feeling chipper. There was a holiday atmosphere around the hotel and on the set, fueled mostly by the tourists staying at the hotel, who got to watch the filming and even be part of the "atmosphere." All of Jim's scenes were around the hotel, the pool, and the beach, except for his very last scene, which had him getting into a limousine and leaving the hotel. That was shot in the parking lot. Maybe it was the salt air or the way the hotel, the hotel guests, and the cast and crew treated him, or maybe it was simply the stimulation of working with April Clough. Whatever it was, he was really enjoying himself, and was generally the "old," pre-illness Jim.

JIM FORGETS TO BE SICK

The weather was great, and when Jim wasn't working, we took long walks along the shore. Working with April Clough, the girl who played his secretary, made him perk up. She had a magic effect on every man there. Wherever April walked, men were sucking in their stomachs and puffing out their chests. She was very good for the posture of all the males around the hotel.

Jim played one of his scenes with April in the hotel swimming pool. He was dressed in a bathing suit, Hawaiian print shirt, and a coconut straw hat, and lying supine on a rubber raft at the edge of the pool. In the scene, he is talking on the phone to Tommy, who is his employee, while April, in a crocheted bikini, is fussing around him doing something immaterial.

At the end of his conversation, he was supposed to turn towards her and give her a hug. Only Jim, being very "method," ad-libbed. He literally threw himself at her, tumbled off the raft on top of her as she backed away in real surprise, lost his hat, and they both sunk out of sight. The director loved it, the guests at poolside loved it, I loved it—and the camera kept on rolling.

JIM GETS AWAY FROM ME

One night, the film's backers decided to have an honest-to-goodness southern-style dinner for the cast and crew at the home of one of the film's backers. They served collard greens, hominy, black-eyed peas, southern fried chicken, yams, home-made-salted-in-the-shell peanuts, key lime pie, lord-knows what else, and lots of champagne.

I had been busy socializing with our hosts, when I realized that Jim and Tommy were nowhere to be found. I checked the grounds, around the gardens, and throughout the house, but they were gone. Finally, someone told me they had commandeered a car and driver and had returned to the hotel, claiming fatigue. They weren't too tired to take a couple bottles of champagne with them, so I got myself a ride and set out to find them because Jim's medication and alcohol were not a good mix.

They weren't at the pool, or in the lobby, or in Jim's room, so I presumed rightly that I would find them in Tommy's room. By the time I got there, the second bottle was just about to become the second dead soldier, and they were feeling no pain. I managed one drink, and then tossed the empty out with its brother.

I helped Jim, who by that time, was not very steady on his feet, back to his room and put him to bed. Fortunately, he didn't have any morning scenes, so breakfast on the hotel patio put him back in shape. From there, we could watch other actors down on the beach, where Jim later had a scene running along the sand, and could also watch Graham Stark taking pictures of April.

When the director finally wrapped Jim's part of the film, we flew on home. He was feeling better than he had in more than a year. On the airplane back, he said, "Jack, you know, I think I can trace my illness back to 1975 when I canceled that job in Dallas." He didn't mean the illness was a result of his concussion, but from the guilt of having canceled out.

JIM HAS ANOTHER MOVIE OFFER

In 1982, Jim was approached by a young filmmaker, Steven Paul. Steven had been an actor working on Broadway, where he starred in Kurt Vonnegut's *Happy Birthday, Wanda June.* He also played the same part in the movie version and was so good that Vonnegut told him, "You were the best thing in the picture. If there's ever anything I can do for you, just let me know."

And Steven said, "I want you to give me *Slapstick,* Vonnegut's most recent book, "for a movie."

Vonnegut said, "If you're ever in New York, drop in and we'll talk about it."

Steven took the "red-eye" flight that very night and knocked on Vonnegut's door early the next morning. He not only talked Vonnegut into giving him the book, but into writing the screenplay. After assembling the financial backing, something for which Steven had a real talent, he set about casting the major roles. He contacted Jim for the part of the President of the United States. Jim wanted to do the film, but was once again having reservations about his physical ability to work a fairly long part. He asked me to come by the house, pick up a script, and then give him my opinion.

Steven had already met with and received commitments from Madeline Kahn, Jerry Lewis, and Marty Feldman for the other key roles, and Jim desperately wanted to be in a film with them, but once again, the old doubts were rearing their ugly heads. He wanted me to assure him he could do it.

I read the book from which a section had been culled for the script. It was, like much of Vonnegut's work, very strange. Then, after re-reading the script to be sure of my feelings, I went to see Jim.

"Jim," I said, "two things can happen with this movie. Like *Slaughterhouse-Five*, it can become a cult film, or it can go right in the dumper. However, it might be fun to do, and it will get you out of the house. So, I think you should accept. Besides, I want to meet Jerry and Marty Feldman."

And so I agreed, as they say in the business, to "get him up in the part," rehearse him, and spend every day of the shoot with him.

That meant picking him up early in the morning and driving to a vacant Gothic-style two-story mansion in the West Adams district of Los Angeles, where most of the action is set, a house right out of Charles Addams cartoons. They couldn't have constructed a more perfect set.

Briefly, the story is set "some time" in the future. The plot revolves around fraternal twins, one boy, one girl, born so grotesque they are shunted off to an old mansion in some very remote and isolated location, and provided with a coterie of servants to care for all their needs. The parents are very wealthy, and seemingly, judging by their offspring, the products of a few generations of in-breeding.

The twins, who were supposed to be long dead by this time, have reached their fifteenth year and have not only survived, but have grown incredibly. Marty Feldman played the lecherous butler in charge of the orgy-minded servants, responsible for raising the twins.

Everything by this time in the twenty-first century has become so expensive that gasoline now costs $2,000 a pint, and everything in the world, to quote the script, is "powered by chicken shit." Jim, as President of the United States, is, for some unexplained reason, flying to see these strange children, as are their parents and their doctor. The scene in a mockup of Air Force One has Jim seated in luxury on one side of the airplane, while the other side is lined with cages full of chickens.

Jerry and Madeline played the dual roles of the parents and the children, now grown to seven feet, two inches. I must say that even though I didn't think the film would do well, both Jerry and Madeline were marvelous. Marty Feldman was . . . Marty Feldman, and that's saying a lot.

Dorothy Paul, mother of Steven, and the casting director for the film, even wanted me to play the part of a soldier in scenes shot at a nearby army base, but I told her I wouldn't shave off my beard. Besides, to be honest, I'm sure I would have been lousy.

Jerry, Madeline, and Marty each had trailers, but Jim, having a smaller part and at the set only part of each working day, had only a small dressing room in one of the "honey wagons." Marty Feldman, however, insisted that Jim use his trailer whenever he wanted. Jerry offered his trailer, too, but as he was accompanied by his new wife, the former Sandy Pitkin, and their dog, Jim didn't want to be in the way. Jerry and Sandy met on the set of *The Nutty Professor*. She danced with him in one scene and that started it all.

Jerry Lewis, realizing that Jim was not well, instructed the crew that when "Mr. Backus is not on camera, I want someone to put a chair wherever he is."

Our normal regimen when Jim wasn't working on the set was to relax, read lines, or take walks around the block. Jim was having difficulty with the mechanics of walking, one of the typical aspects of Parkinson's Disease, having forgotten that arms swing in opposition to the legs, the result of which was that he walked like a zombie. We practiced walking every day with me behind him moving his arms in the proper sequence. Jim was particularly concerned about his ability to get from one mark to another quickly enough, particularly in one scene where there is gun-play and where the script called for him to "dive" out of the way. Jerry had them change the action so all Jim had to do was crouch behind a close-by potted plant.

Jerry, incidentally, was not directing this picture, Steven Paul was, but he asked Jerry for help from time to time, and whatever Jerry recommended was exactly right. He was so solicitous of Jim, and so physically and emotionally helpful that no one can ever say anything bad about Jerry Lewis to me. I found him to be a real *mensch*.

I eventually saw the screening of a rough cut, and knew that the picture would not be a hit or even a cult film. Jerry did whatever he could to salvage it, including re-editing and appearing on talk shows, but nothing ever came of the film that I know of, although I heard it did pretty good business in Europe where Jerry is a giant star.

Slapstick, later called *Slapstick of Another Kind*, was the next-to-last picture I worked with Jim, if you don't count his brief appearances in the last two *Gilligan's Island* television movies, where he really struggled to do as much as walk through a set. We continued to do jobs together, mostly commercials and a very few casuals. Of course, I continued seeing Jim regularly at home, going for drives, and professionally whenever any sort of work came along, but work was not coming that regularly any more.

MOOCH

As I've mentioned *Mooch* at least twice, I ought to tell you something about it. The film, was written by Jim's friend, Jerry Devine, and financed by E. E. "Buddy" Fogelson. According to a promo sheet, the story follows an "adorable mutt" who ". . . brazenly romances Vincent Price, carries on a beach blanket affair with James Darren; then after crashing the gates of a movie studio, is tutored and glamorized by Jill St. John and offered stardom by Jim Backus as Mr. Magoo."

There is a festive party in Bel Air, where Mooch mingles with, in cameo appearances, Janet Blair, Phyllis Diller, Rose Marie, Edward G. Robinson, Cesar Romero, Marty Allen, J.C. Flippen, Sam Jaffe, Dick Martin, Mickey Rooney, David Wayne, and Darren McGaven.

The film was narrated by Richard Burton and Zsa Zsa Gabor. Jim had co-starred with Burton in *Ice Palace* and they had become close friends. When Backus was in Europe, he asked Burton if he would record his role. Burton was agreeable, but said he wouldn't have time to do it in a studio. Jim invited him up to his hotel room where he had an engineer ready to go, and Burton did his reading in the bathroom which made for great resonance.

With a cast such as this, it shouldn't have had much difficulty in getting air time, but Jim and Jerry Devine had miscalculated. The film was only one hour long; too short to be sold as a feature which required a minimum of eighty-five minutes.

Chapter 27
I'm Weaned off Management

I was now mostly filling my life doing public relations and entertainment consulting, keeping busy, but no longer doing much in the way of personal management. I was producing celebrity golf tournaments for various charities, something I started in the late 1970s and had increased (with my friend, Fred Ex) to at least ten tournaments a year. Even though those were all celebrity events, there is little reason to delve into them to any extent. There was, however, a series of three events I did in Morocco, North Africa worth mentioning. One of "my" golfing celebrities was Martin Milner, who you might remember for two television series, *Adam-12* and *Route 66*. He had been invited by a friend to play in the annual *Hassan II* (the King) tournament and was asked if he could bring more celebrities. Martin told them to contact me.

MOROCCO COMES CALLING

The event, including side activities, was held every year in Rabat, Morocco. The men's tournament, officially called *The Hassan II*, had civilians (like me), pros, and celebrities and was played over three days, while the wives/girlfriends, et al., went on sight-seeing trips to places like Fez (Morocco's oldest city) and Casablanca.

The first year, I was asked to bring ten celebrities. Because so many of the celebrities I invited were working, that number was eventually cut to six. The first "name" who agreed to the trip was actor Leslie Nielsen, who immediately called his agent and issued orders that he accept no work for that period. Actor/singer/game show host, Peter Marshall asked me if I would be interested in his friend, Astronaut Admiral Alan Shepard. I said, "You bet." Alan will always be remembered for being one of original astronauts and one who hit a golf ball off the moon. It didn't take much longer to add Arte Johnson, the little German soldier on *Laugh In*, television host/announcer Dennis James, actor/comedian Tom Poston, plus wives, or in Leslie's case, his girlfriend whom he eventually married.

Our Los Angeles group flew first to New York and checked into a hotel for a day, while we waited for the Shepards, who flew in from Texas. From New York we, along with the paying players, and a few pros, flew aboard the King's private 747 to Marrakech and the La Mamounia Hotel, one of the great hotels of the world, complete with a Las Vegas-style casino.

The first full day there, we, along with other American guests, were feted at a glorious poolside luncheon, and then, those of us who wanted, were taken on a guided tour of the Marrakech souk, a gigantic shopping area consisting of a huge open-air market and a partly covered, convoluted area of stalls selling everything from hand-made chess sets to caftans to knock-off watches, luggage, and purses. Without a guide, one might get lost for days . . . or forever.

The next day, one could play a practice round of golf on the local course if you wanted, but the highlight was the luncheon for the Americans and the Europeans, also at the course, all under open-front tents. Every course of the meal was served on silver trays by dozens of costumed waiters. Throughout the lunch, we were entertained by the various tribes of Morocco, each seemingly known for some special talents. Leslie Nielsen was pulled into one tribe's performance. The following year, the late professional golfer, Payne Stewart, got the same treatment.

Speaking of Payne, who was killed when the private airplane in which he was flying lost heating and everyone froze to death, he won the tournament that year and was awarded a huge vase valued at several thousand dollars in addition to the prize money. He was upset at getting the vase because the year before the special prize was a jeweled dagger. He came back the next year, won again, and this time got his dagger.

From the luncheon, we were taken to the airport and loaded into a chartered airplane to take us to the capitol city, Rabat, where we were billeted in the same hotel General Dwight Eisenhower used as his headquarters during World War II.

As to the tournament itself, through some convoluted scoring system, Peter Marshall and Dennis James won silver trays that first year and, as it apparently happened every year, the Crown Prince took first place. The tournament was played on the Dar Es Salaam course, built on the site of Roman ruins. I hit balls from almost every one over the course of three days. The grass was grown over a base of cork cut originally from the cork trees lining the course, which made walking very difficult, like walking on sponges or a mattress.

What no one had mentioned to our group was that we had to walk the course. I found that there were only about twenty golf carts available, ten of which were assigned to the Prince and his party. The man in charge of the carts had lived in the Los Angeles area, and I made it a point to become his pal, so I could get carts for the two oldest celebrities, Leslie Nielsen and Dennis James.

On our last night there, the black-tie Awards Dinner was a serve-yourself buffet, something I found odd considering the number of meals at which there were always dozens of servers.

The second year, I took only cowboy actor/rancher, Dale Robertson, who it turned out had once met with the King and had created a horse breeding program to save the King's stable, and Herb Jeffries, and their wives. Because I had agreed to provide some entertainment on the last night, I had asked for musicians, or at least a pianist who could read music to accompany Herb. No one in the band they hired could read music at all—not even chord charts. Herb finally cornered the band leader and asked what songs he *could* play and they found two that Herb could sing.

For the third year, I brought two people, who again required music, and for more than a month, kept writing to those supposedly in charge for *anyone* who could actually read music. It turned out to be a waste of breath.

MY LAST TRIP FOR THE KING

That third year, I invited singer/actor Len Cariou (who won the Tony Award for *Sweeny Todd*), Gil Gerard (television's *Buck Rogers*), harmonica virtuoso Eddy Lawrence Manson, and once again, Arte and Gisele Johnson, for whom the Federation had asked specifically. Len was going to sing and Eddy would play, only once again, we ran up against the same useless band. Eddy wound up writing a chord chart to "Ol' Man River" for the band's pianist, only he couldn't even read that. So Eddy played piano for Len and went unaccompanied for himself.

I had a long meeting with a member of the Golf Federation in charge of the evening's entertainment. We agreed that my performers would go on before dinner since I had already been through two years of the after-dinner din. By the time dinner was over, the European group was pretty drunk and paid no attention to the entertainment. Just as I was taking the stage to start the show, and as I approached the microphone, Ambassador El Glaoui stepped in front of me and said, "Everybody eat." I was ready to cancel, but Len Cariou said, "What the hell, we just came six thousand miles; we might as well do it anyway."

There was also a problem getting home in that the King apparently decided he needed his airplane and no one had bothered to secure other means of transportation back to New York, where all the Americans would change to whatever planes would take them home. Waiting for our plane in Rabat, about 160 Americans found themselves crammed into a small room, many of them (including some extremely rich folk) sitting on the floor for some three hours. Finally, someone who was a personal friend of the King, called him and asked, "What the hell is going on?" They ended up chartering a 747 from Air France, and, I was told, the King's Director of Transportation got himself fired.

Among the pro golfers with whom I spent some time were Billy Casper, who was the personal golf coach to the King, and Lee Trevino, who when asked if he knew me, replied: "Oh, yes, he and I are old friends." Actually, he was an old friend of José Ferrer's, which was the basis of what friendship Lee and I developed there—that, and because I suggested a way to cure his cough. In order for Lee to make the tournament he had to take six airplanes, starting from the Orient, then to Hawaii, then San Francisco, on to Florida, then New York, and finally via commercial air to Morocco. Not only would he compete for the big prize money, but like a few other pros, he got "appearance money" just for showing up.

I did end up back in Morocco two years later, when a couple of Los Angeles travel agents made a deal with the Golf Federation to try and increase tourism through golf, inviting my partner, Fred Ex, and me, six teaching golf professionals and one celebrity game show host, Tom Kennedy. We played four different courses, traveling by bus from city to city. Our last stop was in Casablanca, where the hotel bar was named *Rick's American Bar*, from the Humphrey Bogart movie, *Casablanca*.

Chapter 28
I Kind of Wrap Things Up

I don't remember exactly when it occurred in the chronology of things, but Jim Backus decided to go to San Francisco and check into a hospital for another complete physical and other tests to determine just what might be wrong with him. He was already being treated with L-Dopa, a specific for the symptoms of Parkinson's, but the side effects were bad and the drug didn't seem to alleviate any of his problems; they only exacerbated them. One of the side effects he didn't have was tremors, one of the more typical symptoms. Aside from his genital problem, I saw no *major* indications of Parkinson's, like difficulty in putting on his pants or shoes and socks. His doctor was constantly fiddling with and adjusting the dosage to no apparent avail.

Jim was always complaining to me, saying, "The head of my joint always feel like I'm ready to come and it's driving me crazy." Even having an ejaculation, with or without help, only provided momentary relief. That was one of the reasons he liked being with hookers; they gave him a little relief and there were no entanglements. Although this is apropos of nothing, and which I may have mentioned somewhere, Jim didn't like thinking he was using professionals and asked that I tell them not to ask him for money. After the deed was done, he wanted to say something like, "Here's fifty bucks . . . go buy yourself something nice." He had a pretty regular girl in the San Fernando Valley—I can't recall who turned me on to her—who was sort of a semi-professional. She had a good, middle-management job, liked sex, and saw no reason she couldn't pick up a few dollars on the side.

Getting back to the San Francisco trip, Henny called and asked if I'd go to with them because she and Jim couldn't possibly make the trip alone. Even though we no longer had any sort of contractual relationship, I said I would. This had to do with friendship, not business.

The three of us flew north together. We dropped Henny at a hotel, and Jim and I went on to the hospital, where I got him settled in. Then, I returned to the hotel and had a couple of drinks with Henny until it was time to catch my airplane back to Los Angeles. I promised to return and get them when the tests were completed.

Jim underwent an extensive series of examinations over a period of a week or so, and then Henny called. I caught an airplane the next morning, went directly to the hospital, got him moved out, and we took a cab to the hotel, where Henny was waiting at the curb, having already checked out.

On the ride from the hospital to the hotel, Jim said, "Jack, I think I've got AIDS."

"How the hell did you get AIDS?" I asked incredulously.

"You remember my night nurse?"

"Yeah," I answered cautiously.

"He's gay."

I said, "Did you fuck him?"

"No, of course not," Jim replied.

"Jimmy, you can't get AIDS from breathing the same air, so just forget about it. You don't have AIDS. You have to have sex with someone who's infected, and you haven't done that."

IT GETS HARDER FOR JIM

From that time on, even though we saw one another on a very regular basis, even working a job or two, Jim seemed to go down hill. He'd have good days and bad, and some in-between, but I could see a continuous and gradual decline. There were still days we could go to Comstock Park for a walk, or hit wiffle balls over the swimming pool in his back yard, tearing holes in Henny's gorgeous lawn, and we talked about our being on the golf course together again one day, but I think we both knew that was very unlikely.

Henny and Jim continued to have their annual "*New Years Eve Party You Go To On The Way To Your New Year's Eve Party*," and still had regular contact with their celebrity friends, particularly people like Donald and Gloria O'Connor (until they moved to Arizona), George Burns (until he died), Cesar Romero (until *he* died), Steve and Jayne Meadows Allen, Jack and Roxanne Carter, Howard and Judy Keel (until *they* moved down to the desert), Betty White, Mel Torme, David Wayne (until *he* died), and Phyllis Diller.

I recall what may have been the last New Year's party while Jim was still alive (Henny kept having them in Jim's honor and memory, although the number of "names" kept decreasing). George Burns was sitting in his usual seat in their living room, holding court with one story after another. I walked over to him and asked, "George, are you going to sing a couple of songs tonight?" His conductor/pianist, Morty Jacobs, had been playing for the guests, some of whom were still gathered around the piano quietly singing along. Comedian Jack Carter was sharing the piano bench.

George said, "I don't think I'll sing tonight."

I said, "If you don't, Jack Carter will."

George said, "We can't have that now, can we? Someone help me up."

He got up, shuffled over to the piano and sang parts of three or four songs—he almost never actually finished a song—when Donald O'Connor walked over and said, "George, do you remember this step?" and danced a few quick movements.

George said, "Certainly do," and proceeded to imitate him.

They sang a song together, danced a little together, and then Morty played a song Donald had written many years before, which Donald sang. That was the kind of affair Jim and Henny had every year.

By the way, I don't mean to imply that Jack Carter is not a good singer, because he is *very* good, indeed. It was just my way of getting George to entertain. Those were the days when celebrities still entertained one another at their house parties. Things—and times—have changed.

By the early 1980s, Jim was in really bad shape, spending almost every day in his den or his bedroom, writing. I have a memory of some television crew in the den with an interviewer when one of their books—perhaps their last—came out. He wrote about his illness, but that was pretty much the extent of their activity. Jim and Henny talked about going on a book tour, and I agreed to go with them, but I never really believed they would do it, and of course, they didn't.

Once in awhile, they would go to dinner at Mateo's, Chasen's, The Brentwood Inn, or Madame Wu's, their favorite restaurant hangouts. They tried to attend social functions whenever Jim was up to it, but they accepted fewer and fewer. Henny reminded me that when the Pacific Pioneer Broadcasters honored Jim, she went in his stead and made a speech, while I stayed home with him.

Jim was trying his best to improve his condition, undergoing hypnotherapy, and even attending a ballet class to improve his movement. Under hypnosis, I saw him make a standing jump on to a desk top. Coming home from therapy that day, he was in excellent spirits, but in the time it took to walk from the car port to his front door, he was back to his usual state of depression.

ALL THINGS MUST END

I was out of town when I heard the news that Jim died on July 3, 1989. Henny later told me that he was in a local hospital for a few more tests, and while there, he was completely off medications. She felt that he was getting better every day, but that towards the end of his stay, he caught pneumonia, and that was what killed him. I've always said that a hospital is the worst place to be when you're sick, because when you're sick you're susceptible to germs, and hospitals, as everyone knows, are where all the germs are.

When Jim died, Henny had a memorial for him—just what Jim would have liked. Among the speakers were Phyllis Diller, Milton Berle, Red Buttons, and Jan Murray. The tone was pretty funny, although there were a few serious moments with words from Cesar Romero, radio and television executive Perry Lafferty, and Natalie Schafer.

Working with Joe Ferrer had pretty much dwindled to nothing since he was doing less and less. His tenure as Director of the Coconut Grove Playhouse was over, and he was spending much of his time shuttling back and forth between Florida and New York where they still kept an apartment and office, although they had long since moved from 57th Street to Central Park South.

In June 1992, I was once again planning my annual trip to Lexington, Kentucky, for that celebrity golf tournament. I called Joe to make sure he was going to be there. At first, he hesitated, making up some silly excuse, but I told him he had to come because I missed him and it was pretty unlikely that I would be coming to Florida any time in the near future.

I learned later that Stella, by then his wife, insisted he meet me there. Joe told me she said, "You have to go. You haven't seen Jack in ages. There's no real reason why you shouldn't be there." And so he came.

When I first saw him in Lexington, I was surprised. He had lost a lot of weight. I said, "What happened to you? How did you take it off?"

He said, "You know I have an allergy to celery. (I didn't know it, but I nodded in agreement). Well, we were in London (Stella's home) at a party and someone put out a plate of celery, which I love. So, I tried a stalk and didn't feel anything, and I ate the whole plate. Later that evening, I began to throw up and couldn't stop. When I did stop, I couldn't keep any food on my stomach except milk shakes."

"How are you now," I asked?

"Great. I can eat anything." Over the next few days, he proceeded to prove it, eating everything in sight. He put away gargantuan breakfasts, and never skipped a meal. We played every practice round and he played another round by himself at six-thirty on the morning of the tournament. I refused to get up that early; besides, there was no way I could play thirty-six holes in one day. He could, and did frequently.

On Sunday, our last day in Lexington, he, I, and entertainer Dick Kerr went to breakfast, where Joe ate two full breakfasts, *starting* with biscuits and gravy and a four-egg omelet.

I never saw him again, although we continued to speak until less than two weeks before his death. He never once let on that he was ill, although he did have what he called "an attack of laryngitis." A month or two before our last conversation, he had to cancel a Broadway show because his voice wasn't improving.

During our last conversation, on his birthday, January 8, 1993, he explained, "The doctors say I'm dehydrated, that's why I still talk this way. They're trying to rehydrate me." I accepted that, but maybe I should have known he was more seriously ill than he admitted.

In January 1993, my wife, Phyllis, and I went with Henny Backus to Las Vegas for George Burns' ninety-seventh birthday bash at the Riviera Hotel. We saw George's show and spent every late evening while we were there with Morty (George's conductor) and Madeline Jacobs, returning home on January 26. No sooner had we walked in the door than there was a telephone call from Herb Jeffries, the great singer from the 1940s. He said, "Is it true what I heard on the radio?"

I said, "I have no idea what you're talking about. Is what true?"

"Joe," he said. "I just heard he died."

"I don't believe it," I said, "I just talked to him a couple of weeks ago and he seemed fine. I'll call Stella."

Stella answered the telephone in Florida, and I said, "Stella, what happened?" She said, "I can't talk about it now. I left a message on your answering machine."

I checked and heard Stella's voice: "Jack, I didn't want you to hear it from someone else first." That was it. I still had no idea what happened other than the story being reported on television news shows. All they knew was that he died. There was no mention about the cause of death.

I called Stella again and told her I wanted to go to Florida for the funeral, but she insisted I stay in Los Angeles because there wasn't going to be a funeral—just she and the children for a very brief memorial.

In retrospect, I realized that Joe was probably in the hospital the last time we spoke, because as far as I can tell, that's where he died. He obviously didn't want to burden any of his friends with his impending death.

I'm not sure whether his first child, Letitia (with Uta Hagen), was there, but his five children with Rosemary Clooney were at his birthday party, as were his two sisters, one coming from Illinois, the other from Mexico City, and his brother Rafael, who came from New York. I suspect they must have known how ill he was when they gathered for his eightieth birthday.

I thought about the party in Los Angeles when he turned seventy-five. He said to me, "Is it okay to be a curmudgeon now?"

I answered, "Why the hell not? You've been one since I met you."

I finally had to learn from his son, Miguel, that Joe died of cancer. He and I have never spoken any more about it, and although I speak with Stella regularly, we don't talk about it either. There is no purpose in pursuing it. His death left a large void in my life, which conversation will not fill.

I GET A NEW HOBBY—CELEBRITY GOLF

And so, I basically quit the management business, except for a pseudo management arrangement with the aforementioned Herb Jeffries, who would move in with me from time to time—whenever he broke up with his wife—actually "wives," because he had two of them during that period of time. Herb, who was born in 1912, the same year as Joe, continues singing and still has one of the best voices in the business. He is ninety-six as I write this, and is once again contracted to sing at the Sweet and Hot Music Festival in September 2010, when he will turn ninety-seven.

It was more or less through Herb Jeffries that I ended up doing more celebrity golf tournaments. Joe Ferrer and I had been at a local golf driving range when we heard someone call out Joe's name.

Joe turned to me and said, "Turn around and tell me if that's Herb Jeffries," presuming I would recognize him. I said, "Yep, that's who it is."

Joe said, "I know him, but he can be an awful pest. I guess I can't ignore him."

Well, that was okay by me, because I had never met Herb and was a big fan ever since I heard his recording of "Basin Street Blues," not to mention his multi-million selling recording of "Flamingo," back in the 1940s.

The end result of our meeting was that Herb asked me to go to Riverside, California with him and meet with General John Hinton. Hinton, stationed at March Air Force Base, was in charge of their annual Bob Hope Celebrity Golf Tournament.

On the drive there, we got into a conversation about "equal

rights." I said that I was all for equal rights just as long as no one group was more equal than any other. I was pretty much talking about the way Blacks were not being well-treated in the area of college admissions.

Herb stopped me by saying, "I don't want to disappoint you, but I'm not Black."

I said, "Then what the hell are you?"

You have to realize that Herb had pretty much built a career on being Black. He was, after all, the featured male singer with Duke Ellington, and had appeared in a series of motion pictures as "The Bronze Buckaroo." The idea for the pictures originated with Herb, who had talked to a movie producer about Blacks' history in the settling of the West.

I repeated the question, and he told me he was Irish and Italian. His Irish mother had been in a relationship with an Italian millinery salesman, resulting in Herb. When that relationship ended, she met the man with whom she had two sons, Donald and Harold Jeffries (or Jeffrey, I'm not sure). Herb was raised by that surrogate father. Years later, Herb introduced me to his half-sister, who had come to the US from Ireland. I asked him when his mother had time to have another child, especially one in Ireland. He replied that she wasn't always having sex in Detroit.

Herb told me that his first big job was as featured vocalist with the Earl "Fatha" Hines orchestra, which had bookings in Europe. For the trip, he had to secure a passport. After checking with the proper authorities in Detroit to get a copy of his birth certificate, he came home practically in tears. He told his mother that they didn't have his certificate, whereupon she told him to go back and ask for "Humberto Ballentino," which is how he discovered that he wasn't at least partly Black. I never met his half brothers, Donald and Harold, but was told by people who knew them that one could have passed for white, while the other was very dark skinned.

Herb later concocted a story about how there might *possibly* be some Black in his background. He told me something that went pretty much like this: "If you remember, the Italians were always invading Ethiopia and would bring back slaves. Somewhere in my ancestors' lives, one of them must have had sexual relations with one of those Ethiopians." He had a short version as well: "There must have been an Ethiopian in the fuel supply."

Herb, by the way, had more than a few wives and children. Eventually, I met all his children, although when I asked him if there might have been more he didn't know about, he responded that "I never throw a stone into a school yard . . . just to be on the safe side." If Herb had any Black in him, he had the whitest kids you ever saw.

Among his wives was the famed stripper, Tempest Storm. The marriage caused both of them trouble. Herb, who was believed to be Black, for marrying a white woman; Tempest for marrying a "Black" man in a society that pretty much frowned on "mixed" marriages. The result was that they moved to Paris for several years, where Herb ended up being a partner in a jazz club. They had a beautiful daughter together, Patricia, who for a short time in her life, also worked as a stripper in Hawaii.

To say that Herb was a lady's man would be the understatement of this volume. He once worked on a cruise ship, where three sisters tried to get him interested in their mother, a recent widow. Herb was about sixty-eight at the time. He ended up marrying the youngest of the sisters and producing a son, Michael.

There was also a woman, who offered him $3 million to marry her, but he turned her down in favor of a much younger and sexier woman with whom he did not have children. That's a story for another book.

Getting back to the Air Force golf tournament, one of the problems they were having was securing celebrities for their "Celebrity" golf event. I asked General Hinton if I could see their list, and saw immediately that their main problem was that most of the names were either people who were dead or who had long since moved away from the addresses the Air Force had. I took their list, which I used not only to greatly increase my own list, but when combined with mine, was able to invite enough to have a full celebrity field.

It had been, for years, their practice of producing a show on the evening before the tournament, and Herb and I agreed to continue the event from among the celebrities we invited, with the admonition from Hinton that the comics would not use "blue" material. That was never a problem with my shows since I never used off-color comics. I once came close with Buddy Hackett, but he begged off at the last minute saying, "You know me, Jack, when I get started I don't always know where I'm going."

Herb decided we needed to bring in a female singer from outside the playing celebrity group. He chose the gorgeous Fran Jeffries (no relation). She was a monster hit. That was the beginning of a regular attraction for the next dozen or so years. I stopped doing their tournaments when the new committee asked for just five or six celebrities. What they really wanted was a small group of performers who would do the show. I said that if what they really wanted was a show, they should consider paying for the talent. End of association.

SO I'M NOT QUITE DONE

I did find it pretty hard to completely divorce myself from show business, and when the late comedian Buddy Lester called to tell me about this "great swing band" he heard, I had to go with him to their Wednesday morning rehearsal. I became a regular visitor to rehearsals, until one morning when I walked in on the end of a band meeting and was told, "Congratulations, Jack, you're our new manager."

At any rate, the time came when I pretty much stopped any more entertainment consulting, golf tournaments and I pretty much backed away from those particular aspects of show business. Until I retired in 1993, I continued writing publicity and doing public relations, but without Joe or Jim, I have had no desire to go back into personal management.

I will never have two dearer friends than Joe and Jim, and trying to work with anyone less than those two giants would only be anticlimactic. There was no sense in working with anything less than the best, and you can't beat working with the best of friends.

Portrait Gallery #2
Jim Backus

Sitting in Jim's hotel room in Troy, Ohio before the "Kitchen Aid" show. This picture became Jim's publicity photo.

With Vikki Carr at the taping of *The Mike Douglas Show* in Philadelphia.

Mike Douglas, Billie Jean King and Jim.

Mike Douglas, Artie Shaw and Jim.

Mike Douglas, Kay Stevens, co-host of the week Jim Backus, Amy Vanderbilt and Artie Shaw on *The Mike Douglas Show*.

Mike Douglas, actress Gale Storm and Jim Backus.

Mike Douglas, actress Natalie Schafer of *Gilligan's Island*, Jim Backus and Gale Storm.

Actress Molly Picon and Jim Backus.

Mike Douglas, Billy de Wolfe, Jim Backus and Molly Picon.

My room in Vero Beach, Florida where Backus co-starred in *There Goes The Bride* with Tommy Smothers and Twiggy.

English actress Sylvia Syms poolside in Florida.

English actor Graham Stark.

Jim Backus and Floridian actress/model April Clough who played Jim's secretary in *There Goes The Bride*.

April Clough and Tommy Smothers, the funny one of the Smothers Brothers.

Jim Backus and April Clough relaxing between takes.

Jim Backus on the phone in the hotel pool.

Before Jim took an unscripted dive under water.

Jim and April coming up for air while the camera kept rolling.

Oh how tough it is working on location.

Jim's last scene in the worst possible clothing combination—his own.

Jim and singer J.P. Morgan on set in Arizona where they were taped as the "hosts" of a previously taped talent show which apparently never saw the light of day, possibly because J.P. wore a see-through blouse.

J.P. Morgan on the Phoenix, Arizona taping.

English actor/comic Marty Feldman in his trailer on location for the Kurt Vonnegut-scripted film *Slapstick*, later retitled *Slapstick of Another Kind*. It still didn't sell.

On the set of *Slapstick* with Marty Feldman, Jim Backus, me and casting director Dorothy Paul.

Jim had a gig at Six Flags Magic Mountain doing shtick as Mister Magoo.

Epilogue

It is obvious to me that no one, or hardly anyone, pays attention to either Prologues or Epilogues. Why do I feel obligated to write an after-piece? Well, it's a good place to stick something in that I forgot earlier. Then, too, the book, as it ended, was really the denouement of that aspect of my life in the entertainment business. My time in the music business as an income producing occupation was short, fun, and when it was over, it was over. Period! Fini! Goodbye and farewell! No regrets. As I am not "over yet," I can't really say there are no regrets because there may be some yet to come.

But the music/entertainment business is ephemeral; it is pictures that fade quickly, life without much substance, and surely devoid of soul food for the mind. It's the toy department of life. I look back fondly on some aspects of it, but mostly because of where it led me. I have often said, "Nothing you experience in life is bad. Even the worst aspects of it teach us lessons, and every step leads somewhere more interesting, if only you pay attention." I have also often said that "None of us is useless. The worst of us can serve as horrible examples," but I think I either stole that or paraphrased someone else.

However, while it was easy to put the "business" and the people I encountered behind me, I don't seem to be able to dismiss the deaths of two of my friends with the mere recounting of our journey together or of their last days—to the extent that I know the details. I could have done extensive interviews with Henny Backus and Stella Ferrer, or any number of people whose lives Joe and Jim touched, but I opted, instead, to avoid writing biographies. Besides, Stella Ferrer has promised me that one day a biography will be written about

José, so I've limited this to what I know first-hand. Jim has several books in print delineating much of his life already.

There is one more person I could have interviewed because he had an impact on José's life for several years, and even after he stopped working seriously, remained a close friend. I have already mentioned his name, but have not given him the proper thanks for the care and consideration he gave Joe. Tom Korman was a super agent, and if you will recall, I interviewed several agents from his office, Contemporary-Korman. I did not, however, meet Tom at that time.

In the sum and substance of their lives, their demise were only punctuation marks at the end of two brilliant books (theirs, not this one). The careers and memories of José Ferrer and Jim Backus will continue to touch everyone with whom they ever came in contact, long after films and books have turned to dust.

Even that wonderful silliness, *Gilligan's Island*, will be running somewhere, and anywhere people are interested in great motion pictures, someone will be watching again and again José Ferrer as Cyrano de Bergerac. No one ever did it better and very likely no one ever will, although many have tried.

One of the few regrets I have is that we were never able to raise the money to produce Cyrano as a musical, because the book he wrote, and the score he had written for it, were far superior to one that eventually made it to Broadway with another star and which closed in a matter of weeks. They used to run his film every year on New York television, billing Cyrano as the "first of the red-hot lovers."

When life ends, I believe, it ends. Nothing more exists, unless you accept the fact that we are all to some extent electrical energy and that we emit that energy as we pass through life. We all know that electrical energy just keeps going and going, like the battery-charged bunny. So, maybe somewhere out in space the power generated by the lives of José Vicente Ferrer de Otero y Cintron (born 1909 or 1912, depending on who you believe, but most likely in 1912), and James Gilmore Backus (born 1913) are traveling endlessly, headed for some distant planet in some other galaxy to brighten the lives of its inhabitants. Unless they come to a stop somewhere, I guess my "energy" will never catch up since, like light, we'll be traveling at the same speed.

Should there be some meeting place after this one, I know we'll get together again because there will be so much to talk about, and if nothing else, I'll have to defend myself through all eternity for writing this thing.

I have one serious problem with this Epilogue: it adds an exclamation point and an end to the book. For me, there will never be an end to my memories of them; so much more than you will find in these pages, but after all, there does have to be a limit.

In the end, regardless of a few bumps along the way, I loved them like brothers, and will miss them as long as I live.

José Ferrer and the author.

INDEX

101 Club 64-65
Adler, "Stretch" 28-29, 33, 35
Allen, Irwin 48-49
Allen, Marty 206
Allen, Steve 214
Amber, Velvet 57-58, 63-64, 70-71, 75, 112-113, 132
American Pharmaceutical Assn. 142-143
Amorous Flea, The 110-111
Androcles and the Lion 130
And They're Off 78
Animals, The 25, 27
L'Auberge 59-60
Backus, Jim
   as Mr. Magoo 2, 109, 182, 197; as Thurston Howell III, 2, 109, 172, 197; early career 109; fear of heights, 126-127; and drinking 127-128; work for La-Z-Boy 133, 187-89; and golf 157, 174, 213; examples of jokes 163-64; as singer 196; Parkinson's Disease 156, 165, 212,-213; daily routine 159-160; hypochondria of 160, 165, 168, 202, 212-213, 215; "voices" of 172; death of 215
Backus, Henny 109-110, 120, 126, 128, 137, 149, 154-156, 165, 170, 173, 176, 182-183, 197-198, 213-215, 217, 239
Baddeley, Hermoine 199
Bailey, Pearl 92
Balsam, Martin 199
Balzano, Jackie 11-12, 30-31, 35
Barrett, Rona 86
Barty, Billy 91
Beach Boys, The 4, 6, 8, 94, 193
Louis Bellson 92
Berle, Milton 174, 215
Bey, Turhan 85-86
Black, Jimmy Carl 179
Blair, Janet 206
Blatty, William Peter 130-131
Bowers, Hoyt 111-112
Borge, Victor 149
Bortz, Neil 138
Blind Faith 10
Bookvich, Steve ("Maruga"), 31-32
Brascia, Tybee 196
Braun, Bob 138
Brubeck, Darius 31-32, 57-58
Bucholz, Horst 48
Burdon, Eric 5, 13, 25-28, 30-31, 84
Burns, George 159, 214, 217
Burton Richard 109, 160, 206
Business Week (magazine) 128, 139
Buttons, Red 88-89, 92, 215
Caen, Herb 86
Campbell, David 57

Campbell, Glen 17
Calvet, Corinne 50
Cariou, Len 209-210
Carr, Vikki 149
Carson, Joanne 19
Carson, Johnny 46, 129-130, 194, 197
Carter, Jack 173, 214
Casper, Billy 210
Cheech and Chong 190
Chong, Tommy 190-191
Christmas Carol, A 59
Clark, Dick 23
Clooney, Rosemary 20, 31, 49, 69, 81-84, 86, 140, 217
Clough, April 199, 201-202
Columbo 50, 64, 86
Condon, Richard 59
Conrad, Barnaby 89
Conrad, Mary 89
Cronyn, Hume 48
Crosby, Katherine 80-81
Crosby, Bing 80-81
Crosby Clambake (golf tournament) 80-83
Curb, Mike 25-26
Cyrano de Bergerac (film) 17, 43, 47, 49, 61
Cyrano de Bergerac (play) 17-18, 42, 240
Cyrano de Bergerac (projected musical) 20, 41-43, 75, 84, 240
Damn Yankees (TV production) 196
Darren, James 205
Davidson, Gordon 20
Davis, Jr., Sammy 110-111
Death in Venice (film) 113-114
Deep in My Heart 49
Denver, Bob 138
De Wolfe, Billy 149
Diller, Phyllis 165, 206, 214, 215
Douglas, Mike 132, 147-149

Duffy, Julia 49
Dunaway, Faye 72
Dusay, Marj 119-120
Eisenhower, Gen. Dwight D. 137, 209
Elektra Records 31
Ellison, Harlan 119
Endless Summer: My Life with the Beach Boys (book) 23
Enter Laughing 43, 49
Evita (TV production) 71-72
Fairchild, Barbara 191
Falk, Peter 50
Feldman, Marty 203-204
Ferrer, José
  awards 2, 42-43, 48, 61; as actor 47-50, 71-72, 84; stage career 42-43; JF film credits 43; TV credits 43-44; and golf 45-46, 51, 59, 62, 79, 80-83, 87, 90-91, 216, 218; childhood of 59; at Princeton 60, 94; as singer 60-61, 66; as ladies' man 68, 85-87; homes of 69; and family, 78, 84; in Rose Parade 85; friendship with jazz musicians 92; letters from 93-94; poems by 115-117; death of, 217-218
Ferrer, Maria 81, 84, 140
Ferrer, Miguel 72, 74, 78, 84, 140-42, 218
Ferrer, Rafael ("Rafi") 72, 78, 84, 92, 217
Fisher, Todd 45
Flippen, J.C. 206
Fogelson, E.E. "Buddy" 197
Fonda, Henry 71, 84
Ford, Glenn 194
Freeman, Morgan 44
French-Atlantic Affair, The 44, 50
Frings, Kurt 160
Gabor, Zsa Zsa 206
Garson, Greer 198

George White's Scandals 156, 176
Gerard, Gil 209
Gershwin, George 31-32
Gershwin, Ira 32
Gideon 43, 71, 185-186
Gideon's Trumpet 43-44, 52, 71, 84
Giffenhagen, George 143, 145
Gilardi, Jack 55-57
Gillespie, John "Dizzy" 92
Gilligan's Island 2, 109, 138, 149, 197, 205, 240
Gold, Steve 4-9, 11, 13-16, 21-28, 30, 34-35
Goldring, Charles ("Charley") 120, 181-184, 187-189, 196
Goldstein, Jerry 4-6, 8, 11, 13, 21-28, 34-35
Gordon, Bob, 10, 13-14
Granz, Irving 19, 23, 61, 118, 124, 193
Granz, Norman 19
Great American Entertainment Show 58
Great Man, The 43, 47, 49, 110
Greco, Buddy 150-151
Griffin, Merv 110, 120-122
Hackett, Buddy 220
Hagen, Uta 69, 217
Hague, Nick 21-22, 34-35
Hall, Jr., Jasper Graham 143-145, 147
Hecht, Beverly 67
Helms, Jesse 93
Hendrix, Jimi 21-22, 34-35
Hill, Phyllis 69
Hoffman, Dustin 70, 146-147
Holliday, Fred 46-47, 54
Hollywood Squares 60, 173-174
Houston, David 191
If This Is Tuesday, It Must Be Belgium 155
In the Rough 157, 159

Jackson, Chubby 54, 92-93
Jacobs, Morty 214, 217
Jaffe, Sam 206
Jagger, Mick 31
James, Dennis 208-209
Jardine, Alan 81-82
Jeffries, Fran 221
Jeffries, Herb 209, 217-221
Johnson, Arte 208
Johnston, Bruce 29
Kahn, Medeline 203-204
Keel, Howard 214
Kerr, Dick 216
King, Billie Jean 149
Korman, Tom 50, 56-57, 186-240
Kragen and Fritz (managers) 184
Kragen, Ken 118, 184
Kupcinet, Irv 138, 149
Lafferty, Perry 173, 215
Lamas, Fernando 173
Lawrence of Arabia 43, 52-53
Lembeck, Harvey 48
Lemmon, Jack 82-83
Leonard, Sheldon 73
Lescoulie, Jack 161
Lester, Buddy 221
Levin, Jeff 57
Lewis, Geoffrey 57-58
Lewis, Jerry 203-205
Linden, Hal 79
Lloyd, Jack
  at Music Tours/The Visual Thing 5- ff; and LSD 13-16; meets JF 17-19; *Endless Summer: My Life with the Beach Boys* 23; becomes JF's manager 40; friendship with JF 47; on state of show business 73-75; becomes JB's manager 120; on "casuals" 154, 155; on personal management, 184-186; concert promotion 190-192; and Peking Opera 194-95; arranging JB's act

197; in Morocco 207-211; last meeting with JF, 216; promotes celebrity golf tournaments 218-ff.
Lloyd, Mike 25
Logan, Josh 2, 60
Love, Susan (wife of Mike Love) 14
Lynde, Paul 60, 174
Magee, Stella 19, 20, 40, 47, 52-53, 62, 68-69, 71, 85-86, 88, 91, 216-218, 239
Man of La Mancha 18-19, 21, 43, 46, 59, 61, 66
Mann, Abby, 111
Manson, Eddy Lawrence 210
Marcus-Nelson Murders, The 43, 71, 77-78
Marie, Rose 173, 206
Marshall, Peter 2-3, 173-174, 208-209
Martin, Dick 206
Mature, Victor 129-130
McGavin, Darren 206
McRae, Meredith 46
Meadows, Jayne 214
Meredith, Burgess 48, 194
Merrill, Bob 47
MGM Records 25-26, 28
Mike Douglas Show, The 131-132, 147-150
Milner, Martin 207
Montalban, Ricardo 61
Mooch 11, 121, 198, 105, 205-206
Morse, Robert 79
Motorola 136-138
Moulin Rouge 43, 47, 49
Murray, Jan 215
Music Tours 4
National Education Alliance (NEA) 37-38
Neilsen, Leslie 79, 207-209
Newport '69:(rock festival) 10-11
Newhart, Bob 50

Newhart 49
Newport '69 (rock festival) 10-11
Oak Records 121, 122, 125, 128
O'Connor, Donald 79, 127-128, 214
O'Curran Charles 194-195
Official Talent & Booking Directory 23, 37-38
Oskar, Lee 27
Ostin, Mo 61
Parks, Michael 65
Paul, Dorothy 204
Paul, Steven 202-205
Peking Opera 192-195
Pleasure Palace 43, 51-53
Plummer, Christopher 42
Picon, Molly 149
Poston, Tom 208
Price, Joe 64, 121
Price, Vincent 92, 205
Puck, Wolfgang 88
Rafaelli, Ron 10, 13, 24, 65
Raitt, John 152-153
Randall, Tony 174
Ray, Johnny 65-66
Reagan, Ronald 48
Reiner, Carl 49
Return of Captain Nemo, The 48-49
Rickles, Don 88-89
Rivers, Joan 130
Robbins, Harold 111, 173
Robertson, Dale 79, 209
Robeson, Paul 42
Robinson, Edward G. 206
Rolling Stones, The 31
Romberg, Sigmund 49
Romero, Cesar 194, 206, 214, 215
Rooney, Mickey 151, 153, 174, 206
Rooney, Jr., Mickey 153
Rosen, Peter 25, 31-32
Ruff, Ray 121, 125
St. John Jill 205
Saperstein, Hank 182

Savalas, Telly 71, 78
Schaefer, George 185-186
Schafer, Natalie 149, 215
Schmockey 139
Sharif, Omar 44, 51-54
Shatner, William 74-75
Shaw, Artie 149-150
Sheep, The 5
Shepard, Adm. Alan 208
Sime, David 136
Sinatra, Frank 61
Sirola, Joe 88
Slapstick (film) 202-205
Sloane, Hal 193-194
Smith, C. Arnholt 137
Smith, Joe 31
Smothers, Tom 199-202
Song of Norway 20
Sorel, Frank (see: Sorienello, Francesco)
Sorienello, Francesco (Frank Sorel) 45-47, 62, 75-76
Stalag 17 43, 48
Stark, Graham 199, 202
Stevens, Kay 149
Stewart, James 60
Stewart, Payne 208
Storm, Gale 149
Storm, Tempest 220
Sunshine Boys, The (play) 86-87
Swarm, The (film) 48-49
Syms, Sylvia 199
There Goes the Bride 199-202
Three Dog Night 12
Tolin, Steve 23-24, 36-40, 73, 190

Tonight Show, The 129-130, 197
Tormé, Mel 214
Trebek, Alex 79
Trevino, Lee 210
Truth of Truths (record album) 121, 125, 138-139, 149, 165
Turner, Kathleen 91
Turner, Lana 85-86
Twiggy 199
Ustinov, Peter 43, 52, 71, 186
Vanderbilt, Amy 149
Visconti, Luchino 113-114
Vonnegut, Kurt 202-203
Walston, Ray 48
War 25, 27, 84
Warwick, Dionne 61
Wayne, David 206, 214
Weiss, Dana 63
Weiss, Martin 63
What's Happening (magazine) 24, 36, 37, 40, 64
What's My Line? 128
Whisky a Go Go 12, 27
White, Betty 214
White, George 156
Whitehouse, Dick 26
White Pelicans (play) 44
Williams, Esther 173
Worley, JoAnne 119, 174
Wynn, Ed 49
Wynn, Tracy Keenan 173
Yeager, Steve 91
Zugsmith, Albert 36
Zugsmith, Michael 36-37, 179

www.ingramcontent.com/pod-product-compliance
Lightning Source LLC
Chambersburg PA
CBHW062014220426

43662CB00010B/1325